PRAYING THE
HEART OF DAVID

PRAYERS FROM
FIRST AND SECOND
SAMUEL AND
FIRST CHRONICLES

BOOKS BY ELMER L. TOWNS

AVAILABLE FROM DESTINY IMAGE PUBLISHERS

PRAYING THE HEART OF DAVID

PRAYERS FROM FIRST AND SECOND SAMUEL AND FIRST CHRONICLES

Praying the Scriptures Series

Elmer L. Towns

Note: *Praying the Heart of David* is based on a text from *The Plain English Bible* edited for *Praying the Scriptures*. *The Plain English Bible*, © 2003 International Bible Translators, Inc. Used by permission from Destiny Image Publishers. This manuscript includes: First Samuel, Second Samuel, and sections from First Chronicles 12:23-40; 15:1-29; 16:1-43; 22:1-29; 30 that cover the life of David. Identical periods in the life of David are covered in First Samuel 16 to Second Samuel 24 and First Chronicles 12-29, but only one story of each event is told. Most of the text for David's life comes from First and Second Samuel, with additions from First Chronicles that are not covered in Samuel.

DESTINY IMAGE® PUBLISHERS, INC.
P.O. Box 310, Shippensburg, PA 17257-0310

"Speaking to the Purposes of God for This Generation and for the Generations to Come."

This book and all other Destiny Image, Revival Press, MercyPlace, Fresh Bread, Destiny Image Fiction, and Treasure House books are available at Christian bookstores and distributors worldwide.

For a U.S. bookstore nearest you, call **1-800-722-6774.**

For more information on foreign distributors, call **717-532-3040.**

Or reach us on the Internet: **www.destinyimage.com**

ISBN 10: 0-7684-3096-8

ISBN 13: 978-0-7684-3096-7

For Worldwide Distribution, Printed in the U.S.A.

1 2 3 4 5 6 7 8 9 10 11 / 13 12 11 10 09

CONTENTS

Preface

PRAYING THE HEART OF DAVID

Both First and Second Samuel are written to focus on the establishment of God's people as a Kingdom on earth, and no one can discuss the Kingdom without focusing on the greatest king Israel ever had—David.

Abraham, who began it all, didn't establish a kingdom; he was just a Bedouin in a clan living in tents at various places in the Promised Land. So, God put His people under the covering of Egypt so they became a large ethnic-people of three million slaves. Under Moses God led them out of Egypt, and under Joshua God conquered the many inhabitants of the Promised Land. But God's people compromised their worship, lusted after sin, and rejected God's commands. Over a period of 300 years, God had to deliver His people from bondage time and again by different judges.

So, First and Second Samuel begins with the birth of Samuel, the king-maker. Samuel's two greatest achievements were establishing the monarchy and he will be forever remembered for anointing David king over Israel.

David probably was more gifted than all of the Old Testament leaders in that he brought together a group of hardheaded, arguing, mean-spirited Jews into a kingdom recognized by the other kingdoms of the area. He nurtured the knowledge of Jehovah to its highest level in the Psalms in spite of his human frailties.

David was a complex man to understand. He was at all times compassionate, tender, generous, and "a man after God's own heart" (1 Sam. 13:14), yet he was fierce in battle and devious in his double sin with Uriah and Bath-Sheba.

David was a godly harpist because he had the Divine within his heart. But David was a poet first and foremost, and will always be remembered for his greatness of Psalm 23. Every time a child in Sunday school repeats "The Lord is my Shepherd," the influence of David's passion to know God will live on. David was a poet, soldier, shepherd, spokesman for God, statesman, devoted father, and consummate leader.

The dynasty founded by David will continue forever. Remember, the angel Gabriel told the Virgin Mary, "The Lord God will give Him (your son Jesus) the throne of his father David" (Luke 1:32). Jesus will sit on David's throne in the millennium for a thousand years.

David brought us close to nature in Psalms 19, 23, and 29, then he lifted us close to Heaven in Psalm 139. David introduced us to the Messiah Jesus in Psalms 2, 22, and 24. David taught us to worship God vigorously.

Psalm 103

I bless you, Lord, from the bottom of my soul;
With all that is within me,
I bless Your holy name.

And I don't forget any of Your benefits;
You, Lord, forgive my sins,
You heal all my diseases,
You, Lord, redeem my life from death.

You crown my life with Your love and mercy;
You, Lord, satisfy me with good things;
My life is renewed like an eagle.

If David had not sinned, we might have made an angel out of him. But his compassion for people corrupted his thinking and he sinned with Bathsheba. No prayer for forgiveness is greater than David's prayer for forgiveness after the conviction and accusation of Nathan the prophet, "Thou art the man." For all who have sinned, these words of David express their guilty souls.

Psalm 51

Lord, have mercy on me according to Your loving nature;
Because of Your mercy blot out my transgressions,
Wash me completely from my sin,
So I will be clean of my guilt
For I acknowledge my terrible deed;
I cannot get it out of my mind;
Against You and no one else have I sinned
In doing what was evil in Your sight.

You are absolutely right to convict me,
And Your punishment is just.

I was born a sinner,
Hide my sin from Your face.

Cleanse my guilty conscience from guilt;
O God, create in me a clean heart,
And renew a right spirit in me.

Don't kick me out of Your presence,
And don't take Your Holy Spirit from me;
Restore to me the joy of Your salvation,
And give me a new spirit to obey You
Then I will tell sinners how to be saved,
And they will turn to You.

David's influence will continue throughout eternity. There will be no offering for sin in Heaven so the forgiveness of sin will cease. But God's people will continue to praise Him with the words of David. There will be no problems in Heaven about which we will pray, but we will worship with the words of David. We will constantly seek God's heart, like David who was "a man after God's own heart."

Therefore, *Praying the Heart of David* could be the greatest book you'll ever read because you see the word of God in David's heart, or you want

God to work in your heart. You will be drawn to God as you see David—a fellow human like you—seek to know God more deeply. May God touch your heart as you expose yourself to the heart of David.

Sincerely yours in Christ,
Elmer Towns
Written from my home
at the foot of the Blue Ridge Mountains

Introduction

SAMUEL THE AUTHOR

Samuel loved his home in Ramah, located on a high plateau. The name *Ramah* meant "to be high." There he enjoyed cool mountain breezes in the hot summer, and everywhere he looked, Samuel saw rows of olive trees and fruitful vineyards of grapes. The old man sat at a large table in the shade of a fig tree, it was the place he came to pray. But today Samuel prepared to write. He would write the story of his life.

Just yesterday a friend compared him to Moses, saying, "You're the next Moses." The humble Samuel was embarrassed with the comparison. He thought, *I've just been faithful to God, I'm no Moses.*

Yet the friend persisted, "Moses delivered Israel from Egypt, you've delivered Israel from the Philistines."

The friend persisted, "Moses closed out the old order of patriarchs, and you've closed out the old order of judges." Samuel thought to himself, *I am the last of the judges.*

Samuel knew he did things that judges did. He knew people came up to him to Ramah when they needed decisions from God. Sometimes God spoke inwardly to Samuel, at other times Samuel relied on his accumulated wisdom.

The friend knew the Pentateuch and quoted Moses who said, "The Lord would raise up a prophet like Moses." Since Moses sometimes predicted the future when he spoke for God, and Samuel could do the same thing, the friend concluded, "You are the second Moses. You are the prophet that Moses predicted would come." This made Samuel all the more uncomfortable.

But the friend was not finished in his comparison. "Moses led Israel from the age of the patriarchs…many family heads, to the age of the judges."

Samuel shook his head in agreement, so the friend continued, "For three hundred years different judges led different tribes, but none of them unified Israel like you, Samuel. So you, Samuel, must be the second Moses."

That was yesterday. But Samuel didn't want to compare himself to Moses. Moses' mantle hadn't fallen on him. He decided to write a book (scroll) to tell an accurate story of his life. Samuel decided, *I won't brag*, but he also knew God had done great things through him, so he concluded, *I won't minimize my accomplishments.*

Samuel knew he was a priest—so was Moses—they were both from the tribe of Levi. So each year Samuel went on a circuit as a priest from Bethel, to Gilgal to Mizpah to sacrifice for the people (see 1 Sam. 7:16). Samuel's traveling was his way of reuniting the people around worship at the Tabernacle and the Ark of the Covenant. His home was at Ramah, only a few miles from Shiloh, where the Tabernacle had its permanent home (see 1 Sam. 1:3).

But Samuel also allowed the people to come sacrifice at his house, "There was his house...and there he built an altar" (1 Sam. 7:17).

Samuel also knew he was a judge, for people came to him to find the will of God for the lives. He wore the ephod, where the Urim and Thummim were located. These stones gave God's decision to the people. "And Samuel judged Israel all the days of his life" (1 Sam. 7:15). After his circuit, he "returned to Ramah, for there was his house, and there he judged Israel" (7:17).

Samuel also knew he was a prophet. He could speak for God, he was a prophetic foreteller. But he could also predict the future, he was a foreteller. And because he denounced the idolatry and evils of the nation, he was a forthteller.

His prophet's office began when he as a boy was sleeping in the Tabernacle, God called him by name, "Samuel." Three times the boy thought it was old Eli, but the last time Samuel answered, "Speak for thy servant heareth" (1 Sam. 3:10). God told Samuel what would happen to Eli in the future, and as a result, "Samuel was established to be a prophet of the Lord" (1 Sam. 3:20).

As Samuel anointed first Saul, then David to be king over Israel, he must have known the day of judges was over. Each judge was raised up to deliver a different tribe from a different attacking enemy nation. But the new king Samuel anointed would permanently sit on the throne. Samuel remembered what the people asked, "Give us a king to judge us" (1 Sam. 8:6). They also requested a king who will "go out before us, and fight our battles" (1 Sam. 8:20).

Samuel had first written a book—the Book of Judges, to tell that in the time of the judges, "There was no king in Israel, every man did that which was right in his own eyes" (Judg. 21:25). But Samuel stood on the hinge of history; with one foot in Judges, he stepped into the future monarchy. Samuel introduced the earthly kingdom.

Samuel would not write sweeping paragraphs of a glorious introduction of the kingdom. No! He would scratch out the story on parchment, giving details of lost donkeys that divinely led Saul to his house. He would not glorify the past, no; God's work sloshes from partial victory by Jonathan, Saul's son, to his ignominious defeats in battle. God's story trudges from Saul's refusal to destroy the Amalekites, to the courage of a 16-year-old David's defeat of the giant Goliath.

Samuel was an honest man who would tell the whole story of the compromise by Eli the high priest, and the sin of his sons: the truth, all the truth, and the unedited truth.

As Samuel sat to write what God had done, he would begin with his own birth. Hannah, his mother, was a godly woman who fasted for a son. Eli was fat (with an undisciplined appetite), half blind from diabetes, and so used to sin and compromise; he didn't realize Hannah was interceding to God. He accused Hannah of being drunk. What you accept is what you expect.

From that prayer, Samuel got his name, which means "to ask of God." The ending "El" signifies the child was from God—Elohim. But the addition of a few letters *sh mu'el* made it "to ask of God." Samuel was an answer to prayer.

Samuel didn't write the last of First Samuel, "And Samuel died and all the Israelites were gathered together and lamented him, and buried him at Ramah" (1 Sam. 25:1). Another finished the book.

In nobility of character...in bringing Israel together...in introducing the monarchy...in faithfulness to God...Samuel is not unworthy to be placed next to Moses. Yet in his greatness, Moses' sin kept him from the Promised Land. In contrast, the record of Samuel is not marred by any act or word whereby he displeased God, nor is there a record of any sin by him.

Looking at First and Second Samuel

As you come to the two Books of Samuel, you see a change from the failed judges to the triumph of God's kings, from a collapsed theocracy (because the people didn't obey) to a triumphed monarchy—King David sits gloriously on the throne.

As you see transitions, don't just look for human failures and excesses. Rather look for God's divine working with His people, and God's progressive revelation of Himself. Ask, "What more can I learn about God from these books?" Also ask, "How can I become more intimate with God as I pray the message of David into my life?" What is the theme of the Samuels? *How God powerfully works through details to establish the throne of His anointed.* Of course the word *anointed* is a reference to King David, but ultimately it is a reference to Jesus Christ the son of David. The word *Christ* means anointed. Look at Psalm 89:19-29 to see God's purpose. When you read the pronoun *him*, ask if it is a reference to David or to Jesus Christ. Also, notice the emphasis on "my" and "I."

Psalm 89:19-29

You once spoke to Your followers;
  You said, "I have helped one who is mighty,

> *I have exalted My chosen one from among the people,*
> *I laid hold of David, My servant.*

> *I anointed David with My holy oil,*
> > *My hand established his life and service.*

> *My arm will strengthen him;*
> > *His enemies will not get anything from him*
> > *Nor will the son of evil afflict him.*

> *I will crush his enemies before him*
> > *And will strike down those who hate him.*

> *My faithfulness will walk beside him;*
> > *My lovingkindness will protect him*
> > *And he will exalt My name.*

> *I will cause the sea to obey him*
> > *And the rivers will run according to his will.*

> *He will say, 'You are my Father,*
> > *My Rock and my God.'*

> *I will make him My begotten first-born,*
> > *The highest king on earth.*

> *My lovingkindness will protect him*
> > *And My pledge will confirm him.*

> *So, I will establish his children forever;*
> > *He will rule from His throne*
> > *As long as the heavens will endure."*

The same writing style will be seen in the two Samuel books that was seen in Judges and Ruth. However new themes arise; the importance of the Ark of the Covenant, the emergence of the prophetic office, the emergence of a unified monarchy, the decline of separate political power of individual tribes, and a new role for the king of Israel.

First Samuel 1-9 deals with the life of Samuel, First Samuel 10-15 covers the rule of Saul, and First Samuel 16-31 describes the growing influence of David. The Book of Second Samuel tells of David's role as king.

Notice the contrast of how God used people in Judges from how he used leaders in First Samuel. In Judges God used unlikely leaders in spite of their weaknesses or flaws. Gideon was from the weakest family in the weakest tribe, Jephthah was a half-breed son of a harlot, Ehud had a physical deformity, and Samson was a womanizer.

In First Samuel God rejects Saul because of his poor decisions, ill temper, and rebellion. God chooses in Saul's place, David: a man after God's own heart.

In Judges no leader could rally all Israel together, in First Samuel, Samuel rallies unity of worship and David rallies unity of military and spiritual purpose.

If you've ever lived in a period of change, you know it's unsettling. That was Judges. In these books, God raises up Samuel to unify the nation spiritually, then Samuel becomes the "king-maker" who anoints first Saul, then David, to unify the nation politically and militarily.

Now let's read how God prepared David to be His king. Let's pray the heart of David.

1

Hannah Prays for a Son

First Samuel 1

There was a man named Elkanah, the son of Jeroham, from
Ramathaim-Zuphim (a twin city) in the hill-country of Ephraim.
Elkanah had two wives. (Though polygamy was often practiced
in the Old Testament, God created one woman for the first man
Adam. Therefore, monogamy was the divinely approved plan.)
One wife was named Hannah, and the name of the other was
Peninnah. Peninnah had children, but Hannah did not have children.

Every year, Elkanah left his town and went up to Shiloh to worship the
Lord of the armies of Heaven and offered sacrifices to Him.
Shiloh was where Hophni and Phinehas served as priests to the
Lord. They were the two sons of Eli. Whenever Elkanah offered
sacrifices, he always gave a share of the meat to Peninnah, his
wife, and to all her sons and daughters. Even though Elkanah
loved Hannah very much, he could only give her one share of
the meat. Hannah could not have children. Yahweh had closed
her womb. But Peninnah, her rival, taunted Hannah to the point
of humiliating her, because Hannah couldn't have children, so
much that Hannah trembled. This happened every year when
they went up to the Tabernacle of the Lord at Shiloh. Peninnah
would taunt Hannah until Hannah wept and could not eat anything.
Elkanah, Hannah's husband, would say, "Hannah, why are you

weeping? Eat something. Why are you so sad? Don't I mean more to you than ten sons?"

One time, after their meal in Shiloh, Hannah went to make her special appeal directly to God. Now Eli, the high priest, was sitting on a chair near the entrance to the Lord's Tabernacle. In the bitterness of her soul, she prayed to the Lord, and travailed. She made a vow, saying, "O Lord of the armies of Heaven, surely You can see that I am absolutely miserable. Remember me. Don't forget me. If You will only give me a son, then I will give him back to You to live his entire life. And, no one will ever cut his hair (he will become a Nazarite). While Hannah kept on praying in the presence of the Lord, Eli watched her mouth moving. Hannah was praying silently in her heart, only her lips moved; her voice was not heard. So Eli thought she was drunk. He said, "Stop getting drunk! Get rid of your wine." Hannah answered, "Not so, my lord, I have not drunk any wine or beer. I am just a woman who is deeply troubled about all of my problems. I am not an evil woman. Until now I have been praying because of my many troubles and grief."

Eli answered, "Then go in peace. May the God of Israel give you whatever you asked of Him." Hannah said, "I want to be pleasing to you." Then she left and ate something, nor was she sad anymore.

Samuel Is Born

Early in the morning, Elkanah's family got up to worship in the presence of the Lord. Then they returned home to Ramah. Elkanah had sex with his wife, Hannah, and the Lord did not forget Hannah. So, Hannah became pregnant, and, in time, she gave birth to a son. She named him "Samuel," meaning "asked of God." She said, "His name is Samuel because I asked the Lord for him."

Every year, Elkanah went up to Shiloh to offer sacrifices and keep his
vow to God. And he brought his whole family with him. But
Hannah did not go up with him. (Only men were required to go
up to the festival, see Exod. 23:17). She told her husband,
"When the boy is old enough to eat solid food, I will take him
to Shiloh and present him in front of the Lord. Then he will
always live there at Shiloh. Elkanah said to her, "Do whatever
you think is best. You may stay home until the boy is old
enough to eat solid food. May the Lord confirm His word." So,
Hannah stayed at home to nurse her son until he was old
enough to eat solid food.

When Samuel was old enough to eat solid food, Hannah took young
Samuel up with her to the Holy Tabernacle of the Lord at
Shiloh. She also brought along a 3-year-old bull, half a bushel of
flour, and a leather container filled with wine. They killed the
bull for the sacrifice. Then Hannah brought the little boy to Eli,
saying, "As surely as you live, my lord, I am the same woman
who stood here near you, praying to the Lord. I prayed to give
birth to this child. The Lord has answered my prayer. Now, I
give him back to the Lord. He will belong to the Lord his entire
life." And they worshiped there in the presence of the Lord.

My Time To Pray

Keep Praying Till You Get Through First Samuel 1

*And she (Hannah) was in bitterness of soul, and prayed to the Lord
and wept in anguish. Then she made a vow..."if You will indeed
look on the affliction of Your maidservant and...will give Your
maidservant a male child, then I will give him to the Lord all the
days of his life"* (1 Samuel 1:10-11).

Have you ever prayed for something you didn't get? Maybe it was something you wanted in the worst way, but the answer didn't come? Maybe you need something right away from God, but you don't know how to get it. Look at how Hannah got what she wanted from God. *Lord, teach me how to get answers to prayers.*

First, is your request a deep need? Hannah was "in bitterness of soul" (1 Sam. 1:10). Hannah's husband had two wives, Hannah and another woman. Hannah was barren, "The Lord had closed her womb" (1 Sam. 1:5.) But look what the other woman had, "all her sons and daughters" (1 Sam. 1:4). Barrenness was a stigma on the *femininity* of a Hebrew wife. So Hannah prayed out of deep anguish. Have you ever hurt so much that you prayed with all your heart? *Lord, I pray deeply.*

Second, have you ever wanted something from God so much that you cried when you prayed? Hannah, "wept sore." Why was she weeping? Apparently it was not over her husband's bigamy. While the Bible never approves of bigamy, some of God's servants (Jacob, Hannah, David) found themselves in this predicament, and had to live for God the best they could under the circumstances. Hannah didn't seem to object to the other wife; it was her own barrenness that motivated her tears. *Lord, motivate me to pray.*

Third, Hannah fasted. She went to the presence of God, the Tabernacle, and fasted for God to answer her prayers. When your answer doesn't come, fasting will take your petitions to a higher level. How do we know Hannah fasted? When she was confident God would answer her petition, she ate (see 1 Sam. 1:18.) You probably wouldn't fast about everything, but when you're pounding on the windows of Heaven, remember the words of Jesus, "This kind does not go out except by prayer and fasting" (Matt. 17:21). *Lord, I will fast.*

Fourth, Hannah "vowed a vow," which is another way of saying she made a life-changing promise. She wanted a son more than anything else. Notice she didn't ask for many sons and daughters like the other wife. All she wanted was one son. One son would satisfy her heart's desire,

"Delight yourself also in the Lord, and He shall give you the desires of your heart" (Ps. 37:4). *Lord, give me one thing.*

What did Hannah promise to do with her son? She promised to give the boy to God! She didn't pray for selfish reasons, nor did she ask for the companionship a mother wants with her son. No! She didn't even ask for a son to keep up with the other wife. Hannah wanted a son for the glory of God. When God gave her a son, she planned to give him back to God. Maybe God is not answering your prayers because your motives are wrong. If you're willing to give the answer completely to God, maybe you'll get your prayers answered. *Lord, I yield to You.*

Hannah prayed so intently and she wept so openly that Eli the high priest thought she was drunk. Hannah was praying so hard that she didn't care what other people thought about her. Is your reputation more important than answers to your prayers? No wonder you don't get answers from God. *Lord, I don't care what others think of me.*

How does God answer prayers? Sometimes He supernaturally reverses the laws of nature. Sometimes He uses circumstances, and at other times He uses the laws of nature. Notice how God answered Hannah's prayers. "And Elkanah knew Hannah, his wife, and the Lord remembered her...Hannah conceived" (1 Sam. 1:19-20.) God used both the natural law of procreation and supernatural intervention. Therefore, it was only natural that Hannah named her son Samuel which means, "asked of God." Every time Hannah called her young son, she remembered asking God for him. *Lord, teach me to remember the times you've answered.*

Amen.

2

HANNAH PRAISES GOD

FIRST SAMUEL 2

Hannah praised God:

"The Lord has filled my heart with joy;
>I feel very strong in the Lord.

I can laugh at my enemies;
>I am glad because You, Lord Who Is Always Present,
>have rescued me!

There is no one holy like You, Lord;
>There is no God but You,
>There is no Rock like our God.

Don't keep on bragging, my enemy,
>Do not boast with your proud words.

Why? Because the Lord is a God who knows everything;
>Actions are weighed by Him.

The bows of warriors break,
>And weak people become strong.

Those who once had plenty of food must now work for it
>And people who were once hungry now flourish.

The woman who was unable to have children now has had seven children
>   But the woman who had many sons is now sad.

The Lord kills,
>   And He keeps alive.

He brings people down to the grave,
>   And He raises them up.

The Lord makes people poor,
>   And He makes people rich.

He makes some humble;
>   He even makes some people great.

The Lord raises the poor up from the dust
>   And, He picks up the needy from the ash heap.

He causes some to sit with princes;
>   Yes, He makes them inherit a throne of honor.

The foundations of the earth belong to the Lord;
>   The Lord sets the world on top of them.

He protects His holy people;
>   But those who do evil will be silenced in darkness,
>   Their power will not give them victory.

The Lord smashes His opponents;
>   He will thunder in heaven against them.

The Lord will judge all the earth;
>   He will give power to His king,
>   He will make His anointed strong."

Then Elkanah went home to Ramah. But the little boy continued to
>   serve the Lord under the supervision of Eli the high priest.

The Corrupt Sons of Eli

However, Eli's sons were evil men—"sons of Belial." They did not respect the Lord. This is what they did: every time someone brought a sacrifice, the meat was first cooked in a container. The priest would then come with a three-pronged hook (a big fork) and plunge the hook into the pan or the pot. Whatever that hook brought up out of the container belonged to the priest. That is how they were compensated by the Israelites who came to Shiloh to offer sacrifices. Moreover, even before the fat began to smoke, the sons would come over to the one who was offering sacrifices and say: "Give the priest some meat to roast. The priest won't accept boiled meat, he only accepted raw meat" (these evil priests wanted to cook the meat their own way).

But the one offering the sacrifice would say: "Let the fat begin to smoke first, then you may take whatever you want." However, the priest would answer, "No! Give me the meat now! If you don't, then I will take it by force." (Hophni and Phinehas wanted to take more than the Law of Moses allowed.)

So the sin of the sons was very great in the presence of the Lord. They did not show respect for the offerings which were being made to the Lord.

However, Samuel was serving faithfully in the presence of the Lord. He wore a sacred apron made out of linen. Every year, Samuel's mother would make a small robe for him. She would take it to him when she went up to Shiloh. She went there with her husband for the annual sacrifice. And Eli would bless Elkanah and his wife, Hannah. Eli would say: "May the Lord reward you with even more children through Hannah. Those children will take the place of the boy for whom Hannah prayed and donated him back to the Lord." Then Elkanah and Hannah would go back home where the Lord was kind to Hannah. She became the mother of three sons and two daughters. But the boy Samuel grew up in the service of the Lord.

Now, Eli was very old. He heard about everything that his sons were doing to all the Israelites. He also heard about how his sons had sex with the women who served at the entrance to the Tabernacle. Eli said to his sons, "The people here tell me about the terrible things that you are doing. Why do you do such evil things?

"If someone sins against another person, God can act as a go-between for him. But if that individual sins against the Lord Himself, there is no one who can pray for him!" Eli's sons would not listen to their father's advice. The Lord decided to put them to death.

The boy Samuel kept growing; he pleased the Lord and the people.

A man of God (a prophet) said to Eli, "This is what the Lord says: 'I plainly revealed Myself to the family of your ancestor, Aaron. (Eli was a priest, and all Jewish priests descended from Aaron, the first high priest [see Exod. 28-29].) That was when they were in Egypt, at the house of Pharaoh. I chose them from all the tribes of Israel to be My priests. I wanted them to go up on My altar, to burn incense, and wear the holy vest before Me. I also gave to the family of your ancestor all the offerings of the Israelites which are made by fire. So, why then look with greedy eyes at My sacrifices and My offerings which I commanded in My dwelling place? You honor your sons more than Me. Your priests have become fat on the best parts of all the meat which the Israelites bring to Me.' (Eli indirectly condoned what his two sons were doing because Eli enjoyed the good meat along with his sons. Perhaps this is how Eli became so obese [1 Sam. 4:18]. Eli may have been grieved at his sons' behavior, but he was unwilling to give up the abundance which flowed to his priestly office.) So the Lord, the God of Israel told him, 'Indeed I promised that your family and your ancestor's family would serve Me forever.' (But all of God's promises are conditional, depending on the faithfulness of people who received God's promises.) But now the Lord says, 'That will never be! I will honor only those who honor Me and I will take away honor from those who do not honor Me. The time is coming when I will destroy the descendants of both you and your father. No man will grow old in your family. You will see trouble in My dwelling place. Good things may happen to Israel, but there will never be an old man in your family. However, I will save one man to serve as priest at My altar. (The man from your family whom the Lord will not cut off from My altar is Abiathar [1 Sam. 22:20-23; 23:6].) He will wear out his eyes and use up his strength. But the rest of your descendents will die by the sword. (See the dramatic fulfillment of this prophecy in First Samuel 22:17-18.) And this will be the sign to you. Both of your sons—Hophni and Phinehas—will die on the same day. (This was fulfilled in First Samuel 4:10-11.) I will choose a loyal priest for Myself. He will listen to Me and do what I want. I will make his family strong. He will always serve in the presence of my anointed king. Then anyone in your family who survives will come and bow down to him. They will beg for a little money or a loaf of bread. They will say, 'Please, give me a job as priest, so that I can have a little bit of bread to eat!'"

My Time to Pray

A Study in Contrast

Now I (Hannah) am giving him to the Lord, and he will belong to the Lord his whole life (1 Samuel 1:28 LB).

Now Eli was very old, but he was well aware of what his sons were doing: (1 Samuel 2:22 LB).

Hannah was a godly woman who fasted and prayed for a son. When God answered her request, she gave the most precious thing she had to God. She carried Samuel to the Tabernacle and left him there to serve God his whole life. Hence, a godly parent produces a godly child. *Lord, I will be godly so I can bear godly children.*

Eli was a study in contrast. He was physically blinded because of diabetes, so he thought Hannah was drunk when she was praying with all her heart. Maybe Eli was physically blind because of an undisciplined diet. He ate too much, got too fat, and diabetes set in. His physical blindness reflected his spiritual blindness. He should have thrown his sons out of the priesthood for stealing and adultery. All he did was rebuke them, which was not enough. Eli never learned "tough love." *Lord, I will be tough on sin in my life before I try to be tough on sin in my children's lives.*

God asked old Eli, "Why do you kick at my sacrifice?" (1 Sam. 2:29). He was kicking God because he let his sons "steal" to get the best of food that Eli probably ate. He was kicking God by not recognizing the extreme importance of the blood sacrifice for sin. He was kicking God by allowing the priesthood to be corrupted by his own sons. *Lord, I will not kick at Your commandments, I submit to You.*

One more practical lesson to influence your prayer life. Did the husband praise God? Nowhere do we read that Elkanah the husband praised God. Most would think that a father would rejoice in the birth of a son. What father doesn't love to have sons? But Elkanah was silent. Watch for this practical lesson. Those who are the most burdened in intercessory prayer will be those who praise first and worship deeply. *Lord, I will worship and praise You when my prayers are answered.*

Amen.

3

THE LORD CALLS SAMUEL

FIRST SAMUEL 3

The boy Samuel (about 12 years of age at this time) was serving the Lord under the supervision of Eli. (Samuel performed both prophetic [1 Sam. 3:19-20] and priestly [1 Sam. 7:9-10; 10:8; 16:2,5] duties.) In those days, the Lord did not speak directly to people very often. There were very few visions coming from God. Eli's eyes were so weak that he was almost blind.

One night, Eli was lying in bed. Samuel was also in bed near the Lord's Holy Tabernacle. The Ark of the Covenant was in the Holy Tabernacle. God's lamp was still burning because it was very early in the morning. Then the Lord called out to Samuel. Samuel answered, "Yes, I'm here." Samuel ran to Eli and said, "Yes, I'm here. Did you call me?"

But Eli said, "I didn't call you. Go back to bed." So, Samuel went back to bed.

The Lord called again, "Samuel." Samuel got up and went to Eli and said, "Yes, I'm here. You called me?"

Again Eli said, "I did not call you, my son. Go back to bed."

Samuel did not yet really know the Lord, because He had not yet spoken directly to him.

And the Lord called out to Samuel for the third time. So, Samuel got up from his bed and went to Eli. He said, "Yes, I'm here. You called me?"

Then Eli realized that Yahweh was calling the boy. So, Eli told Samuel, "Go back to bed. If God calls out to you again, say, 'O Lord, speak; I am Your servant, and I am listening.'" (The attitude which shows that Samuel was willing to do whatever God said.)

So Samuel went back to lie down on his bed. The Lord came and stood there, and He said, "Samuel, Samuel."

So Samuel said, "O Lord, speak; I am Your servant, and I'm listening."

Then the Lord said to Samuel, "Listen, I am going to do something in Israel. It will shock those who hear about it. At that time, I will confirm to Eli everything that I promised regarding his family. I will not stop until I have finished. I have told Eli that I will forever punish his family line. I will do this because Eli knew that his sons were doing evil things, and he did not control them. So to Eli's family line, this is what I vow: 'Your guilt will never be covered by any sacrifice or any offering.'"

Samuel lay down until morning. Then he opened the doors of the Holy Tabernacle of the Lord. Samuel was afraid to tell Eli about the vision. But Eli summoned him and said, "Samuel, my son."

Samuel answered, "Yes, I'm here."

Eli asked, "What did the Lord say to you? Please don't hide it from me. May God punish you terribly if you hide from me anything that He said to you!"

So Samuel told Eli all the words God told him. Samuel did not hide anything from him.

Then Eli said, "He is the Lord, let God do what He thinks is best."

The Lord continued to be with Samuel as he grew up. The Lord did not let any of Samuel's messages fail to come true. (In Acts 3:24, Samuel is mentioned as the first of the series of prophets.)

Then all Israel, from Dan to Beer-Sheba knew that Samuel was confirmed as a true prophet of the Lord. And the Lord continued to appear to Samuel at Shiloh, revealing Himself to Samuel through His Word.

My Time to Pray

Listening to God's Voice ⌁ First Samuel 3

Samuel slept in the Tabernacle to keep the lamp of God from going out because the presence of God dwelt in the Ark of God. The Lord called Samuel and he answered, "Here am I." Then Samuel ran to Eli because the boy thought the old priest had called him (1 Samuel 3:3-4, author's translation).

Has God ever called you, but you didn't recognize His voice? Do you think there could have been times when God was calling you, but you missed Him? Young Samuel was assigned to keep the light in the Tabernacle from going out and was faithfully doing that task when God called him. At first Samuel thought Eli the high priest had called him. The young boy ran twice to Eli, but each time the old priest told him to go back to sleep. The Bible gives this comment, "Now Samuel did not yet know the Lord, nor was the word of the Lord yet revealed to him" (1 Sam. 3:7). *Lord, forgive me when I miss Your call.*

After God called three times, the old priest told young Samuel to respond, "Speak Lord, for Your servant hears" (1 Sam. 3:9.) When Samuel responded to God, the young boy got his first assignment from God. When God speaks to you, He has words of comfort if you're hurting, or words of encouragement to serve Him, or words of rebuke if there is sin in your life. God may call you for a new assignment. *Lord, speak to me.*

Samuel was close to the presence of God. He was sleeping near the Tabernacle, near the Ark of the Lord. If you are close to God's presence, you may hear His voice call you. He was keeping the lamp in the Tabernacle lit. He probably had to make sure there was enough oil and the wick was trimmed. Because Samuel was faithful in little jobs, God called him to a bigger task. Do you want to do something big for God? Be faithful in small tasks like Samuel, it's then you'll hear the voice of God calling you. *God, give me a little job.*

Samuel had ears to hear God's voice. You must have spiritually trained ears to hear God. Too many people have their ears plugged up with the wax of sin. Or they're listening to other voices. Or they're not paying attention to any voice because they are self-centered. Do you have spiritual ears to hear God? If He spoke, would you recognize His voice? *Lord, I'm listening.*

Samuel responded immediately when God called. As soon as Samuel heard the voice, he replied, "Here am I." He answered three times with the same response. What would you have done? Would you have responded three times? God speaks to those who are responsive. Maybe God hasn't spoken to you because you've never responded in the past. Why should God call those who are too busy to listen to Him? *Lord, I'm not listening for anything else but You.*

When God called the first time, why did Samuel not recognize the Lord's voice? Are you like Samuel, sometimes the Lord calls you, but you don't recognize His voice? Maybe Samuel thought he was too unworthy for God to call him? Is that your problem? Maybe Samuel thought he was too young. Maybe Samuel didn't recognize God's call because he was still sleepy, after all God called him in the middle of the night. Have you let circumstances or your physical condition hinder your hearing God's call? *Lord, I will listen carefully for Your call today. Do You have something for me to do?*

It's obvious Samuel didn't respond to God because he didn't recognize God's voice. "Samuel did not yet know the Lord" (1 Sam. 3:7.) Here was a young boy who served God faithfully. He was obedient and he was constantly around spiritual things. Yet he didn't recognize God's voice.

Maybe you're like Samuel. You've attended church and you've even joined the church; but if God spoke you would not recognize His voice. *Lord, help me recognize Your voice.*

Notice God didn't call in the morning, afternoon, or at high noon. God called Samuel in the night. Why does God often speak to us in the night? Perhaps because there are no other distracting voices in the night. Or maybe it's because we have nothing else to do. We're not running around doing busy things. So in the night, we can focus on one thing, we can focus on God's voice and God's message. What goes through your mind at night?

There's another thing about the night. Darkness scares us, or at least at night we are never as sure of ourselves as we are in the day light. It's hard to find our way in the dark and in the night we need more help. So God called Samuel at night to get all of the young boy's attention. What does it take for God to get your attention?

One other thing about darkness. When your eyes can't see, your ears become more sensitive to the sounds around you. When young Samuel was awakened in the night, he was sensitive to one thing—God's voice. Are you ready to focus on God's call? *Lord, I'm ready to listen.*

There's another lesson in this story—persistence. God called Samuel three times, and three times young Samuel ran to the older priest. Samuel didn't turn over in his bed and go back to sleep. Samuel was conscientious and persistent. Is God calling you? Is His call persistent? Perhaps you need to do something about God's call before He quits speaking. Three times young Samuel responded, "Here am I." That's a good beginning for you to respond to God. But willingness is not enough. If you are willing to hear God's voice, that's a good start, but that's not enough.

Old Eli taught young Samuel the next step. The priest told the young boy to respond, "Speak Lord, for your servant is listening." Yes, God calls, but you must respond correctly and seek to find out what He wants you to do. *Speak to me Lord, I want to do what You tell me!*

Amen.

4

THE PHILISTINES CAPTURE THE
ARK OF THE COVENANT

FIRST SAMUEL 4

News about Samuel spread throughout Israel.

At that time, the Israelites went out to fight the Philistines. The Israelites camped at Ebenezer, and the Philistines camped at Aphek. The Philistines engaged the Israelites, and as the battle spread, the Philistines defeated the Israelites. They killed about 4,000 Israelite soldiers on the battlefield.

Then the Israelite army went back to their camp. The elders of Israel asked, "Why did the Lord allow the Philistines to defeat us today? Let us bring here the Ark of the Covenant of the Lord (these leaders were superstitiously treating the Ark as a good luck charm to guarantee a quick victory over the Philistines) from Shiloh, so that it may go with us and save us from the hand of our enemies."

So the army sent some men to Shiloh to bring back the Ark of the Covenant of the Lord of the armies of Heaven, who is enthroned above the cherubim. Eli's two sons, Hophni and Phinehas, were there with the Ark of the Covenant of the one true God. When the Ark of the Covenant of the Lord came into the Israelite camp, all the Israelites were yelling with a tremendous shout. The ground shook.

When the Philistines heard the roar of the shouting, they asked, "What's the meaning of all this shouting in the Hebrew camp?" Then the Philistines found out that the Ark of the Lord had come into the Hebrew camp. So the Philistines were afraid. They said, "A God has come into the Hebrew camp! We are in trouble. This has never happened before. We are in big trouble. Who can save us from these powerful gods? They are the gods who struck down the Egyptians with all kinds of disasters in the desert. Be brave, you Philistines. Fight like men. In the past, they were our slaves. So fight like men, or you will become their slaves."

So the Philistines fought hard and defeated the Israelites. Every Israelite soldier ran away to his own home. It was a huge defeat for Israel, because 30,000 Israelite foot soldiers were killed. And the Ark of God was captured by the Philistines. And Eli's two sons, Hophni and Phinehas, were killed.

The Death of Eli

That same day, a man from the tribe of Benjamin ran away from the battle line (about 18 miles) and came to Shiloh. He tore his clothes and put dust on his head. When he arrived at Shiloh, Eli was sitting on his chair, facing the road. He was worried about the Ark of the one true God. When the Benjaminite man entered Shiloh, he reported the bad news. Then all the people in town cried out.

Eli heard the noise of the outcry and asked, "What does all this noise mean?"

The Benjaminite hurried to Eli and told him what had happened. Eli was now 98 years old, and he was blind, not able to see at all.

The Benjaminite man told him, "I have just come from the battle line. I ran away today."

Eli asked, "Well, what happened, my son?"

The Benjaminite man told him the news, "Israel has run away from the Philistines. The Israelite army has suffered heavy losses. Your two sons, Hophni and Phinehas, are both dead. And the Philistines have captured the Holy Ark of the one true God."

When the Benjaminite man mentioned the Holy Ark of the one true God, Eli fell off his chair backward, falling beside the gate and broke his neck, because he was old and fat. When Eli died, he had been the leader of Israel for 40 years.

Eli's daughter-in-law, the wife of Phinehas, was pregnant, and it was nearly time for her baby to be born. She heard the news that the Holy Ark of the one true God had been captured. She also heard that Eli her father-in-law and Phinehas her husband were both dead. She immediately went into labor. She was having great difficulty in giving birth. She named the baby "Ichabod" and said, "God's glory is gone." She said that because the Holy Ark of the one true God had been captured. It was also because her father-in-law and her husband were dead. As she was dying, the women who helped her to give birth said, "Don't worry, you have given birth to a son." But she did not answer or pay any attention to it, but said, "The glory has departed from Israel, because the Ark of the one true God has been taken away. (In 1926, 1929, 1932, and 1963, Danish archaeologists conclusively discovered that Shiloh was violently overthrown by the Philistines about 1050 B.C. It lay in ruins for centuries after that time.)

My Time to Pray

Losing the Presence of God ⌒ First Samuel 4

Then she named the child Ichabod, saying, "The glory has departed from Israel!" because the ark of God had been captured (1 Samuel 4:21).

How do you feel when the presence of God leaves you? Have you ever enjoyed fellowship with God, then felt empty when He was gone? Do you know anyone who used to be a regular worshiper of God, but now they are far from Him? Israel had experienced the power of God's deliverance through the Judges like Deborah, Gideon, and Jephthah, but the nation lost God's presence under the weak leadership of Eli. *Lord, I feel terrible when You are not near.*

How do you lose God's presence? Obviously by outward obstinate sins of rebellion, filthiness, heresy, or following other gods. At other times you lose God's presence by inward subtle sins such as pride, greed, or lust. But what about carelessness. Can you lose God's presence when you do nothing? Eli was indifferent to spirituality; he couldn't tell if Hannah was drunk or praying intently. Eli did nothing when his sons committed adultery and he looked the other way when they stole from the offerings sacrificed to God. His indifference to God's standards made him lukewarm. *Lord, forgive me for being indifferent in the past.*

Then Israel faced an invasion by the fierce Philistines, who were robbers, rapists, and murderers. The Jewish farmer-militia went out to fight, but was afraid when they saw the number of Philistine soldiers and the size of their men. They remembered the Ark of the Covenant won the battle at Jericho. They thought the Ark was the key to victory. But they were blind to spiritual warfare. It was not a *thing* that gave them victory. The battle was not won by the *Ark of the Lord*, but the battle was won by the *Lord of the Ark*. God who dwelt between the cherubim, gave them victory. Eli allowed his sons to take the Ark into battle, treating it like a good luck charm. But God can't be treated like a thing, and He is jealous when we put our faith in religious instruments, programs, or even our religious practices. God wants us to put our faith in Him, He wants our fellowship. *Lord, I will trust You.*

Israel was defeated even though they took the Ark into battle. Thousands were killed. When the messenger arrived to tell him the Ark had been captured by the enemy, Eli fainted. The impossible had happened; God was captured by the Philistines. Eli, who was fat and elderly, struck the ground with such force that his neck broke. He died. His daily sterile worship of God led to the nation's empty strength in warfare. God is not pleased with your half-hearted worship, nor compromising ministry. *Lord, forgive me when I've offered empty worship.*

The wife of one of Eli's son's was in birth labor when the terrible news arrived. Her husband had been killed in battle and the Ark was captured by the enemy. She gave birth to a son, calling him *Ichabod*, meaning "The glory hath departed." The great power of Israel was in the God they served. But when Israel compromised their obedience to Him and worshiped Him wrongly, God allowed a vicious enemy to overpower them. The nation's spiritual weakness was reflected in its physical weakness. The same thing can happen in your personal walk with God; when you weaken your inner faith, eventually your outer strength unravels. *Lord, I want to grow strong inwardly.*

The birth of a newborn baby should have been a time of joy...hope...ideals. But the mother understood what the future would be like when the Ark of God was gone. *Ichabod!* The thought is repulsive, even the word sounds sinister—*Ichabod*—God is gone. So she didn't give her baby a cute name or a biblical name like families in the Bible. She named the baby *Ichabod.* The baby, like the nation, had little hope. God was gone; the glory was departed. *Lord, I will hang on to Your glory.*

Ichabod's mother didn't have a choice. God was gone, the defending army was destroyed. She was captured by the enemy of God and living in an occupied territory, a POW. Her situation determined her choice. So she chose to call her son, *Ichabod.* She resigned herself to the inevitable. *Lord, I will not resign.*

But you have a choice. You can worship God and follow Him with all your heart. "And you will seek Me and find Me, when you search for Me with all your heart" (Jer. 29:13.) *Lord, I choose You.*

Amen.

5

TROUBLE RESULTED

FIRST SAMUEL 5

After the Philistines had captured the Holy Ark of the one true God,
they took it from Ebenezer to Ashdod (located 33 miles west of
Jerusalem, and three miles from the sea). They carried it into
Dagon's temple and put it next to Dagon. (Samson had once
destroyed Dagon's temple at Gaza, see Judg. 16:21-30.) (The
Philistines probably did this to show that Yahweh was a subordi-
nate deity to their own god.) The people of Ashdod got up early
the next morning and found that the statue of Dagon had fallen
to the ground on its face. It was lying in front of the Holy Ark of
the Lord. Then the people of Ashdod picked up Dagon and put
it back in its place.

Early the next morning, the people of Ashdod got up and again found
the statue of Dagon face down on the ground in front of the
Holy Ark of the Lord. Its head and hands were broken off, lying
on the doorway. Only the torso of Dagon was still in one piece.

So even today (at the time the Book of First Samuel was written) the
priests of Dagon and all others who enter its temple at Ashdod
refuse to step on the door sill.

The Lord punished the people of Ashdod and their neighbors by allowing their territory to swarm with rats. The Lord gave them a lot

of trouble, causing them to have terrible hemorrhoids. (Many scholars believe that this was a severe outbreak of the bubonic plague—"the black death.")

When the people of Ashdod saw what was happening, they said, "The Holy Ark of the God of Israel must not stay with us. God is punishing us and Dagon, our god." So, the people of Ashdod called all the lords of the five main cities of the Philistines together. They asked, "What should we do with the Holy Ark of the God of Israel?"

The rulers answered, "Move the Holy Ark of the God of Israel over to Gath." So the Philistines moved the Ark of the God of Israel.

However, after they had moved it to Gath, the Lord punished that city, also causing a tremendous panic. He afflicted the people of the city, the unimportant and the important ones with terrible hemorrhoids.

Then the Philistines sent the Holy Ark of the one true God over to Ekron. But when it arrived, the people of Ekron yelled, "Why are you bringing that thing to our city? Do you want to kill us and our people?"

Then the people of Ekron called all the lords of the Philistines together. They said to those rulers: "Send the Holy Ark of the God of Israel back to its original place. Do this before it kills us and our people." There was a deathly destruction throughout the entire city. God's punishment was severe there. The people who did not die were plagued with terrible hemorrhoids. So the people of Ekron cried loudly to Heaven.

My Time to Pray

God in the Wrong Place ᔓ First Samuel 5

When the Philistines took the ark of God, they brought it into the house of Dagon and set it by Dagon. And when they arose early the next morning, there was Dagon, fallen on its face to the ground before the ark of the Lord. The head of Dagon and both the palms of its hands were broken off on the threshold; only Dagon's torso was left of it (1 Samuel 5:2,4).

Have you ever tried to take God where He shouldn't go? Obviously, we're talking about your going where you should not go, taking God's presence to an evil place. We're not talking about taking God Himself into some place, because God is everywhere present at the same time. God is in hell, He is present everywhere; including places where sin is committed. God is present even in heathen temples. But it's different when you carry His "localized presence" there, than His omnipresence being there. What happens when you carry God's presence to a place to sin? Because Christ lives in your heart, you take God into an evil place. What happens when you go there continually? Does God leave you? *God, I will not carry You anyplace where I can't magnify You.*

The Philistines defeated Israel and occupied the Promised Land. They captured the Tabernacle and enslaved God's people. But their worst blasphemy was taking the Ark of God into the heathen temple of Dagon, their god. Their egotistical purpose gave them "bragging rights." They wanted to show their god was greater than Israel's God. When you visit a place of sin, for the purpose of sin, do you realize satan brags that he has captured you? *Lord, I won't go there.*

Since God's people were powerless to stand before their enemies—they were spiritually anemic—God had to act independently of them. When the Philistines placed the Ark of God in their temple, they didn't realize they were putting God Himself next to Dagon. But God will not share His glory, and no idol can stand in God's presence. The next morning,

Dagon was on his face before God. What's going to happen when you take God into an unholy place? *Lord, I will not take You to a place of sin.*

The Philistines probably thought an earthquake tipped over Dagon. Maybe they thought someone sneaked into the temple to play a prank. So they re-set Dagon in its place. The next morning, Dagon was again on his face before the Lord, but this time his head and hands were broken off. The heathen priests were so frightened they wouldn't approach where the broken head and hands were found. Then a plague of painful hemorrhoids spread across the Philistines nation, and they recognized it was the judgment of the Lord. When God punishes because of sin, can you recognize it? Can the unsaved recognize it? *Lord, I know when You've punished me.*

But there is also a lesson of worship here. When the Ark was placed in the heathen temple, the demonic spirits of the idols recognized they were in the presence of the living God. And idols can't compare with the almighty God, nor can the demons that empower them stand in God's presence. They are forced to bow in recognition of God's sovereignty. The next morning, the stone idols that represented satanic power, were prostrate before the presence of God. If idols bow in His presence, how can you do otherwise? *Lord, I bow to You this day.*

When you read the whole story, you see the patience of God, along with His permission. He allows His people to grow cold and stray. He allows His leaders to sin. God doesn't stop the sin of His people, nor does He intervene when they stray. Because God wants us to love Him freely and to love Him devotedly, He has allowed us a choice. God has allowed us to love sin freely and to serve sin devotedly, but He doesn't stand idly by while we head for hell. God sends roadblocks to hinder us, and preachers to remind us, and the Holy Spirit to convict us. But if we belligerently choose not to serve Him, God will allow us to be captured by the Philistines. By the way, has the enemy occupied your territory? Are you enslaved? Are you in Dagon's temple? *Lord, I love liberty.*

The only thing you can do when you live in the enemy's territory is worship. If Dagon ended up on his face before God, isn't that where you should be? Notice the irony of today's Scripture: Israel should have been worshiping God, but the nation couldn't do it because she was weakened by compromise. The only worship the Lord received was from a heathen god. *Lord, I fall on my face now before You.*

Look into the temple to see a heathen god before the presence of the true Lord. Don't be amazed, because this is what will happen in the future judgment. Look into the future to see everyone bow before the Lord in worship, saved and unsaved. "That at the name of Jesus every knee should bow, of those in heaven, and of those on earth, and of those under the earth, and that every tongue should confess that Jesus Christ is Lord, to the glory of God the Father" (Phil. 2:10-11). Since everyone will bow in the future, *Lord, I worship You now.*

Amen.

6

THE PHILISTINES RETURN THE ARK OF THE COVENANT

FIRST SAMUEL 6

The Holy Ark of the Lord was with the Philistines for seven months. Then the Philistines called for their priests and magicians, and asked, "What should we do with the Holy Ark of the Lord? Tell us how to send it back home."

The priests and magicians answered, "If you send back the Holy Ark of the God of Israel, do not send it away empty. You must offer a penalty offering so that the God of Israel will heal you. Then you will discover why He has continued to punish you."

The Philistines asked, "What kind of penalty offering should we send to the *Lord*?"

The priests and magicians answered, "Make five golden images of your hemorrhoids. And make five golden figurines of rats. The number of these replicas must be the same number as the number of Philistine lords. This is because the same plague has come upon all of you and your lords. Make the models of the hemorrhoids and the rats that are ruining the country. Show respect to Israel's God. (The Philistines were attempting to placate an "angry" deity.) Then perhaps, Israel's God will stop punishing you, your gods, and your land. Do not be stubborn like the king of Egypt and the Egyptians. God punished them severely! That is why the Egyptians allowed the Israelites to leave Egypt.

Then you must build a new cart. And get two cows that have just given birth to calves. These must be cows that have never had yokes on their necks. Then hitch the cows to the cart. Take their calves home. Do not permit the calves to follow their mothers. (The two milk cows would normally have a strong urge to return home to feed their calves.) Then put the Holy Ark of the Lord on top of the cart, and put the golden models inside a box beside the Holy Chest. They are your penalty offerings to the Lord. Send the cart back; let it go. Watch the cart. It may go toward Beth-Shemesh, in Israel's own land. If so, the Lord is the One who caused this great sickness to afflict us. But the cart might not go toward Beth-Shemesh. If that happens, we will know that Israel's God did not punish us. We would know that our sickness happened merely by chance."

So the Philistines did what the priests and magicians said. They took the two milk cows. They hitched them to the cart, but they penned up their calves in the barn. Then they put the Holy Ark of the Lord on top of the cart. And they put the box containing the golden rats and the images of hemorrhoids on the cart. Then the cows went straight toward Beth-Shemesh. They stayed right on the road, mooing all the way. They did not turn either right or left. The Philistine lords followed the cows as far as the border of Beth-Shemesh.

Now, the people of Beth-Shemesh were harvesting their wheat in the valley when they looked up to see the Holy Ark; they were happy to see it again. The cart went to the field that belonged to Joshua of Beth-Shemesh. The cart stopped in this field near a large rock. The people of Beth-Shemesh chopped up the wood of the cart, killed the cows, and sacrificed them to the Lord as a whole burnt offering. The Levites (Beth-Shemesh was designated to be one of the Levite towns) moved the Holy Ark of the Lord off the cart. Along with it, they also took down the box that contained the golden images. They put both of them on the large rock. That day, the people of Beth-Shemesh offered whole burnt offerings and made sacrifices to the Lord. From a distance, the five Philistine lords watched them do all these things. Then the lords went back to Ekron that same day.

However, some of the men of Beth-Shemesh peered into the Holy Ark of the Lord. (This was strictly forbidden; see Num. 4:20.) So God struck down 70 of them. The people of Beth-Shemesh cried, because the Lord had punished them so terribly. The men of Beth-Shemesh said, "Who can stand in the presence of the Lord, the one true God, the Holy One? And, where can we send His Holy Ark, to get it away from us?"

Then they sent messengers to the people of Kirjath-Jearim. The messengers said, "The Philistines have brought back the Holy Ark of the Lord. Come down and get it."

My Time to Pray

When Fear of God is Reverential ~ First Samuel 7

Then the men of Kirjath Jearim came and took the ark of the Lord, and brought it into the house of Abinadab on the hill, and consecrated Eleazar his son to keep the ark of the Lord. So it was that the ark remained in Kirjath Jearim a long time; it was there twenty years. And all the house of Israel lamented after the Lord (1 Samuel 7:1-2).

The Philistines were scared to death—literally—of the *Lord* of the Ark. The God of the Israelites was among them, and they felt His sting. Jehovah had humiliated Dagon and we see Dagon on his face in front of Jehovah. That's where you should be voluntarily. Worship comes from the deep recess of your heart. Dagon was not voluntarily worshiping the Lord; he was forced to lie on his face before the God of creation. *Lord, I will worship because I want to worship.*

The religious leaders of the Philistines told the leaders to send the God of the Ark back to Israel before the plague killed any more Philistines. They got what they lived. Authorities tell us the plague is caused by the filth of human feces spread by rats. Part of the first evidence is hemorrhoids—terrible hemorrhoids. Doesn't filthy thinking produce filthy living which leads to the plague? Isn't a god who fosters filth in sexual relations—plus many other forms of debauchery—responsible for people's disease? In opposition, a holy God demands His people live clean, pure lives. *Lord, I will be clean physically, mentally, sexually, and spiritually.*

The Philistines built a new cart and placed their veneration—gold rats and gold hemorrhoids—in a box on the cart, along with the Ark of the Covenant. They separated two milk cows from their calves, and sent them back to Israel. It was the sovereignty of God that guided the cart back to the territory of Israel since God dwells between the seraphim above the Ark. I wonder if He enjoyed the trip home. Since the Philistines didn't know the Ark was to be carried by two poles by Levites, God didn't judge them. The workers in the field recognized the Ark and properly welcomed God back in. *Lord, welcome to my life. I will worship you properly.*

Beth-Shemesh was a Levitical city (see Josh. 21:16), the residents should have known the command by God to carry the Ark on poles. They should have not let their curiosity get the best of them. Who left the top off the box? When they looked inside the box, "The Lord smote the men of Beth-shemesh because they had looked inside the ark of the *Lord*" (1 Sam. 6:19). *Lord, You judge those who should have known better.*

There's a difference between reverential fear and superstitious fear. The Philistines were afraid of God because of the bubonic plague. Their fear did not lead them to saving faith. The workers in the field revered God and sacrificed to God. The blood of the oxen was shed. Saving faith leads a person to approach God through the blood. Today, "the blood of Jesus Christ, God's Son, cleanses us from all sin" (1 John 1:7). *Lord, I come to You through the blood of Christ.*

Amen.

7

SAMUEL LEADS ISRAEL

FIRST SAMUEL 7

The Jewish men of Kiriath-Jearim came and got the Holy Ark of the Lord. They took it to Abinadab's house on a hill. There they consecrated Eleazar, Abinadab's son, so that he could guard the Holy Ark of the Lord. The Ark stayed at Kiriath-Jearim for a long time—a total of 20 years. And all the people of Israel were sorrowful, and they began to follow the Lord again.

Samuel spoke to the whole of Israel, saying, "If you are turning back to the Lord with all your hearts, then you must get rid of the foreign gods which are among you. You must get rid of the idols of Ashtoreth. You must give yourselves fully to the Lord and serve only Him. Then he will save you from the hands of the Philistines."

So the Israelites put away their idols of Baal and of Ashtoreth. And they served only the Lord.

Then Samuel said, "All Israel must meet at Mizpah. I will pray to the Lord for you." So the Israelites met together at Mizpah. They drew water from the ground and poured it out in the presence of the Lord. They fasted that day. (This was probably the Day of Atonement because Israel was commanded to fast on that date.)

There they confessed: "We have sinned against the Lord." And Samuel served as "the judge" of Israel at Mizpah.

The Philistines heard that the Israelites were meeting at Mizpah for the purpose of declaring war on the Philistines. So the Philistine lords came up to attack them. When the Israelites heard that the Philistines were coming, they were afraid. They said to Samuel, "Don't stop praying to our God on our behalf. Ask the Lord to save us from the hands of the Philistines." Then Samuel took a little lamb and offered it to the Lord as a whole burnt offering. He called out to the Lord on behalf of Israel. And the Lord answered him.

While Samuel was offering the whole burnt offering, the Philistines came near. They were about to attack Israel, but the Lord thundered against the Philistines with a loud thunderstorm. The Philistines were so scared that they became confused. The Israelites defeated the Philistines in battle. The men of Israel rushed from Mizpah and chased the Philistines as far as Beth-Car—just below it—killing the Philistines along the way.

After this happened, Samuel took a stone and set it up between Mizpah and Shen. (Shen was a sharp-pointed rock, a craggy outcrop that resembled a tooth.) He named the stone Ebenezer (stone of help), a monument to commemorate this victory which God gave to them. Samuel said, "The Lord has helped us up to this point in time." So the Philistines were beaten. They did not invade the territory of the Israelites anymore. The hand of the Lord was against the Philistines all during Samuel's life.

Earlier, the Philistines had taken some towns from the Israelites, but the Israelites won them back—from Ekron to Gath. They also took back the neighboring lands of these towns from the control of the Philistines. And there was peace between Israel and the Amorites. Samuel continued as the judge of Israel all during his life. Every year, he regularly went from Bethel to Gilgal to Mizpah and back again. He administered justice for the Israelites in all these towns. But Samuel always went back to Ramah where his home was located. He also judged Israel there. And there he built an altar to the Lord. (The Tabernacle and its altar at Shiloh may have been destroyed by this time.)

My Time to Pray

Revival and Victory ~ First Samuel 7

So they gathered together at Mizpah, drew water, and poured it out before the Lord. And they fasted that day, and said there, "We have sinned against the Lord." And Samuel judged the children of Israel at Mizpah (1 Samuel 7:6).

Have you ever faced a problem, and then began seeking the Lord to help you with your problem? But the problem got worse, and your enemy got stronger. The more you prayed, the more the enemy prevailed. Have you ever come to the conclusion that prayer was hurting you; rather than delivering you from your problem? *Lord, forgive my doubts.*

Israel was enslaved to the Philistines. Annually they paid oppressive taxes to their "war-motivated" neighbors. Then Samuel was thrust into the office of High Priest. He challenged Israel to repent of her sin and return to God. "If you return to the Lord with all your hearts, then put away the foreign gods…and prepare your hearts for the Lord, and serve Him only; and He will deliver you from the hand of the Philistines" (1 Sam. 7:3). *Lord, I repent.*

The nation of Israel was tired of their sin, and tired of slavery. The nation listened to Samuel. They destroyed their idols. Why do people abandon their sin? Because sin is a "hard task master." Slaves end up miserable, unhappy, wretched, and addicted. Israel wanted freedom from Philistine taxes, and freedom from sin. The nation gathered at Mizpah to worship the Lord. *Lord, I come to Your presence because I need You.*

Now Israel fasted to know God, whereas they had been going without food because the Philistines stole the best, taking all they could find. Now Israel fasted and wept before God in repentance. When's the last time you cried over sin? If you haven't wept over sin, it doesn't mean you're sinless. It means you're hard-hearted. The closer you get to God's heart, the more insidious sin you see in your heart. *Lord, I am sorry for my sin.*

The Philistines heard that Israel gathered at Mizpah to worship. They immediately prepared to attack. Satan fears when he sees a saint on his knees. Israel probably thought their circumstances would get better if they prayed, but things got worse. Was Israel confident? No! When Israel saw the enemy troops advance, "they were afraid of the Philistines" (1 Sam. 7:7). It's possible to be enjoying God's presence, and then be distracted by the enemy. How did that happen? Israel was still looking at their problem, and not at God. So when you close your eyes to pray for an answer, don't peek to see if the problem is beginning to go away. That's unbelief. Keep looking at God, that's faith. *Lord, I continually look to You.*

Israel went out to fight the Philistines, but implored Samuel, "Do not cease to cry out to the Lord...that He may save us" (1 Sam. 7:8). Samuel offered a blood sacrifice for sins, that's symbolic of confessing all sin and rooting evil out of the heart. Then God gave Israel a victory in two ways. First, hailstones pelted the Philistines. This was not just rain. The Philistines worshiped Baal and Molek, the gods of the sun and weather, so they interpreted the hailstones as the divines' displeasure.

Then Israel fought with new determination. Wouldn't you fight better if you knew an intercessor as effective as Samuel was begging God for victory? The Philistines ran away with Israel chasing them—being killed as they retreated—all the way home. When you deal with sin in your life, slay it completely; get it out of your life. "The Philistines...did not come anymore...all the days of Samuel" (1 Sam. 7:13). If you want "revival-victory," you must fast, search out iniquity, and remember Samuel offered a blood sacrifice. So you must put your sin under the blood, "the blood of Jesus Christ His Son cleanses us from all sin" (1 John 1:7). *Lord, cleanse me by the blood.*

But once you sacrifice dearly to get victory, be just as vigilant to keep victory. Samuel set up a memorial stone called Ebenezer, which means, "Thus far, the Lord has helped us" (1 Sam. 7:12). *Thus far* means "up to now." Remember God has helped you in the past, but don't rest on past victories. You have to trust Him this very minute for present victories for this very day. If you want to live in the past, look to the Ebenezer memorial stone. It will remind you to trust God for today's victory and for tomorrow's blessing. *Lord, I'll live for You today, because yesterday's victories remind me of Your promise of victory for tomorrow.*

Victory feels good. Israel had her cities restored (1 Sam. 7:14) and the Philistines retreated. They didn't return during the life of Samuel. That doesn't mean evil men *never* return. Your victory today feels awesome. You think you'll never again be bothered with "that temptation." It might not come back for awhile, but it will return eventually. As long as you live in your physical body, you'll struggle with sin. When you get victory over one area of temptation, there will be another one. The cost of constant spiritual victory is continual vigilance. *Lord, I will keep guard.*

The next time you're attacked, look to your Ebenezer memorial stone. Remember, the God who gave you victory in the past, is the same God who can come to your rescue today. *Lord, I call on You now.*

Amen.

8

The People Insist Upon Having a King

First Samuel 8

When Samuel became old, he appointed his sons as judges over Israel. His oldest son's name was Joel, and his next son's name was Abijah. Joel and Abijah were acting as judges in Beer-Sheba. However, Samuel's sons did not live the same way as he did. Instead, they tried to get money dishonestly. They took bribes. They twisted justice to obtain money. Therefore, all the leaders of Israel gathered themselves together and came to Samuel at Ramah and said to him, "You are old, and your sons do not live as you have always lived. Give us a king to lead us—like all the other nations."

When the elders said that, Samuel knew this was a very bad idea. So he prayed to the Lord. But the Lord told Samuel, "Listen to whatever the people say to you. They have not rejected you. They have rejected *Me*; they do not want *Me* to rule over them. They are doing as they have always done. Since the day I brought them out of Egypt until today, they have always abandoned Me. They have served different gods. They are also treating you the same way. Go on, listen to the people. But give them a very stern warning. Tell them what the ruling king would do—he will exercise his special privileges over them."

Samuel answered those who were asking him for a king. He repeated all the words of the Lord to them. Samuel said, "If you have a king ruling over you, then these are the kinds of special privileges that he will get: he will take your sons to make them serve him with his chariots and his horses. They will run ahead of his chariots. The king will appoint some of your sons to be commanders over groups of 1,000 men or captains over groups of 50 men. He will force more men to plow his ground and to harvest his crops, to make weapons of war and weapons for his chariots. This king will take your daughters, too. Some of your daughters will make perfume. Others will cook and bake for him. He will take over your best fields, your best vineyards, and your best olive trees. And he will give them to his servants. He will put a ten percent tax on your grapes, and he will give that to this officers and servants. He will take your servant boys and servant girls. He will take your best cattle and your donkeys. And he will use them all for his own work. And he will put a ten percent tax on your flocks. And, you yourselves will become his servants. When that time comes, you will cry out for relief because of the king you chose for yourselves. However, the Lord will not answer you at that future time."

But the people refused to listen to Samuel. "No," they cried, "we want a king to rule over us. Then we will be like all the other nations. Our king will lead us. He will be our hero and he will go out ahead of us and fight our battles."

Samuel heard all that the people said, then he reported everything to the Lord. The Lord answered Samuel, "You must listen to them. Put a human king over them."

So Samuel told the men of Israel: "Everyone go back home."

My Time to Pray

Asking for the Wrong Thing ⌐ First Samuel 8

Nevertheless the people refused to obey the voice of Samuel; and they said, "No, but we will have a king over us, that we also may be like all the nations, and that our king may judge us and go out before us and fight our battles" (1 Samuel 8:19-20).

Have you ever prayed for something that God didn't want you to have? What should you do when God says "No!" Israel kept asking for a king, even when God said "no." Did you persist because you thought you knew more than God? Did you persist because your request was selfish, or your request satisfied fleshly desires? Some people keep asking when God says "no" because they are blind to God's plan. Some people are too far from God to hear His voice saying "no." *Lord, teach me when it's wrong to pray.*

When Samuel got old, the people began looking for another leader. They realized Samuel's sons were not spiritually qualified. Samuel's boys took bribes and didn't follow Samuel's example. So what did the people ask, "Now make us a king to judge us like all the nations" (1 Sam. 8:5). *Lord, I don't want to be blinded to Your will.*

Israel had two problems. First they got their eyes off God. They were not looking to Him for protection and guidance. What is it about "time" that makes us forget the nearness of God? Why do we take Him for granted? Have we forgotten there is an enemy—a roaring lion—who walks about to eat us up. *Lord, keep reminding me about the enemy.*

Israel's second problem was looking at their neighbors. Israel had the "green grass" syndrome. They wanted what the heathen had. The heathen had a mighty king to lead them into battle. Israel had a God to lead them whom people couldn't see. Notice what Israel said, "That our king…may fight our battles for us." There's the fly in the ointment. They wanted someone to do it all for them. They wanted a king to fight for them, so they wouldn't have to fight. Do you realize that when you want the government to do something for you, that you are the government? That when you want the church to do something for you, that you are the church? God fought battles *through* His people, and *strengthened* His cause through people, but Israel wanted a king to do it for them. *Lord, I will work for You.*

There was another problem. The people wanted a king to *judge* them. Had God not done this through His laws and commandments? Were the people rejecting God's Word? The king in other nations had elaborate courts for judgment. Was Israel looking at a heathen "Supreme Court Building" with its majestic image and awesome power? Had Israel forgotten God was the source of all law and that the law is an extension of the nature of God? *Lord, I will remember Your laws.*

Maybe Israel liked the king's smile, or his crown, or his regal robe and train. Whatever it was, they liked the idea of a human king, and rejected God. The Lord knew this, but He wanted to make sure they understood. God said plainly, to Samuel, "They have not rejected you, but they have rejected Me" (1 Sam. 8:7). When you continue to beg God to do something against His will, be careful; you're rejecting God. What happens when you ask God to break his natural laws—"I want to fly," or "I want to smoke but not get cancer"? To reject God's law is to reject God. When you know God commands to tithe, but you don't do it, you're rejecting God. *Lord, I will keep Your Law.*

God tried to warn the people. God reminded them their king would draft their sons into the army (1 Sam. 8:11), a king would tax them for his pleasures, a king would confiscate their property (1 Sam. 8:14) and a king would make them his servants. Isn't it ironic that God took them out of servitude to the Philistines—but they didn't want God's rulership—they chose to be a servant to the king of their own choice. Everyone is a slave to someone or something; whose slave are you? In their ignorance, Israel was choosing to be in bondage to their own king. *Lord, I want to be Your slave.*

What does it mean to have a king? He's more powerful than a president or prime minister that can be voted out of office. Once you get him, you can't get rid of him. Like a sinful addictive habit, a king will take your money and strength, and make you work to get more for him. Like an addiction, a king is never satisfied. *Lord, I don't want to be a slave to sin.*

If you had been there, would you have chosen an earthly king or the Lord? David the righteous king recognized who was the real King. He cried out, "My King and my God" (Ps. 5:2). When you choose God, His "yoke is easy and his burden is light" (Matt. 11:30). When God asks for your tithe, He promises to "open for you the windows of heaven and pour out for you such blessing that there will not be room enough to receive it" (Mal. 3:10). When you give your time or talent to God, notice His return, "Give and it will be given to you" (Luke 6:38). *Lord, I choose to be ruled by You.*

Amen.

9

SAUL MEETS SAMUEL

FIRST SAMUEL 9

There was a man from the tribe of Benjamin whose name was Kish. He
was a warrior, the son of Abiel, the son of Zeror, the son of
Becorath who was the son of Aphiah, a Benjaminite. Kish had a
son whose name was Saul. Saul was a good-looking, young
man. There was no Israelite that was more handsome than he
was. Saul stood a head taller than anybody else.

The donkeys that belonged to Kish, Saul's father, got lost. So Kish said
to Saul, "Take one of the servant boys with you, and go search
for those donkeys." Saul went throughout the hill-country of
Ephraim and the land of Shalishah. However, he and the servant
could not find the donkeys. They crossed into the land of
Shaalim, but the donkeys were not there, either. They went all
over the territory of the tribe of Benjamin, but they still did not
find the donkeys.

When they arrived in the region of Zuph, Saul said to his servant boy,
"Come, let us return home. My father has probably quit being
concerned about the donkeys and started to worry about us."

But the servant answered, "There is a man of God in this town. People
have much respect for him, because everything he says comes

true. Let us go there, perhaps he could tell us which way we should go."

Saul said to his servant, "Yes, but if we go into that town, what could we pay him? The food in our bags is gone. We have no gift to give to the man of God. Do we have anything left?"

Again the servant said, "I have $1/10^{th}$ of an ounce of silver. I will give that to the man of God. Then he will show us our correct path." In earlier times, if someone in Israel wanted to ask for something from God, he would say, "Come, let us go to the Seer." (What we now call "a prophet" was previously called "a seer.")

Saul said to his servant, "That's a good idea, let's go." So, they went toward the town where the man of God was located. Along the way, they found some young women coming out to get water. Saul and the servant asked them, "Is the seer in this place?"

One of the young women answered, "Yes, he is here, he is straight ahead, in the direction you are going. Hurry, because he has just arrived in town today. The people will offer a sacrifice at the place of worship today. When you go into that town, you will find him, before he goes up to the place of worship to eat. The people will not begin eating until the seer comes. He must bless the sacrifice. After that, the invited guests will eat. So go on now, and you will find him today."

So Saul and the servant went up to the town. Just as they were entering the town, they saw Samuel. He was coming out of town toward them. He was on his way up to the place of worship.

The day before Saul came, the Lord had told Samuel: "About this time tomorrow, I will send a man to you. He will be from the tribe of Benjamin. You must anoint him as prince over my people, Israel. He will save My people from the domination of the Philistines, because I have seen My people suffer, and I have listened to their cry."

When Samuel first saw Saul, the Lord told Samuel, "This is the man I told you about. This is the one who will rule over My people."

At the gate, Saul came close to Samuel, and asked, "Could you please tell me where is the seer's house?"

Samuel answered, "I am the seer. Go ahead of me to the place of worship. You and your servant are supposed to eat with me today. Tomorrow morning I will send you home and I will answer all your questions. Do not worry about the donkeys that you lost three days ago. They have been found. The people of Israel now desire you and your father's entire family."

Saul answered, "But I am from the tribe of Benjamin. It is the smallest tribe in Israel. And my clan is the least important one within the tribe of Benjamin. Why have you spoken like this?"

Then Samuel took Saul and his servant boy and brought them into a large banquet room. He gave them the important place at the head of the table, over the invited ones at the table. There were about 30 guests. Samuel said to the cook, "Bring the meat which I gave you. It is the portion which I told you to set aside."

So the cook got the leg and placed it on the table in front of Saul. Samuel said, "Look, this is the meat which was reserved for you. Eat it, because it was set aside for you for this special time. I have invited these people for this occasion." So Saul ate with Samuel that day.

Later, they came down from the place of worship into the town. Then Samuel talked with Saul on the roof of his house. They got up early—at dawn—and Samuel called to Saul who spent the night on the roof. Samuel said, "Get up, so that I may send you on your way." So Saul got up. Along with Samuel, Saul left the house. Saul, the servant boy, and Samuel were getting close to the edge of town, so Samuel said to Saul, "Tell the servant boy to go on ahead of us. But you stop here for awhile. I have a special message for you from God."

My Time to Pray

Saul Began Well ~ First Samuel 9

"Come let's go to the Seer, who we now call a prophet" (1 Samuel 9:9).

At the beginning of Saul's ministry, he went searching for a prophet to hear from God. At the end of his ministry he went searching for a witch because God wouldn't hear his prayers. Saul began well but ended up in spiritual bankruptcy. Read carefully the life of Saul to see the seeds of backsliding, then determine to do things differently and be different. *Lord, I will study carefully how this man corrupted himself, and I will think differently, and do things differently, so I will not backslide.*

God gave Saul a number of confirming signs that should have convinced Saul to diligently seek the Lord. First, when Saul was coming into the town, Samuel met him coming out of the town. A special meal was prepared for him and a banquet before Saul planned to be present. Saul got to eat with the prophet, then slept on the roof of the prophet's home. *Lord, I will look for Your hand working in my life in small circumstantial ways.*

God loves weak things, He chose Saul from the smallest tribe—Benjamin. Also, Saul was from the least family in the tribe—the family of Kish. "When you Saul were little in your own eyes" (1 Sam. 15:17). Doesn't the Scripture tell us, "God has chosen the weak things of this world…that no flesh should glory in His presence" (1 Cor. 1:27,29). *Lord, I know I am not strong; use me in Your plan. I know I am not wise or mighty; use me to accomplish Your will, then get all the glory.*

If God will choose a young man who goes looking for his father's donkeys, God can use you. Probably, God has a greater plan for your life, than you have even thought about. Seek God's plan and when you find it, do God's will with all your heart. *Lord, I want to be used of You; use me today. Lord, I want to accomplish something greater with my life than what I'm doing now; anoint me for service. Lord, stretch me...fill me...guide me...and use me.*

Amen.

10

SAUL BECOMES KING

FIRST SAMUEL 10

Then Samuel took a small container of olive oil, and he poured the oil on Saul's head. (This act is the Jewish inauguration of a man to be king, thus making him the earthly representative of the heavenly King, God. The word "Messiah" ["Christ"] means "the anointed one.") He kissed Saul and said, "The Lord has just appointed you to be the leader of His people Israel. After you leave me today, you will meet two men. They will be near Rachel's tomb, on the boundary line of the tribe of Benjamin at Zelzah. They will tell you: 'The female donkeys that you were searching for have been found. But now your father has stopped being concerned about his donkeys. He is worrying about you. He is asking, "What should I do about my son?"'"

Samuel continued, "Then you will go on from there until you reach the oak tree at Tabor. Three men will meet you there. They will be on their way up to worship the one true God at Bethel. One man will be carrying three little goats. One man will be carrying three loaves of bread. And the third man will be carrying a leather bag of wine. They will greet you and they will offer you two loaves of bread. You must accept the bread from them. After that, you will go to Gibeah-ha-Elohim, 'the Hill of the One True God.' There is a Philistine fort there. When you come near this town, a group of prophets will come out, going down from the place of worship. And they will be playing a harp, a tambourine, a flute, and a lyre. And they will be prophesying. The Spirit of the Lord will be powerful on you—and you will prophesy with these prophets. You will be transformed into a different person. After these signs come true for you, do whatever you find to do. (This means that Saul was supposed to take whatever appropriate action deemed by God.) God will help you.

Go on down to Gilgal ahead of me. I will come down to you later. Then I will offer whole burnt offerings and sacrifice peace offerings. But you must wait for seven days. Then I will come to you and tell you what you are to do."

When Saul turned his back to leave Samuel, God changed Saul's heart. All of these signs came true that day. When Saul and his servant arrived at Gibeah, Saul did meet a group of prophets. And the Spirit of God came over Saul in a powerful way. He did prophesy among the prophets. People who had known Saul in the past saw him prophesying with the prophets. They asked each other, "What has happened to the son of Kish? Is Saul also one of the prophets?" (This was a proverbial statement of surprise. Saul was known for becoming the first king of Israel; he was not known for being a prophet.)

A local man answered, "Who is his father?" This became a famous saying: "Is Saul also one of the prophets?" When Saul finished prophesying, he went to the place of worship.

Saul's uncle asked him and his servant boy, "Where did you go?"

Saul answered, "We were searching for the female donkeys. When we could not find them, we went to talk to Samuel."

Saul's uncle asked, "Tell me what Samuel said to you."

Saul answered his uncle, "He told us plainly that the female donkeys had already been found!" However, Saul did not tell his uncle what Samuel had said about his becoming king.

Then Samuel called for all the people of Israel to meet with the Lord at Mizpah. (The purpose of this assembly was to reveal God's choice to the people of Israel and to define what the new king could and could not do.) Samuel said to the Israelites, "This is what the Lord, the God of Israel, says: 'I brought Israel up out of Egypt. I saved you from the power of the Egyptians and from the power of all the other kingdoms that oppressed you.' However, today, you have rejected your God. He saves you from all your troubles and problems. But you said to Him, 'No, put a human king over us.' Now come, stand in the presence of the Lord—arrange yourselves by your tribes and by your clans."

So Samuel brought all the tribes of Israel near. And the tribe of Benjamin was chosen. Samuel made them pass—clan by clan. And Matri's family was chosen. Then he caused each man of Matri's family to pass by, and Saul, the son of Kish, was chosen. But when they searched for Saul, they could not find him. Then they inquired from the Lord again: "Has Saul come here yet?"

The Lord said, "Yes. Look, he is hiding behind the baggage."

So they ran and got him out of there. When Saul stood among the people, he was a head taller than anyone else. Then Samuel said to all the people, "Do you see the man whom the Lord has chosen? There is no one like him among all the people."

Then all the people shouted, "Long live the king!"

Samuel explained the duties of being king. He wrote down the rules in the charter, and placed the book in the presence of the Lord. (This legal document was preserved in the sanctuary of the

Tabernacle.) Then Samuel told all the people to go to their homes.

Saul also went to his home in Gibeah. God touched the hearts of some brave men to join Saul. But some troublemakers (sons of Belial) said, "How can this man save us?" They hated Saul and refused to bring gifts to him. However, Saul kept silent.

My Time to Pray

First Samuel 10

Whose name was Saul, a choice young man and a godly: there were not among the children of Israel a godlier person than he (1 Samuel 9:2).

Samuel begins writing a detailed description telling how wise the choice was for Saul to be the first king of Israel. The author goes into vivid detail to demonstrate that Saul *could* have been a great choice for God's people. Did you see that conditional word *could*? Saul *could* have been a great king, but by the time we come to the end of First Samuel we will see how a meek and humble Saul turns selfish, mean, and under the influence of a "demonic" witch. *Lord, thank You for this explanation.*

The story of Saul demonstrates the power of sin. At the beginning, Saul prophesizes (1 Sam. 10:6,11) singing joyfully the psalms and praising God. At the end, he sneaks into the home of a demonic witch because God will no longer hear Saul or speak to Saul. *Lord, may I never depart from You.*

Saul began as a good man, no one in Israel was better than him. God gave Saul confirmatory signs that should have kept Saul on a narrow track. First, God told him he'd find two men at Rachael's tomb (1 Sam. 10:2). Second, God told him he'd meet three men going to Bethel who would give him two loaves of bread (1 Sam. 10:3). Third, God told Saul he would prophesy among the prophets (1 Sam. 10:5-6). What happened, "All the signs came about that day" (1 Sam. 10:9). Saul should have been able to trust God because of these confirmatory signs. *Lord, I will obey You whether or not You give me signs.*

Do we see doubt early on in Saul? When Saul met his uncle, the uncle asked, "Tell me what Samuel said to you" (1 Sam. 10:15). When we are silent about what God is doing in our lives, is that the first sign of backsliding? "Saul did not tell him what Samuel had said about the matter of kingship" (1 Sam. 10:16). *Lord, may I always speak for You.*

Samuel brought all of Israel to Mizpah for the election of a new King. Saul hid among the baggage. Is that any way for a man to act who has been anointed by God? A representation for each of the 12 tribes walked in front of Samuel and the lot was cast. God chose the tribe of Benjamin, then each family head of Benjamin walked in front of Samuel and again the lot was cast; God chose the clan of Matri. When all the Matri family heads appeared, God chose Kish and when the lot was chosen for the sons of Kish, Saul was chosen. Was it humility for Saul to hide? Probably not. Was Saul denying the will of God? Probably. *Lord, I will appear where I am supposed to be.*

When God calls, your only answer is "Here am I." When God has a job to do, your only answer is "Send me." *Lord, send me.*

Amen.

11

SAUL RESCUES JABESH-GILEAD

FIRST SAMUEL 11

About one month later, Nahash the Ammonite and his army surrounded the city of Jabesh in Gilead. All the people of Jabesh said to Nahash, "Make a treaty with us, and we will serve you (pay taxes to you)."

But he answered them, "I will make a pact with you...on one condition—that I can gouge out the right eye of each one of you. I want to humiliate all Israel."

The elders of Jabesh said to Nahash, "Leave us alone for seven days. We still send messengers throughout all the territory of Israel. If there is no one to come save us, we will surrender to you."

The messengers came to Gibeah, Saul's hometown. When they told the people the news, the people cried loudly. They wept. Saul had just finished plowing in the fields with his oxen. When he heard the people crying, he asked, "What's wrong with them? Why are the people crying?" Then they told him the words of the people of Jabesh. When Saul heard these words, the Spirit of God came over him in a powerful way. He became very angry. Then Saul got his team of oxen, killed them, and cut them up into pieces. Then he gave those pieces of the oxen to the messengers. He ordered them to carry the pieces throughout all the land of Israel.

The messengers made this announcement to the people: "This is what will happen to the oxen of anyone who does not follow Saul and Samuel." In this way, the Lord shocked the people. They all came together as if they were one man. Saul gathered them together at Bezek. The Israelites numbered 300,000 strong; the men from the tribe of Judah alone was 30,000.

They said to the messengers who had come, "Tell this to the people at Jabesh-Gilead: 'When the day gets hot tomorrow, you *will* be rescued.'" So the messengers went and reported this to the people of Jabesh. They were extremely happy. The people of Jabesh said to Nahash and his army, "Tomorrow we will come out to you, and you can do whatever you want to us."

The next morning, Saul separated his soldiers into three groups. They broke into the Ammonite camp at dawn, and they struck down the Ammonites until the day got hot. The Ammonites who were still alive were scattered. Not even two of them remained together.

Then the people said to Samuel, "Who said: 'Will Saul rule over us?' Surrender those men, and we will kill them."

But Saul said, "No! No one will be executed today, because the Lord has caused this deliverance in Israel today."

Then Samuel said to the people, "Come, let us go to Gilgal. We will recommit ourselves to the kingdom." So all the people went to Gilgal. And there, in the presence of the Lord, the people confirmed Saul as king. They also offered peace offerings in the presence of the Lord. And there Saul and all the men of Israel had a big banquet.

My Time to Pray

More Seeds of Backsliding

There was Saul, coming behind the herd from the field (1 Samuel 11:5).

When Saul became king, he should have acted like a king, and done the work of a king. But the chapter begins with him plowing in his father's field with oxen. Doesn't sound like a king to me. Could we call Saul the *reluctant king?* Could we say that if Saul had taken the authority of king and raised an army, the opposing king—Nahash of Ammon—would have attacked the city of Jabesh-Gilead? Shouldn't Saul have been reigning on a throne and with his strong presence, protecting his people from an attack by an evil king? *Lord, I not only will try to wipe out sin, I will also try to prevent sin from attacking me and other believers.*

Next we see the anger of a king. Now it's all right to get mad at sin, but why was Saul angry? People should follow their king out of love and respect, but in the story they follow because, "The people were afraid of Saul's anger" (1 Sam. 11:7 LB). A leader who makes people fear him only gets fellowship for a limited realm and for a limited time. While fear is a great motivator, there are better, positive ways to motivate followers. *Lord, I will follow You because I love You. Out of gratitude I will serve You whole-heartedly. After all Christ has done for me, how can I do less than give Him my best?*

God works through our strengths and weaknesses. God used King Saul to deliver the city of Jabesh-Gilead. Saul got his first great victory in battle, and the enemy was defeated, "No two of them were left together" (1 Sam. 11:11). No one is perfect, and we all serve God through our imperfections. The wonderful thing about the grace of God is that He takes who we are, and He fills what we give Him, then uses it in His service. *Lord, I don't have much but what I have I give to You. Use me according to Your usefulness. Make me better than I am, and help me to accomplish more than I could without Your power working through me.*

Notice the result of Saul's victory, "They went to Gilgal and in a solemn ceremony before the Lord and they crowned him king" (1 Sam. 11:15). It took a victory for the people to fully recognize Saul as their king. First, Samuel had anointed him at God's direction (1 Sam. 10:1). Second, the people proclaimed him king when God used the Urim and Thummin to find Saul hiding among the baggage (1 Sam. 10:22-24). Think what a victory will do for your life and ministry. A victory will make you realize that God is working in you. But also, a victory will demonstrate to others that God is working through you. *Lord, give me victory over sin in my life. Then give me victory over circumstances, and finally, give me victory in my service for You.*

Amen.

12

SAMUEL MAKES A SPEECH TO ISRAEL

FIRST SAMUEL 12

Then Samuel said to all Israel, "Behold, I have listened to everything
you wanted me to do. I have put a human king over you. Now,
look, the king is leading you, but I am old and gray. Look, my
sons are with you, too. Since I was young, testify against me in
the presence of the Lord and his anointed king. Have I stolen
anyone's ox? Whose donkey did I take? Since very young—until
today—I have led you. Have I done anything wrong, cheated
anyone, or taken advantage of anyone? Did I ever secretly take a
bribe and then pretend not to see that something was wrong? If
I did any of these things, I will pay it back to you."

They answered, "You have not cheated us. You never took advantage of
us. You have never taken a bribe from anyone."

Samuel said to them, "The Lord is witness to what you have said. His
anointed king is also a witness today. They are both witnesses
that you have not found anything wrong in me."

They said, "Yes, that is true."

Then Samuel said to the people, "It was Yahweh who chose Moses
and Aaron. He brought your ancestors up out of the land of
Egypt. Now, stand there, so that I can remind you regarding all

the good things that Yahweh has done for you and for your ancestors:

After Jacob entered Egypt, your ancestors cried out to the Lord for help. So the Lord sent Moses and Aaron. They brought your ancestors out of Egypt, and the Lord caused them to live in this place.

However, they forgot the Lord their God. So he allowed them to become the slaves of Sisera. He was the commander of the army of Jabin, king of Hazor. The Lord also allowed them to become the slaves of the Philistines and the king of Moab. They all fought against your ancestors. Then your ancestors cried out to the Lord for help. They said, 'We have sinned. We have abandoned the Lord. We have served the Baals and the Ashtoreths. Nevertheless, save us now from our enemies, and we will serve You.'

So the Lord sent Gideon. And He sent Barak, Jephthah, and me, Samuel. He saved you from the hands of your enemies who surrounded you. And you lived in safety. But when you saw Nahash, the king of the Ammonites, coming against you, you said to me, 'No, we want a human king to rule over us!' Even though the Lord, you God, was your King. Now, here is the king whom you chose, whom you begged for. Look, the Lord has put a human king over you. You must revere the Lord and serve Him. You must obey His commands. You must not rebel against the Lord's authority. Both you and the king who is ruling over you must follow the Lord, your God. If you do, it will go well with you.

But if you will not obey the Lord, and if you rebel against His authority, then the hand of the Lord will be against you as He was against your ancestors. Now stand still and see the great thing which the Lord is about to do in front of your very eyes. Today, it is the time of the wheat harvest, isn't it? I will pray for the Lord to send thunder and rain. Then you will realize what an evil thing you have done against the Lord when you asked for a human king for yourselves."

Then Samuel prayed to the Lord and that same day, the Lord sent thunder and rain. And all the people became very afraid of the Lord and Samuel. The people then said to Samuel, "Pray to the Lord your God for us. Don't let us die. We have added this evil to all of our other sins when we asked for a human king for ourselves."

Samuel answered the people, "Do not be afraid. It is true that you have done all this evil, but you must not turn away from following the Lord. Serve the Lord with all your hearts. Idols are worthless, so do not worship them. They cannot help you or save you. They are useless. The Lord will not abandon His people, because His name is great. The Lord resolves to make you a special people for Himself. I will certainly not stop praying for you. If I did, I would be sinning against the Lord. I will continue to teach you the path that is good and right. However, you must revere the Lord. You must always serve Him in truth—with all your hearts. Remember the wonderful things that He has done for you. But if you are still stubborn and do evil, He will sweep you and your king away."

My Time to Pray

The Good Testimony

I am old and grey-headed, and look, my sons are with you (1 Samuel 12:2).

Samuel gathered all Israel together and reminded them of his faithfulness. He challenged the people, "Witness against me before the Lord"

(1 Sam. 12:3). Samuel didn't claim to be sinless, but he was blameless. None of us can be perfect, because "all have sinned" (Rom. 3:23). But we can be blameless, which means we don't intentionally sin, and we can seriously try to keep every law of God. Even Paul, probably the man who most tried to live closer to God than anyone else, had to say at the end of his "blameless" life, "I am the chief of sinners" (1 Tim. 1:15). *Lord, I will try to be blameless, but I know my deceitful heart (Jer. 17:11), keep me from presumptuous sins (Ps. 19:13 KJV). Lord, give me strength to overcome temptation, and give me a pure heart. When I do fall into sin, forgive me and cleanse me with Your blood (1 John 1:7).*

Earlier the people criticized Samuel to his face because of the sins of his sons. "Thy sons walk not in thy ways" (1 Sam. 8:5). The Bible says, "His sons took bribes and perverted justice" (1 Sam. 8:3). We don't know how Samuel did it—the story doesn't tell—but Samuel straightened out his "boys." As a result Samuel stood before the people to testify that he and his sons were blameless. This is commendable, because the Book of First Samuel begins with the evil sons of old Eli the high priest. Eli couldn't handle his sons and didn't put them out of the priesthood. So God replaced Eli with Samuel. *Lord, I thank You for Samuel dealing rightly with his sons. Lord, may we all have the testimony of a godly family.*

Did you see the place of prayer in the ministry of Samuel? Samuel says, "Far be it from me that I should sin against the Lord, by ending my prayers for you" (1 Sam. 12:23). Prayerlessness is not a sin against the people you lead; it is a sin against God. Samuel had the integrity to testify that he had continually prayed for those he led. Can you say that? *Lord, I will pray continually for my family, leaders, and those I lead. I want to become effective in prayer; teach me to pray.*

Amen.

13

SAUL SINNED AT GILGAL

FIRST SAMUEL 13

Saul was 30 years old when he became king. He was king over Israel
for 42 years. Saul chose for himself 3,000 soldiers from Israel.
There were 2,000 men who were with him at Michmash in the
mountains of Bethel. And 1,000 men were with Jonathan (Saul's
oldest son) at Gibeah in the territory of Benjamin. Saul sent all
the rest of the men back home.

Jonathan attacked the Philistine fort in Geba. And the other Philistines
heard about it. Saul said, "Let the Hebrew people hear what has
happened!" So he told the men to blow trumpets throughout all
the land of Israel. All Israel heard the news: "Saul has attacked
the Philistine fort. Now the Philistines will truly hate Israel."
Then the Israelite army was called out to follow Saul at Gilgal.

And the Philistines gathered to fight Israel. They had 3,000 chariots and
6,000 charioteers. The number of their soldiers was very large,
like the grains of sand on the beach. The Philistines came and
camped at Michmash, which is east of Beth-Aven. The Israelites
saw that they were outnumbered and that they were in trouble.
So they hid in caves, in holes, in rocky crags, in pits, and in cis-
terns. Some Hebrews decided to cross the Jordan River over to
the land of Gad and Gilead.

However, Saul was still staying at Gilgal. All of his army was trembling with fear, though they still followed him. Saul waited for seven days, because Samuel had said he would meet Saul at that time. But Samuel did not come to Gilgal right away. And Saul's soldiers began to scatter.

So Saul said, "Bring me the whole burnt offering and the peace offerings." Then Saul offered the whole burnt offerings. (It was forbidden for Saul to do this; he was *not* Samuel, who was authorized to do so as a judge and a priest.) Just as Saul finished offering the burnt offering, Samuel arrived. Saul went out to meet and greet him.

Samuel asked, "What have you done?"

Saul answered, "I saw that the soldiers were abandoning me, and you did not come on time. And the Philistines were gathering at Michmash. So I thought, 'The Philistines will come down against me at Gilgal. And I had not asked for the Lord's approval.' Therefore, I forced myself to offer the whole burnt offering."

But Samuel said to Saul, "You have acted foolishly. You have not obeyed the Lord your God's command that He gave to you. If you had obeyed Him, then the Lord would have caused your kingdom to continue in Israel forever. But now your kingdom will not last. The Lord is searching for a man after His own heart. The Lord has given the order that another man be a prince over His people. The Lord is doing this because you have not obeyed His command."

Then Samuel got up and left Gilgal. He went up to Gibeah in the territory of Benjamin. Saul gathered together what was still left of his army—only about 600 men.

Saul and his son Jonathan stayed in Geba in the territory of Benjamin. Saul's soldiers who were still following him stayed there, too. The Philistines camped at Michmash. Three groups of Philistine raiders went out from their camp. One group turned in the direction of Ophrah, toward the land of Shual. The second group turned in the direction of Beth-Horon. And the third group turned in the direction of the boundary line which overlooked the Valley of Zeboyim, facing the desert.

The Philistines Possessed the Technology; Israel Did Not

No metal-worker existed in all the land of Israel, because the Philistines had said, "The Hebrews must not make swords or spears." Therefore, all Israel went down to the Philistine metal-workers so that they could have their plows, hoes, axes, and sickles sharpened. The Philistine metal-workers charged about a quarter of an ounce of silver for sharpening plows and hoes. And they charged one-eighth of an ounce of silver for sharpening picks, axes, and the metal-tipped sticks used for prodding oxen.

So when the day for battle came, the Hebrew soldiers who were with Saul and Jonathan had no swords or spears in their hands (only bows, arrows, and slingshots). Only Saul and his son Jonathan possessed some swords and spears. The outpost group from the Philistine army had gone out to the mountain pass at Michmash.

My Time to Pray

Waiting for God to Show Up ~ First Samuel 13

"When I saw that the people were scattered from me, and that you did not come within the days appointed, and that the Philistines

gathered together at Michmash," then I said, "The Philistines will now come down on me at Gilgal, and I have not made supplication to the Lord. Therefore I felt compelled, and offered a burnt offering" (1 Samuel 13:11-12).

Have you ever done the right thing for the wrong reason? Maybe you attended church for a business deal. Maybe you prayed for someone to get saved to satisfy your selfish desire. Maybe you served the Lord for pride. That was Saul's problem, doing a good thing in the wrong way. He was not supposed to sacrifice, he wasn't a Levite. Only the priests were to offer the blood sacrifice to cover sin. But Saul was in trouble, and his army was in trouble, so he sought the Lord's blessing. He sacrificed, doing a good thing the wrong way. *Lord, keep me from presumptuous sins.*

Samuel was supposed to meet Saul in Gilgal where the old priest would offer sacrifices before King Saul went into battle against the Philistines. The Bible describes Saul's soldiers were "trembling" (1 Sam. 13:7). Can you imagine waiting seven days, all the while not knowing if the Philistines would attack at any moment? To Saul's credit, he didn't want to fight if he were not spiritually ready.

Modern people in the 21st century are *time focused*. We understand keeping schedules. We hate to wait. Saul was no different. He was in a hurry to get God's canopy over his "project." Have you ever been in such a hurry to get God's blessing that you couldn't wait on God the Blesser? Sometimes we put a program before prayer and put an organization before agonizing in prayer. Samuel was late, Saul was anxious; but the issue is not time—it's God. *Lord, teach me patience.*

We talk ourselves into doing the will of God in the wrong way. Saul told Samuel all the reasons why he had to sacrifice. Finally the rebellious Saul said, "I felt compelled" (1 Sam. 13:12). He had convinced himself that *wrong* was *right*. Isn't that what I do and you do; we give our reasons, but we make our choices apart from God. Saul wasn't close enough to God to hear Him speak. Think of all the things you have to do today. You've already got them planned. Your agenda is set. Now you come into *His Daily Presence*. As you pray, don't force your schedule on God. Be quiet before Him. Listen! Let God tell you what He wants you to do today. *Lord, I wait on You.*

Saul's life could have been transformed if he had waited. "Wait on the Lord" (Ps. 27:14). Instead of fretting about Samuel being late, and worrying about the Philistine army that was much larger than his, Saul should have been concerned with God. If Saul were rightly related to God, everything else would have fallen into place. Think about the times you ran ahead of God and did things in the flesh. Have you, like Samuel, gotten yourself in a mess because you didn't wait on God? *Yes, Lord, I've run ahead of You. Forgive me.*

Notice God's timing—"As soon" (1 Sam. 13:10). As soon as Saul disobeyed God, Samuel showed up. Isn't that the way it usually happens? Saul couldn't wait, he just couldn't obey God. Within minutes of Saul's disobedience, Samuel shows up. God was not testing Saul's patience, God was testing Saul's obedience. "As soon" as Saul disobeyed, Samuel walks in to ask "What have you done?" Watch for God's timing in your life. You may not have a patience problem, you may have an obedience problem. *Lord, teach me obedience.*

"What have you done?" Samuel asked. Isn't that God's usual way of confronting us? God doesn't ask questions to find out what we've done wrong. He knows what we've done. God asks a question to get us to think about our disobedience. What have you done today?

This story is about complete disobedience, not partial obedience, nor delayed obedience. God wants to walk with you, and listen to you, and God wants you to wait on Him. It's not our service He's looking for, it's our fellowship. God tells us to meet Him each day, He'll be there. Don't worry about the things we do for God, be concerned with Him. *Lord, I'll obey; I'll meet You each day.*

Amen.

14

JONATHAN ATTACKS THE PHILISTINES

FIRST SAMUEL 14

Then the day came when Jonathan, Saul's son, spoke to the young man who carried his weapons. Jonathan said, "Come, let's go over to the Philistine outpost that is on the other side." (However, Jonathan did not tell his father.)

Saul was sitting under the pomegranate tree at the edge of Gibeah. He had about 600 men with him. One man was Ahijah, who was the son of Ahitub, Ichabod's brother. Ichabod was the son of Phinehas, Eli's son. Eli had been the high priest of the Lord at Shiloh. He had worn the ephod. (No one knew Jonathan had gone.)

Now there were very steep slopes on both sides of the pass. Jonathan planned to go through the pass to the Philistine outpost. The cliff on one side was named "Bozez." The other cliff was called "Seneh." One of the cliffs was facing north toward Michmash. The other cliff was facing south, toward Geba.

Jonathan said to the young man who carried his weapons, "Come, let us cross over to the outpost of those men who are not circumcised. Perhaps the Lord will help us. It does not matter to the Lord whether we have many soldiers or only a few. The Lord can give us a victory."

The one who carried Jonathan's armor said, "Do whatever is in your heart. Go ahead, I am with you. It's your decision."

Jonathan said, "Listen, we will cross over to the Philistines, then we will reveal ourselves to them. If they say to us, 'Wait there until we get to you,' then we will stay put; we will not go up to them. But if they say, 'Come up to us,' then we will climb up farther, because the Lord has given us the victory over them. That will be the sign for us."

Both of them showed themselves to the men of the Philistine outpost. And the Philistines said, "Look, Hebrews are coming out of the holes where they were hiding." Then the Philistines in that outpost shouted to Jonathan and the one who carried his weapons, "Come up here to us, we will teach you something."

So Jonathan said to his helper, "Climb up behind me. The Lord has given the victory to Israel." So Jonathan climbed up high, using his hands and feet. His helper was right behind him. And Jonathan cut them down one by one as he went. And his helper finished them off (gave the death blow) as he followed behind Jonathan. Jonathan and his helper killed about 20 Philistines in that first fight, within an area of about half an acre.

The ground itself shook. All the Philistine soldiers, and those in the main camp and those among the raiders panicked. God caused this general panic to occur.

The lookouts of Saul in Gibeah-Benjamin were watching and saw the Philistine camp was in a state of complete confusion. So Saul said to his army that was with him, "Do a roll call and see who is missing." They did, and found Jonathan and his helper were gone.

Then Saul said to Ahijah, "Bring the ephod of the one true God." It had been restored to the Israelites at that time. And while Saul was

still speaking to Ahijah the priest, the disturbance in the
Philistine camp got worse and worse. So Saul said to the priest,
"Stop what you are doing."

Then Saul quickly organized all the soldiers who were with him and
went to fight the Philistines because there was a great panic
among the Philistines—they were killing each other. Before this
time, there were some Hebrews who were forced to work for the
Philistines. These Hebrews had gone up with the Philistines and
were everywhere in the Philistine camp. These Hebrews servants
joined Israel's army, with Saul and Jonathan. Then all the men of
Israel who had been hiding in the hill-country of Ephraim heard
that the Philistines were retreating. So they also chased the
Philistines after the battle. So on that day, the Lord saved Israel.
And the conflict moved on past Beth-Aven.

Jonathan Eats Honey

Now the Israelites were hard pressed that day. Why? Because Saul
forced his soldiers to take an oath. Saul said, "I must get the victory over my enemies. Any of my men who eats food before
nightfall is cursed. You soldiers must fast." A big forest was
there; and much honey had dripped onto the ground. Saul's
army came into the forest, and saw honey flowing everywhere.
Nevertheless, no soldier ate any of the honey. They were afraid
of Saul's curse. But Jonathan never heard about the oath which
his father made his soldiers vow. Jonathan reached out with the
tip of the rod that was in his hand and dipped it into the honey-
comb. Then he ate some of the honey. Immediately, he felt
refreshed. Later, a soldier told Jonathan, "Your father forced us to
take this vow: 'The man who eats any food today is cursed.'
Because of this, the army is very weak."

Jonathan said, "My father is hurting my countrymen. Look how I have perked up because I ate a little honey. How much better it would have been today if our fellow soldiers had been permitted to eat freely from the plunder which they got from their enemies. By now, we could have killed many more Philistines."

On that day, the Israelites struck down the Philistines from Michmash to Aijalon. However, the Israelites became very weak because of the lack of energy. They had captured plunder from the Philistines—sheep, oxen, and calves. That night, they began killing the animals on the ground, not draining the blood. The soldiers ate the meat raw, with the blood still in it. (This was strictly forbidden by God's law.) This was reported to Saul: "The soldiers are sinning against the Lord by eating the meat with the blood still in it."

Saul said, "You have committed a terrible wrong. Roll a large stone over here for me now." (This was necessary to get the dead animals up off the ground so that the blood could drain out of the carcasses.) "Go out among the soldiers and tell them that each man must bring me his ox or his lamb and butcher them right here to drain off the blood. Then they can eat that meat. But do not sin against the Lord by eating meat with blood still in it." That night, everyone in the army led his ox to that spot and butchered it. Then Saul built an altar to the Lord. (It was the first altar that Saul ever built to the Lord.)

Then Saul said, "Let's go down after the Philistines tonight. We will take more plunder from them until daylight. We will kill them all."

And the soldiers said, "Do whatever you think is best."

But the priest said, "Let us ask God first" (by the means of the Urim and Thummim). So, Saul tried to get an answer from God: "Should I go down after the Philistines now? Will You give us the victory?" However, the Lord did not answer Saul that day.

So Saul said, "Bring all the leaders of the army here. Today we must find out what sin has occurred to cause this silence from God. As surely as the Lord lives, the One who saves Israel, even if the cause is in my son Jonathan, he will surely die." But none of the soldiers said anything to Saul, they knew that Jonathan had eaten some food.

Then Saul said to all Israel, "All of you must stand on one side, and my son Jonathan and I will stand on the other side."

The army said to Saul, "Do whatever you think is best."

Then Saul prayed to the Lord, the God of Israel, "Give me a clear answer." And the lot showed that it was on Jonathan and Saul's side; the army was not chosen. Then Saul said, "Now, show whether it is me or my son Jonathan." And, Jonathan was chosen by lot.

Then Saul said to Jonathan, "Tell me what you did."

So Jonathan told him, "I did taste a little honey with the end of the rod which was in my hand. Here I am. Must I die?"

Saul answered, "Yes. God will punish me if you are not put to death."

But the army said to Saul, "Should Jonathan die? Never. He is the one who won this great victory in Israel. As surely as the Lord lives, nothing bad is going to happen to Jonathan. It was Jonathan who cooperated with God today." So the army rescued Jonathan; he did not die.

Then Saul quit chasing the Philistines, and they retreated to their own territory.

King Saul Fought Other Enemies of Israel

After Saul had taken charge of the kingdom over Israel, he fought
against all his enemies that surrounded him—against Moab,
against the Ammonites, against Edom, against the kings of
Zobah, and against the Philistines. Wherever Saul turned, he
defeated them. Saul was a strong warrior. He also struck down
the Amalekites. He rescued Israel from the control of those who
were plundering them.

Saul's Family

The sons of Saul were: Jonathan, Ishvi, and Malchishua. He had two
daughters, his firstborn was Merab, and the name of the younger
one was Michal. Saul's wife's name was Ahinoam; she was the
daughter of Ahimaaz. The name of the commander of his army
was Abner, the son of Ner, Saul's uncle. Kish was Saul's father,
and Ner was Abner's father. Kish and Ner were sons of Abiel.
Throughout Saul's rule, a bitter war continued against the
Philistines. Whenever Saul noticed any strong or brave warrior,
Saul drafted him into the personal guard.

My Time to Pray

Perceptions Lead to Expectations ᴄ First Samuel 14

*Nothing can hinder the Lord. He can win a battle whether he has
many warriors, or only a few* (1 Samuel 14:8 ELT).

L ife is made up of perceptions and expectations. When we perceive
wrongly, we usually act wrongly. Wasn't that Saul's problem? "Saul
was sitting in the outskirts of Gibeah, under a pomegranate tree" (1 Sam.
14:2). The Philistines were sending raiding parties to ravage the land;

Saul did nothing about it. Saul was anointed king to protect the people, but he did nothing. He didn't blow the sopher for more troops, he didn't attack with the troops he had. It's all right to wait when you wait upon the Lord, but Saul waited in fear. *Lord, You know the reason I'm sometimes frail.*

Saul originally had 3,000 soldiers (1 Sam. 13:2), but he sinned against the Lord in front of his army. Now he has only 600 men (14:2). Look at his *perception*. He felt weak without God, and weak without his larger army. Since *perception* leads to *expectation*, Saul didn't attack the invading Philistine raiding parties. He probably expected to lose. Have you ever waited because you were afraid of losing? Have you ever expected defeat, but you did nothing for God? *Lord, forgive me faulty perceptions.*

Amen.

15

God No Longer Wants
Saul to Be King

First Samuel 15

Samuel said to Saul, "The Lord sent me to anoint you king over His
people, over Israel. Now listen carefully to the sound of the
Lord's words. This is what the Lord of the armies of Heaven
says: 'When the Israelites came out of Egypt, the Amalekites
tried to block their way to Canaan. I will punish the Amalekites
for what they did. Now go attack the Amalekites. Totally destroy
everything that belongs to them. Do not pity them. Do not let
anything live. Put to death the men, the women, the children,
and even the nursing babies. Kill all the cattle and the sheep, the
camels, and the donkeys.'"

So Saul called the army together at Telaim and counted 200,000 foot
soldiers including 10,000 men from the tribe of Judah. Saul
went to the city of Amalek. Then he set up an ambush in the
ravine. He said to the Kenites, "Go away! Get away from the
Amalekites, so that I will not destroy you along with them. You
showed kindness to all the Israelites when they came up from
Egypt." So the Kenites moved away from among the Amalekites.

Then Saul attacked the Amalekites. He fought them from Havilah all the
way to Shur, which is at the eastern border of Egypt. He captured

Agag alive, the king of the Amalekites. But he wiped out all of Agag's army with the edge of the sword. But Saul and the army allowed Agag to live. They also kept alive the best of the flock, the fat cattle, and the rams. They kept every good animal alive. They did not want to destroy them all. But whenever they found an animal that was weak or useless, they killed it.

Then the Lord spoke His word to Samuel: "Saul has turned completely away from following Me. And I am sorry that I made him king. He has not obeyed My commands." Samuel was upset, and he cried out to the Lord all night long.

Early in the morning, Samuel got up to go meet Saul. But someone told Samuel, "Saul has gone to Carmel. And look, he has put up a monument in his own honor. Then Saul crossed over and went down to Gilgal."

When Samuel came, Saul said to him, "May the Lord bless you. I have obeyed the Lord's commands!"

But Samuel said, "Then why do I hear sheep baaing and cattle mooing?"

Saul answered, "The soldiers got them from the Amalekites. They saved the best sheep and cattle to offer them as sacrifices to the Lord your God. But we totally destroyed all the other animals."

"Stop," said Samuel to Saul, "Let me tell you what the Lord said to me last night."

Saul answered Samuel, "Tell me."

Samuel said, "Once you did not think much of yourself. But now you have become the head of the tribes of Israel. The Lord anointed you to be king over Israel. The Lord sent you on a mission. He said, 'Go and completely destroy those evil people, the Amalekites. Make war on them until all of them are dead.' Why didn't you obey the Lord? Why did you take the best things? Why did you do what the Lord said was wrong?"

Saul said, "But I did obey the Lord. I did what the Lord told me to do. I destroyed all the Amalekites. And I brought back Agag, their king. It was the soldiers who took the best sheep and cattle, the best of what was devoted to God, to sacrifice them to the Lord your God at Gilgal."

But Samuel answered, "What pleases the Lord more—burnt offerings and sacrifices? Or obedience to His voice? It is better to obey God than to offer a sacrifice. It is better to pay attention to God than to offer the fat of a male sheep. Refusing to obey is just as bad as the sin of witchcraft. Being stubborn is just as bad as the sin of worshiping idols. Because you have rejected the Lord's command, He now rejects you from being king."

Then Saul said to Samuel, "I have sinned. I did not obey the Lord's commands. I did not do what you told me, because I was afraid of the people. I did what they said instead. Now, I beg you, forgive my sin. Come back with me, so that I may give worship to the Lord."

But Samuel said, "I will not go back with you, because you rejected the word of the Lord. And now He rejects you from being king over Israel."

Yahweh Rejects Saul

As Samuel turned to leave, Saul grabbed Samuel's robe, and it tore. Then Samuel said to him, "The Lord has torn the kingdom of Israel from you today. And He has given it to one of your neighbors, to someone better than you. The Lord is the Glorious One of Israel. He does not lie or change His mind on a whim. He is not a human being, so He doesn't change His mind like people do."

Saul said, "I have sinned! Please show me honor in front of the elders of my people. Please honor me in front of the nation of Israel. Rejoin me, so that I may give worship to the Lord, your God."

Samuel finally decided to reconcile with Saul, and Saul did worship the Lord. Then Samuel said, "Bring me Agag, the king of the Amalekites." Agag was in a good mood when he came to Samuel. Agag thought: *Surely the bitterness of death is gone.*

But Samuel said to Agag, "Your sword has caused mothers to live without their children. Now your mother will be without her son." Then Samuel cut Agag to pieces in the presence of the Lord at Gilgal.

Then Samuel left and went to Ramah. But Saul went up to his home in Gibeah-Saul. And Samuel never saw Saul again for the rest of his life. But Samuel cried for Saul, but the Lord was very sorry that He had made Saul the king over Israel.

My Time to Pray

Listening to the Wrong Voice ᷤ First Samuel 15

So Samuel said: "Has the Lord as great delight in burnt offerings and sacrifices, as in obeying the voice of the Lord? Behold, to obey is better than sacrifice, and to heed than the fat of rams" (1 Samuel 15:22).

When the flesh whispers, do you listen? When the old nature raises up its head, do you enjoy its company? We all have fleshly desires, but as Christians we are not supposed to give in to its temptation. Paul reminds us that we should have "crucified the flesh with its passions and desires" (Gal. 5:24). But we give in to the constant invitations to satisfy the flesh. We're not talking about the physical appetites of food, air, sleep, and the necessities that our body needs. No. The Bible uses the word *flesh* to mean our old nature, to please our ego contrary to the Word of God—sex outside of marriage, addictive alcohol, and drugs that will enslave the body, etc. *Lord, I am a sinner; forgive me.*

The problem was the Amalekites and their King Agag. God told Saul to completely destroy the Amalekites (1 Sam. 15:3). From the beginning, these desert tribes of nomads were a thorn in the side of God's people. They tried to steal the well at Horeb (see Exod. 17) and they attacked a weak Israel when the nation first came out of Egypt (1 Sam. 15:2). Besides that, their filthy sexual practices were a threat to pollute God's people. The Amalekites were to be eliminated once and for all. God's command to Saul, "Utterly destroy all that they have, and do not spare them" (1 Sam. 15:3). *Lord, how can I utterly deny the flesh when I like it so much?*

Amalek, the grandson of Esau (Gen. 36:12) is described in Galatians as the one "born according to the flesh" (Gal. 4:29). Throughout the Bible, the Amalekites are described as a picture of our flesh that tempts us to satisfy its illicit desires. Does the flesh tempt you to sin? How do you deal with your fleshly distractions? *Lord, give me strength to say no.*

Just as God told Saul to get rid of Amalek and all their possessions, so God tells you to get rid of the fleshly appetites that keep you from doing His will. Paul tells us the basis of victory, "Our old sinful selves were crucified with Christ, so that sin might lose its power in our lives" (Rom. 6:6 NLB). Since God put your old flesh to death positionally, why don't you put it to death actually? Why don't you deny the flesh any control over your life? What have you done this week to "crucify" its desires? *Lord, it's so hard to say "no" to the flesh.*

Saul went to battle with the Amalekites and defeated them. That's good. But Saul only defeated Amalek, he did not eliminate him. But God knew about Saul's incomplete obedience. God told his prophet Samuel that Saul had only partially obeyed, so God sent Samuel to confront King Saul. The way that Saul responded to the prophet Samuel is just the way you and I respond to God when He confronts us about the flesh. *Lord, thank You for confronting me when I sin.*

When Saul saw Samuel coming, the king blurts out, "I have performed the commandments of the Lord." It sounds like us singing, "I surrender all," when we actually keep the flesh hidden from God. Notice what Samuel said, "What then is this bleating of the sheep in my ears" (1 Sam. 15:14). God says to you, "If you've crucified the flesh, why do you still feed this sin-animal that you're trying to hide from me?" You keep your sin hidden from family and the church. Yet you sneak off to the pen where it's hidden to play with it. No one knows you're addicted to this fleshly habit, but you're feeding that fleshly animal. *Lord, I've got a problem.*

Samuel doesn't accept Saul's excuses. The old prophet says, "Why then did you not obey the voice of the Lord?" (1 Sam. 15:19). You should answer the same question today, "Why have you not put your fleshly habit to death?" Notice Saul's answer. "The people took of the plunder, sheep and oxen, the best of the things which should have been utterly destroyed, to sacrifice to the Lord your God in Gilgal" (1 Sam. 15:21). King Saul blamed others. Who do you blame for your sin? Do you blame a friend, a family member, or do you blame complete strangers because you are constantly tempted? Saul tried to tell Samuel the people couldn't keep their hands off the possessions, money, clothes, animals. Do you blame something for tempting you to sin when in fact the blame rests with you? You haven't crucified that temptation. You have a little fleshly animal hidden in the pen of your heart. You don't crucify that desire because you like it too much. When you are tempted, it makes you feel good. *Lord, I confess my addiction to sin.*

The "fleshly stuff" of the Amelekites was to be offered to God as a burnt sacrifice. But it wasn't stuff that God wanted. No! "Has the Lord as great delight in burnt offerings and sacrifices?" (1 Sam. 15:22). No! God wants obedience. God wants you to choose His way and to obey His command. The issue is not the fleshly "thing" you have hidden in your heart. The issue is God. He wants your heart. Will you obey Him? *Lord, come into my heart; like in my life, take complete control.*

Amen.

16

SAMUEL SECRETLY ANOINTS DAVID TO BE THE NEW KING

FIRST SAMUEL 16

Then the Lord said to Samuel, "How long will you continue to feel sorry for Saul? I have rejected him from being king over Israel. Fill your small container with olive oil and go, I am sending you to Jesse, who lives in Bethlehem. I have chosen one of his sons to be king."

But Samuel said, "How can I go? When Saul hears about it, he will try to kill me."

Then the Lord said, "Take a young calf with you. Say this: 'I have come to offer a sacrifice to the Lord.' Invite Jesse to the sacrifice. Then I will show you what to do. You must anoint for Me the one I tell you to anoint."

Samuel did what the Lord told him to do. When he arrived at Bethlehem, the elders of the town were afraid. They met him and asked, "Are you coming in peace?"

Samuel answered, "Yes, I come in peace. I have come to make a sacrifice to the Lord. Make yourselves holy for the Lord and come with me to the sacrifice." Then Samuel purified Jesse and his sons, and invited them to come to the sacrifice.

When they arrived, Samuel saw Eliab. Samuel thought: "Surely the Lord has chosen this man standing here before Him to be His anointed king."

But the Lord said, "Do not look at his outward appearance. Do not look at how tall he is. I have not chosen him. I do not see the same way that a human being sees. People look at the outside of a person, but I look at the heart."

Then Jesse called for Abinadab and made him pass by in front of Samuel. But Samuel said, "The Lord has not chosen this man." Then Jesse caused Shammah to pass by Samuel. But Samuel said, "No, the Lord has not chosen this one, either." Jesse had seven of his sons pass by in front of Samuel. But Samuel said to him, "The Lord has not chosen any of these."

Then Samuel asked Jesse, "Are these all the boys you have?"

Jesse answered, "I still have the youngest son, but he is out there taking care of the sheep."

Samuel said to Jesse, "Send for him. Bring him here. We will not sit down to eat the sacrifice until he arrives."

So Jesse sent someone to get David. He was a fine looking young man—all tan and handsome.

The Lord said to Samuel, "Go, anoint him with olive oil. He is the one."

So Samuel took the small container of olive oil. Then he poured the oil on David to anoint him among his brothers. From that day on, the Lord's Spirit came over David in a powerful way. Then Samuel got up and went to Ramah.

David Becomes Saul's Musician and Armor-bearer

But the Lord's Spirit had gone out of Saul. He was always being terrified by times of deep depression. So Saul's servants said to him,
"Look, you are often deeply depressed. Give us the command
and we will search for someone who knows how to play the
harp. Whenever the depression comes over you, he will play
music. Then the depression will leave you alone, and you will
feel better."

So Saul said to his servants, "Find someone who plays well. Bring him
to me."

One of the servant boys spoke up, "Jesse, the man from Bethlehem, has
a son who plays the harp very well. I have seen him play it. He
is a strong warrior, and he fights well too. He is skillful with
lyrics and good-looking. And the Lord is with him."

Then Saul sent messengers to Jesse, "Send me your son, David, who is
with your flock." So Jesse loaded a donkey with bread and a
leather bag full of wine. He also got a young goat. He sent all of
this to Saul with his son David. When David came to Saul, he
stood in his presence. Saul liked David very much, and David
became the one who carried Saul's armor.

Later, Saul sent a message to Jesse: "Permit David to remain here and
serve me. I like him." And whenever the depression hit Saul,
David would get his harp and play it. Then the depression
would leave Saul. When Saul got relief; he felt better again.

My Time to Pray

God Doesn't Need You Anymore ∻ First Samuel 16

Now the Lord said to Samuel, "How long will you mourn for Saul, seeing I have rejected him from reigning over Israel? Fill your horn with oil, and go; I am sending you to Jesse the Bethlehemite. For I have provided Myself a king among his sons" (1 Samuel 16:1).

Have you ever felt like the Lord had abandoned you? You prayed, but Heaven was shut up? You read the Scriptures, but God didn't speak to you. If you've felt that way, search your heart for rebellion against God. Saul did two things—first, he refused to do what God commanded; and second, he did the opposite. What did God say? "Rebellion is as the sin of witchcraft, and stubbornness is as iniquity and idolatry" (1 Sam. 15:23). *Lord, don't leave me.*

It's one thing to feel the door of Heaven shutting you out, but it's even worse when God rejects you. The Bible is filled with illustrations of Saul rejecting the will of God. Finally God said, "I have rejected him." How long has it been since you've intentionally done the will of God? Now a harder question, what are you purposefully doing that's contrary to God's will? If God rejected Saul from ruling over His people, will He reject you? *Lord, forgive me for neglecting You.*

Notice what's missing from today's text. God turned His back on Saul, but the stubborn king didn't notice. He was not aware of what God had done. His heart has been hardened, and there were no tears, no concern—Saul didn't care. So what about you? If you're concerned about your spiritual condition, then probably God hasn't cut you off. If you're scared of losing God, or you're searching desperately for answers to prayer, it's not too late. God promises, "And you will seek Me and find Me, when you search for Me with all your heart" (Jer. 29:13). *Lord, I want more of You.*

When God has a job to be done, he uses those who are closest to Him. He looks around to see who is available. (Are you close to Him?) God looks among His servants for someone who is spiritually ready. (Are you available to obey Him?) God looks around to use those who are eager to serve Him. (Are you constantly searching for ways to serve God?) *Lord, here I am.*

In a warfare analogy, God is fighting a battle; the enemy is attacking. He needs someone to counterattack. He'll use the soldiers standing around Him. If you're there and ready and able to defend God's honor, He'll use you. God uses those closest to Him. Will God go looking for a reluctant soldier? No! *Lord, I won't hide.*

Does God have to come searching for you? If God has to come searching for you, He'll send someone else into battle. God is looking for rebellious believers to restore to fellowship, and if a soldier is too rebellious, God has to punish him. What will God see in your heart when He finds you? Are you spiritually ready for service? *Lord, I'm ready.*

When God has a job for you to do, if you're not ready, He'll get someone else to do the job. When you tell God "No!", or when you're too busy with your own schedule, God will use someone else. God had chosen King Saul to rule Israel. But Saul forgot he was to rule for God. First, in front of his army, Saul violated the sacred priesthood and in self-will, Saul tried to sacrifice for God. Later, God told Saul to completely destroy the Amalekites. In a second act of disobedience in front of his army, Saul allowed some Amalekites to live. So God had to finally say, "I have rejected Saul." Why? Because the rebellious king had publicly rejected God. Have you told God "no" quietly? Have you embarrassed God publicly? If so, quickly seek His forgiveness. Ask for restoration. Quickly get rid of all known sin. Immediately begin following God. *Lord, I do it now.*

God was not left empty-handed. God had another to take Saul's place. It was David, "A man after God's own heart." So when you won't do God's work, He has another do it. God told old Samuel to go to Bethlehem because, "I have provided Me a king in Bethlehem." If you won't serve the Lord, He has another who will do it. *Lord, I will serve You.*

Sometimes you think you can serve God better than anyone else. Perhaps you think God needs you, or that God can't get along without you. That attitude will lead you to a downfall, just the way Saul fell. Saul thought he could get away with anything because God had chosen him; therefore, God needed him. Nothing was further from the truth. God didn't need Saul. God had a boy tending sheep in Bethlehem who would be king. As a matter of fact, David was the best human king ever. Does God need you? No! Does God want to use you? Yes! Will God get someone else if you don't serve Him? Yes! *God, I will do Your work.*

Just as God was preparing David to take Saul's place, so today God prepares another to take the place of those who reject Him and embarrass Him. So ask yourself some questions. Am I being used of God today? Is God pleased with my service? Does God have to prepare another to take my place because I've failed Him? *Here am I, Lord, use me. Amen.*

Psalm 23

Written by David About This Time

Lord, You are my Shepherd,
*   I don't need anything.*

You make me lie down in green pastures,
*   You lead me beside still waters.*

You renew my spiritual energy,
*   You guide me in the right paths*
*   To glorify Your name.*

When I walk through dark valleys,
*   I will not be afraid of death shadows;*

Because You are with me,
*   Your rod and staff protect me.*

You prepare a banquet table for me,
*   And my enemies watch me eat.*

You pour oil on my head to honor and heal me,
You fill my cup so it runs over.

Surely Your goodness and mercy will follow me,
As long as I live on this earth;
And in eternity I will live in Your house forever.

Amen.

My Time to Pray

When did David write the 23rd Psalm? Some say it was written toward the end of his life because of its lofty approach to God, because of his full understanding of trials, dangers, death, and because of his desire to go live with God forever in His heavenly home. Maybe! But I think it reflects the deep fiery passion of a *young* man, not the matured wisdom of an older man. This Psalm reflects the yearning of a young boy overlooked by his parents, alone with sheep in the wilderness, and starved for attention, love, and acceptance. *Lord, when I'm most needy, I'll come to You.*

The real measure of David's greatness is seen in his intimacy with nature and God. God was not a deity to be worshiped. The Lord was David's Shepherd who led him, fed him, and protected him. David was intimate with the Lord, and the Lord responded by showing Himself to David. *Lord, I want to know You.*

David knew that the Shepherd was leading his life. He was passionate about his relationship with his *Lord-Shepherd.* David prayed, "One thing I want above all else when I pray…this is my heart's prayer, 'That I may enjoy Your intimacy in Your house all the days of my life, so I can look into Your face to see Your beauty, to worship You in Your Temple'" (Ps. 27:4 ELT). *Lord, I have the passion of David. I want to worship You in Your house.*

David is every man, a study in contradictions. Read carefully the rest of his life to see a "man after God's heart," yet a man driven by ambition, pride, and destiny. David worshiped God, yet in his loneliness, sought out

Bathsheba. David committed to do God's will (monogamy), yet in his passion for companionship married multiple times. David showed his anger against Nabal, yet was patient with the self-willed Joab. David was the permissive parent, yet loved Absalom to a fault. He would have forgiven Absalom even though Absalom would have rebelled again, and tried to kill his father again. *Lord, I am like David, forgive my sin as you forgave David's sin; and bless me as You blessed David.*

Amen.

17

DAVID DEFEATS GOLIATH

FIRST SAMUEL 17

The Philistines gathered their armies for a battle (about 27 years after
their defeat at Michmash; 1 Sam. 13-14). They met at Socoh in
the territory of Judah. Their camp was at Ephes-Dammim,
between Socoh and Azekah. Saul and the Israelites gathered in
the Valley of Elah, and camped there. They drew up their battle-
lines to fight the Philistines. The Philistines stood on one hill,
and the Israelites stood on the other hill. The valley was between
the two armies.

There was a champion named Goliath from Gath who appeared
between the armies, he came out of the Philistine camp. He was
9 feet 6 inches tall. He had a brass helmet on his head. And he
wore a coat of scale-armor that was made of bronze and
weighed 125 pounds. He wore brass shin-guards on his legs,
and he had a small bronze javelin across his shoulders. The shaft
of his big spear was made of wood; it was like a weaver's pole.
The iron tip weighed 17 pounds. A man who carried his shield
walked ahead of him.

Goliath stood and shouted to the soldiers of Israel, "Why have you
taken positions for battle? I am a Philistine, and you are servants of Saul. Choose just one man and send him down to fight
me. If he can fight me and kill me, we will become your slaves.

But if I defeat him and kill him, then you will become our slaves." Then the Philistine giant said, "Today I dare you, army of Israel. Give me one man, and let's fight it out." When Saul and the Israelites heard the words of the Philistine, they were very scared.

David Arrives on the Scene

Now David was the son of Jesse, an Ephrathite from Bethlehem in the territory of Judah. In Saul's time, Jesse was a very old man. Jesse had eight sons, and the three oldest sons followed Saul to war. The names of the sons who went to war were Eliab, Abinadab, and Shammah. David was the youngest of all Jesse's sons. David went back and forth from King Saul to Bethlehem, where he took care of his father's flock.

The Philistine, Goliath, came forward every morning and evening. He presented himself to the Israelite army over and over for 40 days.

Now Jesse told his son David, "Take this half-bushel of roasted grain and these ten loaves of bread, and carry them quickly to your three brothers at the camp. Also, take these ten pieces of cheese. Give them to their commander. See how your brothers are doing. Are they all right? Bring back something to show me that they are all right. Your brothers are with Saul and the Israelite army in the Valley of Elah. They are fighting against the Philistines."

So early in the morning, David left the flock with another shepherd. And David took the food and left as Jesse had told him. When David arrived at the barricade, the army was leaving. They were going out to their battle positions. The soldiers were shouting their war cry. The Israelites and Philistines were lining up their men to face each other in battle.

So David left the food with the man who kept the supplies, then he ran to the battle line. He asked his brothers if they were all right. While David was talking to them, Goliath, the Philistine champion from Gath, stepped out of the Philistine lines. He shouted against Israel, as he usually did. However, this time David heard it. When all the Israelites saw Goliath, they were very afraid, and they ran away.

The Israelites said, "Have you seen this man, Goliath? He keeps coming out to taunt Israel. The king will give a lot of money to the man who kills Goliath. He will also give his daughter in marriage to the one who kills him. And his father's family will be exempt of taxes in Israel."

Then David asked the men who were standing with him, "What will be done for the man who kills this Philistine and takes away this shame from Israel? Who does this uncircumcised Philistine think he is? Does he think he can taunt the armies of the living God?"

These soldiers repeated the same thing to David. They said, "That is what will be done for the man who kills Goliath."

David's oldest brother, Eliab, overheard David talking with those men. He became angry with David, and asked, "Why did you come down here? Who is taking care of those few sheep in the desert? I know you have an arrogant attitude. You have come down here just to be a spectator—to watch the battle."

But David replied, "Now what have I done wrong? Can't I even ask a question?" Then David turned toward the others to ask the same sort of questions. And they gave him the same answer as before. Some men overheard what David was saying, and they informed Saul, and Saul welcomed him.

And David said to Saul, "Do not let anyone be discouraged. I will go and fight this Philistine."

Saul answered David, "You are not able to go out against this Philistine and fight him. You are only a boy. Goliath has been a warrior since he was a young man."

But David replied, "I have been shepherding my father's flock. Whenever a lion or a bear came around and snatched a lamb from the flock, I chased it. I attacked it and rescued the lamb from its mouth. And whenever a lion turned on me, I would seize it by its throat and I would kill it. I have killed lions *and* bears. This uncircumcised Philistine will become like the ones I killed. Goliath has taunted the armies of the living God." David continued, "The Lord has saved me from both lions and bears. God will also deliver me from this Philistine."

Then Saul said to David, "Go, and may the Lord be with you."

David Defeats Goliath

After this, King Saul put his own battle gear on David. He put a brass helmet on David's head and outfitted him with body-armor. David also strapped on Saul's sword. Then David tried to walk around, but he was not comfortable with all this equipment which Saul had put on him.

He said to Saul, "I cannot go with this stuff. I'm not used to it." Then David took off the helmet and the armor. David took his own rod in his hand, and he chose five smooth stones from a stream. He put them in his shepherd's bag, and his sling was in his hand. Then he went closer to meet Goliath. And the Philistine came closer to David. The man who was carrying the shield walked in front of Goliath. The Philistine giant looked at David, and when he saw that David was only a boy—tanned and handsome—he looked down on David with disgust and said, "Do you think I am a dog, that you come at me with sticks?" Using the names of his gods, Goliath cursed David. The Philistine said, "Come here, boy, I will feed your body to the birds of the air and to the wild animals."

But David said to him, "You come to me with a sword, and a javelin, and a big spear, but I come to you in the Name of the Lord of the armies of Heaven. He is the God of the armies of Israel too. You have taunted Him. Today, the Lord will give you to me. I will strike you down and I will cut off your head. Today, I will feed the corpses of the Philistine soldiers to the birds of the air and the living creatures of the earth. Then all the world will know that there *is* a God for Israel. Everyone who is gathered here will know that the Lord does not deliver people by swords or spears. The battle belongs to *Him*. And He will help us defeat all of you."

As Goliath moved closer to attack him, David ran quickly to meet him. Then David reached into his bag and took a stone from it, put it into his sling, and then David threw it with all his might. The stone hit the Philistine in his forehead and stuck there. Goliath fell face down on the ground. Then David ran and stood next to the Philistine, pulled Goliath's sword out of its scabbard, and killed him. David cut off his head.

So David got the victory over the Philistine with only a sling and a stone. David hit him and killed him. David did not carry a sword in his hand. When the Philistines saw that their hero was dead, they ran away. The men of Israel and Judah shouted and started chasing the Philistines. They pursued them all the way to the entrance of the city of Gath (about seven to nine miles from the battlefield). And they chased them to the gates of Ekron (Gath and Ekron were two of the five main Philistine cities).

Many of the Philistines died. Their corpses were lying all along the Shaaraim road as far as Gath and Ekron. Then the Israelites returned from chasing the Philistines. They collected (pillaged) many things from the Philistines' camp.

Years later, David took Goliath's head and brought it to Jerusalem. He also put Goliath's weapons in his tent.

Saul had watched David go out to meet Goliath, the Philistine. Saul said to Abner, the commander of the army, "Abner, who is that young man's father?" (Perhaps David now had a beard, and this accounts for why Saul did not recognize him.)

Abner answered, "As surely as you live, king, I do not know."

The king said, "Find out whose son this young man is." When David came back from killing the Philistine, Abner brought him into the presence of Saul. The Philistine's head was in David's hand. Saul asked him, "Young man, who is your father?"

David answered, "I am the son of your servant, Jesse, from Bethlehem."

My Time to Pray

When It Is Your Time to Fight ⌁ First Samuel 17

You come to me with a sword, with a spear, and with a javelin. But I come to you in the name of the Lord of hosts (1 Samuel 17:45).

The Christian life is not a bed of roses, nor is it just a picnic. Not at all, the Christian life is a battle against the devil who is determined to destroy you. To serve Christ you must constantly struggle against the world, the flesh, and the devil. *Lord, I will get mentally ready to fight.*

There will always be giants that want to defeat you. You may have inner peace, but there will always be another outward struggle. And your giant is 9´6˝ tall. He has a coat of armor that weighs 125 pounds, and has a spear that looks as big as a roof rafter, and its tip weighs 17 pounds. *Lord, give me ingenuity and strength against satan's weapons.*

Remember, your enemy hates you because he hates God. Goliath defied the armies of the living God and "cursed David by his gods." God created the world and everything in it, but people reject God's ownership of them. God wants everyone to worship and serve Him, but people refuse His rulership. People hate God because they love the lust of the flesh, the lust of the eyes and the pride of life. Their motto, "Not God, but I." *Lord, I turn from sin to You.*

God's method to combat the devil is a humble person who serves the living God. God is not looking for giants, dragons, or "superhuman" people. No, God is looking for average people who will allow His presence to indwell them, and allow His power to fight through them. God is looking for an insignificant person, with apparent inadequate weapons, who in threatening circumstances will yield to the Holy Spirit so God can win His battle through him. *Lord, I yield to You.*

When you fight for God, you will probably face criticism from another Christian who does not see what God is doing, and who does not understand how God wins His battles. David's older brother was angry against David and accused him of "pride and insolence." *Lord, I will look to You and not to others.*

When the Lord wants to defeat a giant, He looks for an insignificant person to take up His cause. David said, "Is there not a cause?" *Lord, I take up Your cause.*

King Saul made his armor available to David. It must have been good armor, for it was fit for a king. Also, it was big armor, for King Saul stood head and shoulders above the crowd. But David rejected the armor of another, saying, "I have not tested them." Remember you can't fight giants with the reputation or techniques of another. David took his sling and shepherd's staff into battle. Then he chose five smooth stones as his weapons. *Lord, I'm amazed at the things You use.*

God doesn't use novices to fight His big battles, no; God uses those who have been successful in previous battles. David had fought with a bear and lion and was victorious. When the lion stole a lamb, David ran after the animal and killed it. In the same way, we must win small battles against sin before God puts us in the arena against Goliath. *Lord, I will win today's battles, and not worry about future big battles.*

When fighting the enemy, we must realize our strength is in God, not in human weapons nor human methods, nor human preparation. David told Goliath, "I come to you in the Name of the Lord of the armies of heaven...you have taunted Him." *Lord, I need Your strength today...help me.*

David was confident in the Lord, not in his own strength or weapons. He told Goliath what he was going to do. "I will cut off your head." We should never settle with a halfway victory. We can't just repent of a few little sins. No. God wants us to have a complete victory over sin, over all sin. Note what David did, "David cut off his head." *Lord, I surrender all.*

Amen.

18

Jonathan and David Become Good Friends

First Samuel 18

From that day on, Saul kept David with him. He did not permit David to go back home to his father's house. Jonathan, the son of Saul, admired David very much. In fact, he loved David as much as he loved his own life. Eventually, Jonathan made a pact with David, because he loved David as much as he loved himself. Jonathan took off his robe and gave it to David, also giving him his tunic, as well as his sword, his bow, and his belt.

David went out to fight wherever Saul sent him, and was very successful. Then Saul promoted David, putting him over some of his soldiers. Saul's officers and all the other people were very glad to see this.

After David had killed more Philistines, he and the soldiers would return home. Women would come out from all the towns of Israel to meet King Saul singing songs of joy. They danced and played tambourines and 3-stringed instruments, singing, "Saul has killed thousands of his enemies, but David has killed his tens of thousands!"

This song of the women made Saul very upset. He thought it was a bad thing, saying, "They claim that David has killed tens of thousands, but they say I have killed only thousands. What else will belong to David but the kingdom?" So Saul watched David very closely from that time forward, because he was jealous of him.

On the next day, that same deep depression took hold of Saul. Inside his house, he babbled like a crazy man. With his hand, David was playing the harp as he always did when Saul was depressed. But Saul had a spear in his hand. He raised the spear toward David, thinking: *I will pin David to the wall*. But David dodged him twice.

The Lord was with David, but the Lord had abandoned Saul. So Saul was afraid of David. Saul sent David away from him, making David his commander of 1,000 soldiers. So David led them out to battle. David was tremendously successful in everything he did, because the Lord was with him. When Saul saw how successful David was, he became even more afraid of David. But all the people of Israel and Judah loved David. He was a real military leader.

David Marries Michal

Saul said to David, "You are indeed a brave soldier for me, and you fight the Lord's battles. Look, here is my older daughter, Merab. I will let you marry her." Saul had thought: *I won't have to kill David; the Philistines will surely kill him.*

But David said to Saul, "I am not worthy enough for this great honor. My family is not important enough for me to become the king's son-in-law." However, when the time came for Saul's daughter Merab to marry David, Saul gave her to Adriel of Meholah for his wife instead.

Now Saul's other daughter, Michal, loved David. When they told Saul that Michal was in love with David, Saul was pleased, thinking:

I will let Michal marry David. Then I will use her as a trap for him. And the Philistines will defeat him. So Saul said to David a second time, "Now you will become my son-in-law."

And Saul gave this order to his servants: "Speak to David privately, saying, 'The king is pleased with you, and all his servants like you. You should become his son-in-law.'" So, the servants of Saul told these words to David.

But David answered, "Do you think it is an easy thing to become the king's son-in-law? I'm only a poor man, and no one respects me."

Then the servants of Saul reported to Saul what David said. Then Saul said, "Now say this to David: 'The king does not really want you to pay a large price for the bride. He only wants you to bring him 100 Philistine foreskins so that he can get revenge on his enemies.'" Saul was thinking that the Philistines would surely kill David.

So Saul's servants told David these words. David wanted to become the king's son-in-law. Before the time had expired, David and his men went out and killed 200 Philistines. And David brought all those foreskins to Saul, so that he could become the king's son-in-law. Then Saul gave David his daughter, Michal, to be his wife.

Saul realized that the Lord was with David. He also saw that his daughter, Michal, was in love with David. This caused Saul to be even more afraid of David. And Saul hated David for the rest of his life.

The captains of the Philistines continued to come out to fight. However, David defeated them every time. David was more successful and more honored than any of Saul's officers. David was getting famous.

Psalm 12

Written About This Time by David

Lord, help me to be godly;
There are so few left who are faithful.

The ones I expect to follow You
They are falling away.

They talk with their friends about fleshly things;
They lie about You and the truth,
Telling others it's all right not to follow You.

Lord, one day You will shut them up;
They won't be able to lie about You anymore.

They won't be able to justify their sin,
They won't be able to say anything they desire;
They won't be able to deny Your rule over them.

Lord, come strengthen the weak who are resisting
The enemy's arguments.

Your followers are being knocked down,
They are gasping for spiritual breath.

Lord, I know Your words are better than what the enemy says;
I have repeatedly tried Your promises and they never fail.

Lord, I know You will keep those who trust in Your Word;
You will preserve them from the enemy's lies,
Even when the enemy is all about them.

Amen.

My Time to Pray

Living Under Unjust People ⌁ First Samuel 18

The women sang as they danced, and said: "Saul has slain his thousands, and David his ten thousands." Then Saul was very angry and the saying displeased him; and he said,..."What more can he have but the kingdom?" So Saul eyed David from that day forward...and Saul cast the spear for he said, "I will pin David to the wall!" (1 Samuel 18:7-11).

Have you ever been in the same situation as David? Have you done your job, and done it well, only to be criticized and hated by someone? Perhaps a boss, or a committee chairman over you, or a family member who has power over you? Remember, you are not responsible for what happens *to* you, but you are responsible for what happens *in* you. *Lord, I will not let others make me compromise myself.*

Have you ever noticed that an unjust person usually attacks you when you are most vulnerable? David was in Saul's court and he was going to win battles for Saul, yet Saul was out to get him. If David ran away—returned to sheep herding—he would have left the plan for which God anointed him. *Lord, I will not run away.*

David had to deal with his inner response as he dodged the spear and plots of Saul against his life. David could have become angry, bitter, resentful, or retaliated. But David didn't run away, nor did he try to get even. *Lord, don't let me be ground under someone's feet.*

Saul had a deeper problem than David. He was controlled by an evil urge (jealousy) to get rid of David. But even deeper, there were neurotic problems that controlled his mind, emotions, and even his will. Just as Saul tried to kill David, maybe you feel someone is trying to "kill" you socially or at your job. *Lord, I will deal with my feelings, will You deal with the unjust person?*

David didn't have many options. If David tried to kill Saul, he would be guilty of treason, and he would have sinned against God. If David tried to manipulate Saul out of power, David would be discredited in the eyes of the people and couldn't be worthy of the throne. If David complained and told everyone, the people would reject him. If David tried to hurt Saul or get even with Saul, the guards of Saul could have killed him. *Lord, teach me what to do when I'm hemmed into a corner.*

David was not trapped by an inner desire for position, power, or prestige. He was not motivated by ego or the flesh. But, "David behaved himself more wisely than all the servants of Saul" (1 Sam. 18:30). *Lord, may I always do the right thing, no matter what's done to me.*

David always did the right thing in the right way. He had the greatest accomplishment in life, when no one expected much from him. Instead of praise and compliments, David became the object of the king's hatred, and the object of the king's continued plots to kill him, and the source of the king's neurotic fears. Yet David remained true to his inner walk with God and remained loyal to the crown. And in all of this, David showed exemplary trust in God. *Lord, help me endure hatred and help me glorify You in all I do.*

Amen.

19

SAUL TRIES TO KILL DAVID

FIRST SAMUEL 19

Saul told his son Jonathan and all his servants that they must kill David. However, Jonathan, the son of Saul, cared about David very much, so he warned David, "Saul, my father, is trying to kill you. Please be on guard tomorrow morning. Stay in a secret place. *Hide!* I will go out and stand next to my father in the field where you are hiding. I will talk to him about you. Then I will tell you whatever I learn."

So Jonathan talked to his father Saul. Jonathan said good things about David, saying to him, "You are the king, you must not do wrong to your servant David. He has done no wrong to you. His deeds have been very beneficial to you. David risked his life when he killed Goliath the Philistine. Didn't the Lord cause a great victory for all Israel? You saw it, and you were glad. Why would you harm David? He is innocent. There is no reason to kill him."

Jonathan persuaded Saul not to kill David. Then Saul swore this oath: "As surely as the Lord lives, David will not be put to death."

After Saul left, Jonathan called out to David. Then he told David everything that he and his father had talked about. Later, Jonathan brought David to Saul, so David was in Saul's presence as before.

War broke out again. So David went out to fight the Philistines. He
defeated them badly, and they ran away from him.

However, once again Saul was suffering deep depression. He was sitting
in his house as David was playing the harp with his hand. Saul
had his spear in his hand and tried to run his spear through
David to the wall. The spear stuck in the wall, but David got
away from him. That night, David ran away and escaped.

Saul sent messengers to David's house to watch for him, and kill him in
the morning. But Michal, David's wife, warned him, saying, "You
must run away tonight to save your life. If you don't do this, you
will be killed tomorrow morning." Then she lowered David
through a window, so he ran off and escaped. Then Michal took
a big statue and laid it on the bed. She covered it with a bed-
spread and put a pillow of goats' hair at its head.

Saul sent his men to arrest David, but Michal said, "He is sick."

The men went and told Saul, but he sent them back to get David. Saul
had told them, "Bring me David on his bed, so I can kill him."
When the men went into David's house, they found that it was
merely a statue on David's bed. And the hair was only a pillow
of goats' hair.

Saul said to Michal, "Why did you trick me like this? You sent my
enemy away. He has escaped."

Michal answered Saul, "David told me if I did not help him escape, he
would kill me."

Psalm 59

Carved on Stone About This Time by David

Deliver me from my enemies, O God;
Protect me from those who attack me.

Deliver me from those who rebel against You
And save me from murderers.

They are planning to ambush me;
These violent men are waiting for me
Even though I've done nothing to them.

I am innocent, yet they seek to kill me;
Come see my dilemma and help me.

O Lord God Almighty, God of Israel;
Rise up to punish the lawless,
Don't show them any mercy. Selah!

They come prowling around at evening,
Snarling like hungry dogs.

They belch out threatening words of harm,
And they think no one can hurt them.

But You laugh at them, Lord,
You scoff at the godless heathen.

I wait for You because You are my strength,
O God, You are my defense.

But I will sing of Your power,
Every morning I will sing of Your love.

You have defended me from my enemies,
You protect me in time of trouble.

I sing to You, O my Strength;
You protect me, O my loving God.

Amen.

After David had run away and escaped from Saul, he traveled to Samuel
at Ramah. He told Samuel everything that Saul had done to
him. Then David and Samuel went to Naioth (Some special
building or small settlement for prophets near Ramah. The
Hebrew word is translated as "house of study," that is, the lodg-
ings of students [scribes], dormitories.) and stayed there.
Someone told Saul: "David is at Naioth in Ramah." So Saul sent
some men to capture David. But they met a group of prophets
who were prophesying. Samuel was standing there, leading this
group. The Spirit of God came over Saul's men, and they also
began to prophesy.

Saul heard about this, so he sent some more men, but they also prophesied. Then a third time Saul sent more men, and they also
prophesied. Finally Saul himself traveled to Ramah. He came to
the big well at Secu. He asked, "Where are Samuel and David?"

One person answered, "Look at Naioth in Ramah."

So Saul went to Naioth in Ramah. However, the Spirit of God also
came over Saul. As Saul was walking along, he began to prophesy until he got to Naioth in Ramah. Saul took off his royal
robes. And Saul himself prophesied in front of Samuel. He laid
there that way—without his robes—all day and all night. That is
why people ask: "Is Saul also one of the prophets?"

Psalm 7

Written About This Time by David

O Lord, I trust You with my life;
Save me from those who persecute me.

They want to rip me in pieces like a lion,
Thinking no one will deliver me.

O Lord, let my enemies persecute me if I deserve it;
If my hands have sinned,
If I have attacked those at peace with me,
(Actually, I've done good to my enemies).

O Lord, if I have done evil things;
Let my enemies stomp me under foot,
Let them drag my honor through the dirt. Selah!

O Lord, wake up Your righteous anger
Because my enemies are attacking me;
Awaken to carry out Your judgment.

O Lord, let Your people gather about You;
Return so they can enjoy Your presence.

O Lord, I know You will judge all people;
Judge me first and see that I try to do right,
Examine me to see my integrity.

O Lord, stop the wicked from doing wickedness,
Let the righteous do righteously.

You can do this because You know the hearts of all;
Therefore, You are angry with the wicked
And You are pleased with the righteous.

My enemy is a friend of iniquity,
He thinks constantly of harming others.

He always is digging a trap
But he falls into his self-made destruction.

His attack on others ends up hurting himself,
His wounds are self-inflicted.

But You, O Lord, will I praise
For You always deal with everyone rightly;
I will praise Your name, O Lord, Most High.

Amen.

My Time to Pray

Sin Against an Innocent Person ⌐ 1 Samuel 19

For he (David) took his life in his hands and killed the Philistine, and the Lord brought about a great deliverance for all Israel. You saw it and rejoiced. Why then will you sin against innocent blood, to kill David without a cause? (1 Samuel 19:5).

Saul was God's choice to be the first king over Israel, yet his incomplete obedience and entire disobedience made God say, "I have rejected him from reigning over Israel" (1 Sam. 16:1). *Lord, may I always obey You instantly and completely.*

Saul apparently began as a humble candidate who hid among the baggage because he thought himself unworthy to be king. But Saul the man with weak ego-strength, turned into a man with negative ego-strength, and let his jealousy over David drive him to abuse his power. Saul allowed anger to dominate his thoughts, and like gasoline on fire, he exploded into rage. His spear was always in his hand, whether to protect himself physically, or to give him the appearance of power. Saul threw his spear at David twice, then at his son. His jealousy was out of control. *Lord, may I understand how a good person goes bad, and discipline myself at all times.*

David was wrongly accused and sinfully treated. The jealousy of Saul opened his inner door to an evil spirit. When one is possessed with evil, he will open himself up to pride, anger, murder, and distrust of family, friends, and fellow workers. *Lord, keep me from evil.*

We need to learn from David, a man who did not insist on his rights, nor did he compromise his stance. He was aware of danger and did not needlessly die, nor did he allow false accusations to stand. He ran from Saul, to save his life. He was truthful with friends and was faithful to them. David sought God's direction and used his ingenuity to avoid danger and live to serve another day. *Lord, help me learn from David.*

None of us like to suffer, but God allowed pressure to squeeze David for 13 years. God knew the heart of David, and pressure didn't make him bitter, but rather it made David stronger. If David hadn't been 13 years in the desert, we would never have had some wonderful Psalms by David. *Lord, help me see Your purpose in my suffering.*

Amen.

20

Jonathan Helps David Escape

First Samuel 20

Then David ran away from Naioth in Ramah. He went to Jonathan and
asked, "What have I done? What is my crime? In what way did I
sin against your father? Why is he trying to kill me?"

Jonathan answered, "You will not die. My father does not do anything
without telling me about it first, whether it is a very important
thing or just something small. Why would my father hide it from
me? No, it is not true."

But again David insisted that it was true, saying, "Your father knows
very well that I am your friend. He is thinking to himself:
'Jonathan must not know about this. If Jonathan knew about it,
he would be very upset.' But as surely as the Lord lives, and as
surely as you live, I am only one step away from death."

So Jonathan said to David, "I will do whatever you want me to do."

Then David said to Jonathan, "Tomorrow is the New Moon festival. I
am supposed to eat with the king. But let me hide in the field
until the third evening. If your father notices that I am absent,
this is what you should tell him: 'David begged me to let him
go to his hometown of Bethlehem. Every year at this time his
whole family offers a sacrifice.' If your father says, 'Good,' then

I am safe. But if Saul gets angry, then you will know that he is really planning to hurt me. Jonathan, be loyal to me. You have made a pact with me before the Lord. If I am a traitor, you may kill me yourself. Why would you bring me to your father? Do it yourself."

Jonathan answered, "No, never! If I learn that my father truly plans to harm you, I will warn you."

David asked, "Who will inform me about how your father reacts? What if your father answers you in a harsh way?"

Then Jonathan said to David, "Come, let us go out into the field." So both Jonathan and David went into the field. Jonathan said to David, "Before the Lord, the God of Israel, I make this promise: at this same time, day after tomorrow, I will find out how my father feels, whether he feels good toward you or not. I will send word to you to let you know. My father may indeed have it in his mind to harm you. If so, I will inform you and send you away safely. May the Lord punish me if I do not keep my promise. And may the Lord be with you as He has been with my father. But as long as I live, show me kindness like that of the Lord so that I will not be killed. You must never stop showing your love to my family. Please do not do this, even when the Lord has destroyed each of your enemies from the surface of the earth."

So Jonathan made a pact with the household of David, saying, "May the Lord punish David's enemies." Then Jonathan asked David to repeat his vow of loyalty to him. He did this because he loved David as much as he loved his own life.

Jonathan said to David, "Tomorrow is the New Moon festival. Your seat will be empty. You will be missed. On the third day, toward evening, go down quickly to the place where you hid when all this trouble began. Wait by the big rock called 'Ezel' (a milestone to direct travelers). I will shoot three arrows to the side of the rock, as if I were shooting at a target. Then I will send a boy, telling him to go find the arrows. If I specifically say to the boy, 'Look, the arrows are on this side of you, bring them here,' then you may come out of hiding. As surely as the Lord lives, you may come out, because you are safe. There is no danger for you. However, if I say to the youth, 'Look, the arrows are *beyond* you,' then you must leave, because the Lord is sending you away. Remember what you and I talked about, the Lord is a Witness between you and me forever."

King Saul Throws His Spear at Jonathan

So David hid himself in the field. And when the New Moon festival came, the king sat down at the meal to eat, sitting where he always sat—near the wall. Jonathan sat near Saul, and Abner sat next to him. But David's spot was vacant. Saul did not say anything about David's absence that day. He thought: *Maybe something accidental has happened to David, that he is ceremonially unclean. That must be the reason he is not here.*

However, the next day was the second day of the New Moon festival, and David's spot was empty again. So Saul said to his son Jonathan, "Why hasn't the son of Jesse come to the festival meal, either yesterday or today?"

Jonathan answered, "David begged me to let him go to Bethlehem. David said, 'Please let me go, because our family has a sacrifice in Bethlehem. And my brother is expecting me to be there. Now if I am your friend, please let me get away and visit my brothers.' That is why David has not come to the king's table."

Then Saul became very angry at Jonathan, saying to Jonathan, "You son of an evil and disobedient woman, I know that you are on David's side, that son of Jesse. You are bringing shame on your-self and on your mother who gave birth to you. As long as Jesse's son is alive on this earth, you will never be king or have a kingdom. Now, send for David and bring him to me. He must die."

Jonathan asked Saul, his father: "Why should David be put to death? What crime has he done?"

Then Saul threw his spear at Jonathan, trying to kill him. (So Jonathan knew that his father truly wanted to kill David.)

Jonathan left the table; hot with anger. He did not eat anything for the rest of that day, because he was so upset about the shameful thing that his father wanted to do to David.

The next morning, Jonathan went out to the field to meet David, as they had agreed. He had a young boy with him. Jonathan said to the boy, "Now run and find the arrows that I shoot." As the boy ran, Jonathan shot an arrow that passed over him. The boy got to the place where Jonathan's arrow fell, but Jonathan called out to him, "The arrow is beyond you." Then Jonathan shouted, "Hurry, go quickly, do not stop!" The boy picked up the arrows and brought them back to his master, he knew nothing about what this meant; only Jonathan and David understood it. Then Jonathan gave his weapons to his boy, telling him, "Go back to town."

As soon as the boy had gone, David came out from the south side of the rock. He bowed facedown three times on the ground in front of Jonathan. Then David and Jonathan hugged and kissed each other. They wept together, but David cried the most.

Jonathan said to David, "Go in peace. The two of us have made a vow by the Lord that we will always be friends. We said: 'The Lord will be a Witness between you and me, and between our descendents forever.'"

Then David got up and left, and Jonathan went back to town.

My Time to Pray

So Jonathan made a covenant with the family of David, and David swore to it with a terrible curse against himself and his descendants, should he be unfaithful to his promise. But Jonathan made David swear to it again, this time by his love for him, for he loved him as much as he loved himself (1 Samuel 20:16-17 LB).

What is it about the friendship of youth that we remember our promises for the rest of our lives? David and Jonathan made a vow to each other and many years after the death of Jonathan, David shows kindness to Jonathan's son, Mephibosheth. "Mephibosheth dwelt in Jerusalem, for he ate continually at the king's (David) table. And he was lame in both feet" (2 Sam. 9:13). *Lord, I want to be a person who can be trusted to tell the truth. Convict me of my sin should I "fudge" the truth. Remind me when I forget the truth. Forgive me when I speak wrongly because I am ignorant of the truth. Give me courage to speak up when it will damage me for telling the truth. May I be like Jesus Who is the truth (see John 14:6).*

Can we be faithful when it hurts? Or can we be faithful when it's dangerous? David was to be the next king—not Jonathan who stuck up for David when his father ridiculed him. Jonathan continued to protect David in the face of danger, "Saul cast a spear at him to kill him" (1 Sam. 20:33). *Lord, help me always be faithful to Your principles; help me be faithful to my friends as Jonathan was to David.*

That must have been a difficult parting. "So he (David) arose and departed, and Jonathan went into the city" (1 Sam. 20:42). David didn't realize it at the time, but he would spend the next 13 years as a fugitive in the wilderness of Israel and as a sojourner in a foreign land. He would be separated from home, family, surroundings, and fellowship with God in the Tabernacle. David gave up all to follow God's call upon his life. Will you? *Lord, I give all to You. I will go where You want me to go. I will do what You want me to do. I will say what You want me to say. I am Your servant.*

Amen.

21

DAVID RECEIVES HELP FROM THE HIGH PRIEST

FIRST SAMUEL 21

Then David went to Nob (A town northeast of Jerusalem on the northern part of the Mount of Olives. After the destruction of Shiloh
(1 Sam. 4:2-3, the Tabernacle was relocated to Nob) to see
Ahimelech the high priest. However, Ahimelech trembled with
fear when he met David. (Perhaps Ahimelech was justifiably
worried about the volatile nature of King Saul.) He asked David,
"Why are you alone? Why is no one with you?"

David told him, "The king has given me a special order. He told me:
'No one must know about the secret mission that I am sending
you to do.' I told my young men where to meet me. Now, what
food do you have with you? Give me five loaves of bread, or
whatever you can find."

But the priest answered David: "I do not have any ordinary bread here,
but I do have some holy bread (the bread of the Lord's
Presence) here. You and your men may eat it if your young men
have not had sex with women."

David answered the high priest: "Women have been kept from us. My
men always keep their bodies ceremonially clean, even when we

go on an expedition. And this is especially true when the work is holy."

There was no bread except the bread that had been made holy for the Lord. So the high priest gave the bread to David. (It showed that they were in the presence of God. Each Sabbath day, they took this bread away and put hot bread in its place.)

Now one of Saul's servants was there that day. He was staying there before the Lord. His name was Doeg, the Edomite. He was the chief of Saul's shepherds.

David asked Ahimelech, "Do you have a spear or a sword here? The king's business was very important. I had to leave quickly, and I did not bring my sword or any other weapon."

The priest answered, "The sword of Goliath the Philistine is here. He is the one whom you killed in the Valley of Elah. His sword is wrapped in a cloth under the ephod. Take it, there is no other sword here except that one."

David said, "There is no other sword like Goliath's sword. Give it to me."

That day, David ran away from Saul. He went to Achish, king of Gath. (This was one of the five major cities of the Philistines. It was not uncommon in ancient times for famous men like David to seek asylum with neighboring princes as exiles.) But the servants of Achish said to him, "This is David, the king of that land. He is the man whom the Israelite women sing about when they dance. They sing,

'Saul has killed thousands of his enemies.

But David has killed tens of thousands!'"

David paid attention to these words. He was very much afraid of
Achish, the king of Gath. So David changed the way he
behaved. He pretended to be insane in front of Achish and his
servants. He acted like a crazy man. He scribbled on the doors
of the gate. Spit ran down his beard.

Then Achish said to his servants, "Look at this man, he is insane! Why
do you bring him to me? I do not need any more madmen. Do
I need you to bring him here to act like this in front of me? No!
David must not come into my house."

Psalm 56

Written About This Time by David

O Lord, be merciful to me in danger;
Because my enemy would destroy me,
He daily oppresses me.

My enemy is constantly trying to kill me,
There are many that oppose me, O Lord Most High.

When I am most afraid,
I will trust in Your protection.

I will exalt Your Word
Because that will protect me,
I will not be afraid of what my enemy can do.

Every day he twists my words,
Using everything against me.

My enemy gets others to help him;
He sneaks around behind my back
Looking for ways to destroy me.

Lord, don't let him get away with his sin;
    Judge him by Your wrath.

Lord, You know how I meditate on You;
    Don't forget my tears over this matter.

When I cried to You, my enemies were stopped;
    Therefore I know You are for me.

I have trusted You for protection,
    I will not be afraid of what they can do to me.

O Lord, this is what I promise to do;
    I will praise You for safety.

Because You have protected me from destruction,
    You kept the evil one from me;
    You helped me walk before You in this life.

                    Amen.

22

DAVID'S HIDEOUTS

FIRST SAMUEL 22

So David left Gath and escaped to the Cave of Adullam (a labyrinth of
caves about six to twelve miles west-southwest of Bethlehem).
When David's brothers and other relatives learned about this,
they went down there to visit him. Many individuals joined
David. All those who were in trouble, who owned money, or
who were disgruntled gathered around him, and David became
their leader. He had about 400 men with him.

From there David went to Mizpeh in Moab. He spoke to the king of
Moab. (David's great grandmother Ruth was from Moab.) He
said, "Please allow my father and my mother to come stay with
you Moabites until I find out what God is going to do for me."
So David helped them to get settled with the king of Moab. And
they stayed with the king as long as David was hiding in Moab.

But the prophet of Gad said to David, "Do not remain in the hideout
any longer. Get up and go into the land of Judah." So David left
and went into the Forest of Hereth.

Psalm 64

Written by David About This Time

O God, listen to my request;
    Don't let my enemies terrify me.

Don't let their conspiracy succeed,
    Protect me from their rebellion.

They sharpen their tongue like a sword,
    They aim cutting words at me like an arrow.

They shout at the innocent with their accusations,
    Never considering consequences or reprisals.

My enemies encourage each other to attack me,
    They plan together their deceptive snares;
    They think no one will know.

They devise a cunning trap for me
    Using their creative minds and evil hearts,
    Thinking it is a perfect plan.

But You, Lord, will shoot arrows at them;
    Suddenly, they shall be wounded.

Their lies will be turned against them,
    And all their supporters will abandon them.

Everyone will then fear You, my God,
    Because they will realize what You have done.

The righteous will rejoice in You,
    And Your people will praise You.

                    Amen.

Saul Kills Ahimelech and 84 Priests

King Saul heard that someone saw David and the men who were with
him. Saul was sitting under the tamarisk tree at Gibeah, all his
officers were standing next to him. He had a spear in his hand
(it was being used like a king's scepter). Saul said to those who
were standing there, "Listen you men of Benjamin, do you think
the son of Jesse would give fields and vineyards to any of you?
Would David make you commanders over thousands of men or
captains over hundreds of men? You have all conspired against
me. No one told me when my son made a pact with the son of
Jesse. None of you feels sorry for me. No one told me that my
son had encouraged my servant David to ambush me at this
very moment."

Doeg the Edomite was standing there with Saul's officers. He spoke up,
"I saw the son of Jesse at Nob. David went to see Ahimelech, the
high priest, the son of Ahitub. And Ahimelech prayed to the
Lord for David. He gave him some food, too. Also he gave him
the sword of Goliath the Philistine."

Then the king sent for Ahimelech the high priest, the son of Ahitub. He
also called all of Ahimelech's relatives who were priests at Nob.
All of them came to the king. Saul said to Ahimelech, "Listen
now, O son of Ahitub."

Ahimelech answered, "I am here, my lord."

Saul said, "Why have you and the son of Jesse conspired against me?
You gave him bread and a sword. You prayed to God for him.
David will attack me. He is waiting to ambush me at this very
moment."

Ahimelech answered the king, "No, David is very loyal to you. No other
servant of yours is as loyal to you as David. He is your own son-
in-law. He is the captain of your personal bodyguards. All the

people in your household respect him. Was that the first time I prayed to God for David? Not at all. Do not blame me or any of my relatives for such a thing as that. I knew nothing at all about any of this."

But the king said, "Ahimelech, you and all your relatives must surely die." Then Saul told the guards who stood next to him, "Go and put the priests of the Lord to death. They are on David's side. They knew David was running away, but they did not tell me."

But the king's officers were unwilling to harm the priests of the Lord.

Then the king ordered Doeg, "You go and kill the priests." So Doeg the Edomite went and executed the priests. That day he killed 85 men who wore the priestly clothes. He also killed the people of Nob, the town of the priests. He killed men, women, children, and nursing babies with the sword. He even used his sword to kill some cattle, donkeys, and sheep. (This fulfilled the prophecy against the household of Eli [1 Sam. 2:30-36]).

Psalm 140

Written by David About This Time

O Lord, deliver me from evil people;
Protect me from those who would hurt me.

They think up evil plans in their heart,
They want to fight me every day.

They sharpen their tongue like a serpent,
Their words against me are poison. Selah!

Deliver me from the hands of the wicked,
Protect me from violent people
Who plan to destroy me.

They arrogantly set a trap for me,
>*They plan to trip me up*
>*And catch me in their deceit. Selah!*

O Lord, You are my God;
>*Hear my cry to You for help.*

O Lord, You are the strength of my salvation;
>*Protect me in the heat of battle.*

Do not let the wicked do what they desire,
>*Don't let them become proud before You. Selah!*

Let my enemies be destroyed
>*With the destruction they plan for me.*

May burning coals be thrown upon them,
>*And throw them into the pit never to escape.*

Don't let liars prosper on this earth,
>*May they be hunted down and destroyed.*

I know You will do the right thing to the poor,
>*And protect the rights of the needy.*

Then the godly will praise Your name,
>*And they will live in Your presence forever.*

Amen.

But one named Abiathar escaped. He was a son of Ahimelech, who was the son of Ahitub. Abiathar ran away to join David. He told David that Saul had killed the priests of the Lord. Then David said to him, "Doeg the Edomite was there at Nob that day. I knew that he would be sure to inform Saul. So I am responsible for the death of each person of your father's family. The man who wants to kill you is the same man who also wants to kill me. Stay with me. Do not be afraid. You will be safe here with me."

23

DAVID SAVES THE PEOPLE OF KEILAH

FIRST SAMUEL 23

Someone told David: "The Philistines are fighting against Keilah. They are robbing grain from the threshing-floors." (They wanted to starve the Hebrews into submission.) Now Abiathar, a priest, the son of Ahimelech, had brought the ephod with him. He brought it when he fled to Keilah.

Therefore, David asked (probably by means of the Urim and Thummim through Abiathar the priest) the Lord, "Should I go and attack these Philistines?"

The Lord answered, "Go, attack them, and save Keilah."

But David's men said to him, "We are afraid here in the territory of Judah. We would be even more afraid if we went to Keilah; Philistine troops are there."

So David asked the Lord again, and the Lord answered, "Get up, go down to Keilah. I will defeat the Philistines. You will be victorious." So David and his men went to Keilah, and fought the Philistines and captured their livestock. David killed many Philistines. That is how David rescued the people who lived in Keilah.

Saul Continues to Chase David

Someone informed Saul that David was now at Keilah, so Saul thought: "God has given David to me. He has entered a town with gates and bars." (He is trapped.) So Saul called all his army together for battle. They prepared to go down to Keilah to surround David and his men.

But David found out that Saul was making plans to capture him. So David said to Abiathar the priest, "Bring the holy vest here." David prayed, "O Lord God of Israel, I have certainly heard about Saul's plans, that he is coming to Keilah to destroy the town because of me. Will Saul come to Keilah, as I heard? Will the leading men of Keilah surrender me to Saul? O Lord God of Israel, please tell me."

The Lord answered, "Saul will come down."

Again David asked, "Will the people of Keilah surrender me and my men to Saul?"

The Lord answered, "They will do so."

So David and his men left Keilah. There were now about 600 men who went with David. And they went wherever they could go. When Saul found out that David had escaped from Keilah, he cut short his trip there.

David stayed in the hideouts in the desert. He also stayed among the hills of the Desert of Ziph.

Saul was looking for David all the time, but God did not allow him to capture David.

David was at Horesh in the Desert of Ziph. He learned that Saul had come out to kill him. But Jonathan, Saul's son, went to David at Horesh. He helped David have a stronger faith in God.

Jonathan told him, "Do not be afraid. My father will not find you. You will become the king over Israel, and I will be second in rank to you. Even my father Saul knows this is true." And the two of them made another pact in the presence of the Lord. Then Jonathan went back home, but David stayed at Horesh.

The people from Ziph went to Saul at Gibeah, telling him: "David is hiding in our region. He is among the hideouts at Horesh. He is on the hill of Hachilah, south of Jeshimon. (This Hebrew word means "solitude." It is a barren and wild "wilderness of Judea.") Come down, O king, whenever you desire. It is our duty to give David to you."

Saul answered, "May the Lord bless you for helping me. Please go and learn more about David's location. Find out exactly *where* he is hiding. Learn who has seen him there. I know that David is very clever. Investigate all the hiding places that David uses. Then come back and tell me everything. After that, I will travel with you. If David is in that area, I will find him. I will track him down among all the clans in Judah."

So they went back to Ziph ahead of Saul. David and his men were in the Desert of Maon, which is in the Arabah, to the south of Jeshimon. Saul and his men went to look for David, but some people warned David. Then David went down to the cliff which is in the Desert of Maon and stayed there. Saul heard that David had gone there. So Saul chased after David into the Desert of Maon. Saul was going along one side of the mountain, David and his men were on the other side. (There was a deep, narrow, impassable gorge between the two armies. Saul could see his enemies, but he could not get to them.) They were hurrying to get away from Saul. Saul and his soldiers were closing in on David and his men, and were just about to catch them. But a messenger came to Saul, saying, "Come quickly. The Philistines are raiding our land." So Saul quit chasing David and returned to fight the Philistines. That is why people call this place "the Rock of Escape." Then David left the Desert of Maon and stayed in the hideouts of En-Gedi.

Psalm 17

Written by David About This Time

Listen to the prayer of those who live right;
Answer my request to You, O Lord,
Because I am sincere when I pray.

Examine those who live right
And You will know that I am blameless.

You have listened to the thoughts I think,
You visited me in the night to see if I sin.

You have examined me and found no rebellion,
That's because I determined that my mouth would not
transgress.

I know the evil intent of those who hate You,
So I stayed away from them.

Keep me in the right paths
So that my feet won't slip.

I have called unto You because You are listening,
Answer my request that I make.

Show Your wonderful love to me,
And save me by Your strong hand
From my enemies that attack me.

Keep me as the apple of Your eye,
Hide me under the shadow of Your wing.

Because wicked people are ready to attack me,
They have already surrounded me.

They are big and they are powerful,
They brag that they will eliminate me.

Like a lion ready to pounce on its prey,
They are ready to eat me up.

Come to my rescue, Lord, defend me;
You can defeat the wicked.

Lord, I will be happy when I see Y our face;
Then, I will be conformed into Your image.

Amen.

My Time to Pray

Gratitude Is the Least Remembered ⌐ First Samuel 23

And David and his men went to Keilah and fought with the Philistines, struck them with a mighty blow, and took away their livestock. So David saved the inhabitants of Keilah (1 Samuel 23:5).

David's great victory at Keilah was not without danger and loss. The Philistines had seen the ripe grain in the fields just over their border in Judah. They waited until harvest and spread out over the threshing-floors to steal the harvest. Not only would it leave the people without food to eat, it would destroy their economy. *Lord, my enemy is also great.*

David had 400 fighting men who had defected from Saul's army, and others who opposed Saul and saw David as an opportunity to free Israel from the tyranny of Saul (1 Sam. 23:13). They were untested, and so was David's leadership. Would they fight for David or leave him in battle? *Lord, I'm like David; I'm not always sure about the loyalty of those around me.*

The people of Keilah called for David's help; why didn't Saul come to their rescue? That was the king's job. Do we help people just because they ask? The men of David had some questions, "Behold we are afraid in Judah, how much more if we go to Keilah against the armies of the Philistine" (1 Sam. 23:3). *Lord, teach me when to go help another.*

The priest Abiathar had just joined David, and brought along the ephod. This vest had the Urim and Thummim, a way God was able to answer when questions were asked of Him. (Probably a vest pocket held two stones, a white one for yes, and a black one for no.) David had Abiathar ask God, "Shall I go and smite these Philistines?" (1 Sam. 23:2). God's answer, "Yes." *Lord, help me seek Your will for the things I do.*

David's 400 men were not sure they should fight. David inquired of the Lord again, and God answered, "Go." First David took away the "livestock" of the Philistines, which could have included the cattle they stole, or the animals they rode. Then David "smote them with a great slaughter" (1 Sam. 23:5). David saved the city of Keilah. *Lord, thank You for victory.*

Saul heard about David's victory and saw his chance to kill David. "Saul sought him (David) every day, but God delivered him not into his hands" (1 Sam. 23:14). Even though the city of Keilah had double walls, and double gates—great security—Saul felt David was caged up like a bird. Saul's twisted mind said, "God hath delivered him into my hands" (1 Sam. 23:7). *Lord, keep me safe, and keep me from getting into trouble.*

But David was smart, "David knew Saul was plotting something against him" (1 Sam 23:9). David knew Saul would destroy a Jewish city and its people just to kill him. So David got Abiathar to ask God, "Will the city deliver me to Saul to save themselves?" The Lord said, "Yes." *Lord, people won't be gracious if it's not in their best interests.*

David fled into the wilderness and lived in caves. Yet God protected and led David. "Then Saul went on one side of the mountain, and David and his men on the other side of the mountain" (1 Sam. 23:26). *Lord, I will always show gratitude, because You have been gracious to me.*

Amen.

24

DAVID SPARES SAUL'S LIFE

FIRST SAMUEL 24

After Saul had returned from fighting the Philistines, someone told him: "David is in the wilderness of En-Gedi." So Saul got 3,000 men—he chose them from all Israel—and they went to search for David and his men. They looked near the Cliffs of the Wild Goats (a name for En-Gedi). Then Saul came to some sheep pens beside the road, and a cave was there. So Saul went inside to relieve himself. Now David and his men were hiding in that cave—deep inside it. David's men whispered to him, "Look, today is the day the Lord spoke about. The Lord told you: 'I will give your enemy to you. You can do anything you want to Saul.'"

Then, in the darkness, David quietly crawled up to Saul and cut off a corner of Saul's robe. Saul didn't even notice it. Later David felt guilty that he had cut off a corner of Saul's robe. After David returned to his men, he told them, "May the Lord stop me from doing such a thing to my master. Saul was the anointed king of the Lord, I will not do harm to him, because he is the Lord's anointed king." Using these words, David was barely able to stop his men from killing Saul. David would not permit them to attack Saul.

Then Saul rose up and left the cave, and he went on his way.

David came out of the cave, and called out to Saul, "O my master, the
king." Saul looked behind him. David was bowing down on the
ground. Then David laid down on his face. (He was momentari-
ly in a defenseless position.) David said to Saul, "Why do you
listen to people who say: 'David is trying to hurt you?' Today,
you can see with your own eyes—the Lord has just put you in
my power in that cave. My men told me to kill you, but I refused
to kill you. I took pity on you.' I thought: 'I will not harm my
master, because he is the anointed king of the Lord.' My father
(David is showing respect for the older generation), look at this.
It is a piece of your robe in my hand. I cut off the corner of your
robe, but I did not kill you. Now you must understand and
know for sure that I am not planning anything bad against you
or plan to start a rebellion. I have done nothing wrong against
you, yet you are trying to hunt me down and kill me. May the
Lord judge between me and you. And may He punish you for
the wrongs you have done to me. But I will not fight you. As the
ancient proverb says: 'Evil deeds come from evil people.' So I
will not harm you. Against whom are you, the king of Israel,
coming out? Whom are you chasing after? A dead dog? A flea?
I am harmless. May the Lord be our Judge; let Him render a
decision concerning you and me. The Lord will uphold my claim
and show that I was right. He has rescued me from you."

When David finished speaking, Saul asked, "Is this your voice, O David,
my son?" And Saul wept out loud, and told David, "You are
right, and I am wrong. You have been good to me, but I have
done wrong to you. Today you have declared the good things you
have done toward me. The Lord did put me in your hands, yet
you did not kill me. If a man catches his enemy, he does not let
him get away unharmed. May the Lord reward you with good
things, because you were kind to me today. Now listen, I know
that you will certainly be king. You will rule over the kingdom of
Israel. So vow this to me now: Promise me by the authority of

the Lord that you will not kill my descendants. Promise me that you will not wipe out my name from the family of my father."

Therefore David made that solemn promise to Saul. Then Saul returned home. And David and his men went up to his hideout.

Psalm 11

Written by David About This Time

I trust you, Lord, when trouble comes;
>   *Even though people tell me to hide in the mountains,*
>   *They tell me to fly away like a bird.*

My enemies are getting ready to attack me,
>   *They have their bow and arrows to kill me;*
>   *They will attack anyone who lives right.*

Lord, if Your foundations of truth are destroyed,
>   *What can we do who live by Your principles?*

Lord, I recognize You are in Your holy Temple;
>   *You see everything from Your throne in Heaven,*
>   *You will judge all people by what You see.*

Lord, examine both those who live right
>   *And those who hate Your principles.*

Lord, punish those who rebel against You
>   *With the fire and brimstone of hell;*
>   *Give them what they deserve.*

Because You are a righteous God,
>   *You love those who do right;*
>   *You favor them with Your presence.*

>   *Amen.*

My Time to Pray

What Makes a Kite Fly? ∂ First Samuel 24

When Saul had returned from following the Philistines, that it was told him..."David is in the wilderness of En Gedi.' Then Saul took three thousand chosen men from all Israel, and went to seek David (1 Samuel 24:1-2).

What makes a kite fly or an airplane soar? Resistance! Wind blowing into the face of a kite lifts it from the ground. And the stronger the wind, the higher the kite flies. Was it resistance that made David a man of even greater character? Look at all the problems he faced. He was the youngest left to tend sheep, and he learned from them— enough to write the most remembered chapter in Scripture—the 23rd Psalm. *Lord, I will learn from problems.*

Then again, look at the ridicule from his brothers when David wanted to fight Goliath. Also remember Saul tried to dissuade David from fighting Goliath. Even Goliath himself was a formidable obstacle in David's predetermined march to the throne. God chose David because, "He was a man after God's own heart." *Lord, see in me a desire to serve You.*

But a desire to serve God is not enough, the best must have character to go with desire. So God allowed King Saul to live another 13 years, which means God allowed David to be hunted like an outlaw for 13 years. Can you imagine looking over your shoulder for 13 years, knowing any day may be your last day? Any day you may be killed? During those 13 years David learned to trust God more than if he sat around waiting for Saul to die. Resistance made David a greater man of God because he had to yield to God...trust God for protection...and follow God closely. *Lord, I will seek You when resistance comes.*

Wind doesn't make a good kite, and resistance doesn't make just any kite fly higher. No, a kite must be a good kite for the resisting breeze to lift it into the sky. Wind didn't make David great. No, David was great long before he first met Saul. But wind resistance makes a good kite even greater. And so 13 years of running from Saul makes the great David even greater. *Lord, I would be greater.*

The *kite-maker* must have skill to build into his kite all the qualities to make it fly. God was the *king-maker* who built into David all the qualities he needed to be a great king. For 13 years, David learned more leadership qualities by leading 600 men to do right. Difficult wind allowed David to *soar* even higher. *Lord, help me learn the lessons I need when the wind is blowing hardest.*

Amen.

25

SAMUEL DIES

FIRST SAMUEL 25

Samuel died. (According to Josephus, Samuel lived for 18 years of King
Saul's reign. Samuel played a pivotal role, transitioning from the
time of the judges to the Jewish monarchy. God gave His law
[Torah] through Moses, but it was Samuel who prepared the way
for the prophets.) All the Israelites gathered and mourned over
him. In Ramah, they buried him at his home. Then David got
up and moved down to the Desert of Paran.

Abigail and David

There was a very rich man in Maon. He did business at Carmel. He had
3,000 sheep and 1,000 goats, and he was cutting the wool off
his flock at Carmel. The name of this man was Nabal (the word
means "fool"), and he was a descendant of Caleb. His wife's
name was Abigail. She was a beautiful woman, and smart too.
But Nabal was cruel and unfair in his business dealings.

When David was in the desert, he heard that Nabal was cutting the
wool from his sheep. So David sent ten young men, telling
them: "Go up to Nabal at Carmel and greet him on my behalf.
Say this to Nabal: 'May you and your family have good health.
And may all who belong to you have good health. Now I have

heard that your shearers are cutting the wool from your sheep. When your shepherds were with us, we protected them. And the whole time your shepherds were at Carmel, we took nothing from them. Ask your servants, and they will tell you that this is true. We come at a time when things are going well for you. So for this reason, I would like for you to share some of your blessings with my young men. Please give them anything you can spare. Please do this for your son David.'"

When David's young men arrived, they delivered David's message to Nabal faithfully. Then they paused, but Nabal insulted David's servants, answering them: "Who is David? Who is the son of Jesse? These days, many slaves are running away from their masters. I have bread and water. I butchered the animals for my shearers who cut the wool. And the meat belongs to *me*. I will not give it to men I do not know. Where do they come from?"

David's men turned away. They went back and told David everything that Nabal had said. Then David commanded his men, "Let each one of you strap on his sword." So they put on their swords, and David put on his sword, too. About 400 men went up with David, but 200 men stayed with the supplies.

One of Nabal's young servants informed Abigail, Nabal's wife, what had happened. He said, "David has sent messengers from the desert to greet our master, but Nabal yelled at them to go away; he would not share anything with them. Yet those men were very good to us. They always protected us. We never found anything missing during the whole time we were out in the field with them, going in and out among them safely. They have protected us night and day—like a wall—while we were with them, taking caring of our sheep. Now, think carefully about what you should do. It is a major decision. Big trouble is headed for our master, Nabal, and for his entire household, including us. Nabal is such a worthless man; he won't listen to anyone."

Then Abigail hurried, and took 200 loaves of bread, two leather bags full of wine, and five cooked sheep. She also took about one bushel of roasted grain, 100 bunches of raisins, and 200 cakes of pressed figs. She loaded all these things on donkeys. Then she told her servants, "Go on ahead of me. I will follow you." But she did not tell her husband, Nabal. Abigail rode her donkey, and was coming down into the ravine when she met David and his men coming toward her.

David had just said, "What a waste of time it was. I have watched over Nabal's property in the desert. I made sure that none of his sheep was missing. I did nothing but good to him, but Nabal has paid me back with insults. May God punish me terribly if I permit any male of Nabal's household to live until tomorrow morning."

When Abigail saw David, she scrambled off her donkey and bowed down low in front of David. Her face touched the ground. She lay there at David's feet, pleading, "O my master, put the blame on me alone. I beg you, let me talk to you. Please listen to what I have to say. O my master, don't pay any attention to that worthless man, Nabal. He is the same as his name. His name means 'fool,' and he is truly foolish. But I, your servant girl, did not see the young men whom you sent. The Lord has now prevented you from unnecessary bloodshed and personally punishing anyone. As surely as the Lord lives, and as surely as you live, may your enemies and all who intend to harm you become like Nabal. I have brought this gift to you. Please allow it to be given to the young men who follow you. Please forgive my error.

The Lord will certainly make your family into a dynasty that lasts, because you have fought His battles. As long as you live, people will not find anything wrong with you. You have integrity. Even though someone is chasing you to kill you. The Lord your God will keep you alive. He will fling the lives of your enemies away, as one would throw a stone from the pouch of a sling. The Lord will keep all His promises about good things which are in store for you. God has decreed that you will be the prince over Israel. Then you will not have any guilt on your conscience. You will have no serious consequences for killing innocent people and avenging yourself. Please remember me when the Lord brings you success."

David answered Abigail, "Praise the Lord, the God of Israel for sending you to meet me today. May you be blessed for your insight. May you be blessed because you have kept me from killing innocent people and avenging myself by taking matters into my own hands. As surely as the Lord, the God of Israel, lives—He has kept me from hurting you. If you had not hurried to meet me, not one male that belongs to Nabal would have remained alive by dawn tomorrow morning."

Then David accepted Abigail's gifts—what she had brought to him. He told her, "Go up to your home in peace. I have heard your words, and I will do what you have asked."

When Abigail got back to Nabal, he was in the house, having a banquet, eating like a king. He was in a good mood—he was drunk. So she did not tell him anything until the next morning.

In the morning, when Nabal was sober, his wife told him everything that had happened. Then Nabal's heart failed him, and he became rigid, like a stone. About ten days later, the Lord struck down Nabal, and he died.

When David heard that Nabal was dead, he said, "Blessed be the Lord. Nabal insulted me, but the Lord has supported me. God has prevented me from doing wrong. And the Lord caused Nabal's wrongdoing to come back on his own head."

David sent a message to Abigail that he wanted her to marry him. David's servants went to Carmel, and spoke to Abigail, telling her, "David has sent us to bring you to him; he is asking you to become his wife."

Abigail got up and bowed herself down, with her face touching the ground. She said, "I am your servant girl. I am ready to serve him. I am willing to wash the feet of David's servants." Abigail got on a donkey quickly and went with David's messengers. Her five servant girls followed her. And she became David's wife.

David had married Ahinoam of Jezreel, so both women were wives of David. Michal, Saul's daughter, was also David's wife, but Saul had given her to Palti, the son of Laish, from Gallim.

Psalm 120

Written by David About This Time

I called to You, Lord, when I was in trouble;
You heard me when I prayed.

Save me, O Lord, from liars
And from deceitful people.

God, what will You do to the liars
And how much will You punish them?

Inflict them with the pain of sharp arrows,
And with the torment of burning coals.

I am suffering because I live in Meshech,
And stayed in the tents of Kedar.

I have lived too long
Among those who hate peace.

I am a lover of peace,
But they are all men of war.

Amen.

My Time to Pray

Samuel Mourned in Death ᴐ First Samuel 25

Then Samuel died; and the Israelites gathered together and lament-
ed for him, and buried him at his home in Ramah. And David arose
and went down to the Wilderness of Paran (1 Samuel 25:1).

The Bible scholars say Samuel was between 92 and 96 years of age when he died. He had served his Lord faithfully, he had served his people with equal faith. He was buried in the city where he was born, Ramah. *Lord, may I die well and be buried just as Samuel. In my grave I will wait for the return of Jesus Christ.*

The death of Samuel appears to be peaceful, and when he was gone, there was no singular prophetic voice to take his place. Samuel had trained a group of students to speak for God, but none of them became notewor-thy. Yet the greatness of some leaders is not in a solitary follower, but his greatness is leaving an army of followers who do the same thing he did, but without notoriety. *Lord, carry on my work when I'm gone.*

Samuel was buried in the yard of his home. We don't know anything about his wife, but she probably preceded him to death. Samuel was the last judge (1 Sam. 7:6,15) and closed out that era when "every man did that which was right in his own eyes" (Judg. 21:25). Samuel was the first preaching prophet and the first writing prophet. He delivered to the peo-ple God's word. In the transition, Samuel closed out the Judges, and introduced the monarchy. He anointed Saul as the first king, and when Saul's rebellious nature disqualified him from the throne, Samuel anoint-ed David, a man after God's heart. *Lord, thank You for Your great leaders.*

What was Samuel's lasting influence? He reinstituted worship at the Tabernacle. Samuel put the Levites back in charge of ministry. He called for a national celebration of the Passover (1 Sam. 7:6 ff) and there led the people in the first revival in history. When the Philistines attacked Israel, Samuel prayed while the army got a great victory over the Philistines. *Lord, help me be as influential to my generation as Samuel was to his.*

But most of all we remember Samuel as a man of prayer. He was born because of fasting and prayer by his mother. When Israel faced a battle, they cried, "Cease not to cry unto the Lord our God for us, lest He will save us" (7:8). *Lord, teach me to pray like that.*

David probably could not attend Samuel's funeral. But most Bible teachers think David wrote at the passing of Samuel. "Help, O Lord! For the godly man is gone, the faithful are vanishing from the earth" (Ps. 12:1 ELT).

Amen.

26

David Spares Saul's Life Again

First Samuel 26

The people of Ziph went to Saul at Gibeah and said to him, "David is hiding himself on the hill of Hachilah at the edge of Jeshimon" (another word for the desert).

So Saul got up and went down to the Desert of Ziph. He had 3,000 chosen men of Israel who went with him to search for David in that desert. Saul made his camp on the hill of Hachilah, beside the road, at the edge of Jeshimon. But David was still staying in the desert. (He had learned that Saul was coming after him into the desert.) So David sent out spies, and learned that Saul had arrived.

Then David went to the place where Saul was camping. He saw where Saul and Abner, the son of Ner, were sleeping. (Abner was the commander of Saul's army.) Saul was sleeping in the middle of the camp, with the whole army around him.

David talked to Ahimelech the Hittite and Abishai, the son of Zeruiah. Abishai was Joab's brother. David said, "Who will go down into Saul's camp with me?"

Abishai answered, "I will go with you." So that night David and Abishai sneaked into Saul's camp and saw Saul lying there asleep in the middle of the camp. His spear was stuck in the ground near his head. Abner and the army were sleeping all around Saul. Abishai whispered to David, "Today God has let you defeat your enemy. Now allow me to pin Saul to the ground with the spear, just one time. I will not need to hit him twice."

But David whispered back to Abishai, "Do not kill Saul. No one can harm the Lord's anointed king and still be innocent." As surely as the Lord lives, the Lord Himself will punish Saul. Perhaps Saul will die naturally, or he will go into battle and be killed. But the Lord keeps me from harming His anointed king. Now, pick up the spear and the water jug that are near Saul's head and let's get out of here."

So David got the spear and water jug near Saul's head and left. No one saw them. No one knew about it or woke up. The Lord had caused them to stay asleep.

David crossed over to the other side of the hill. Then he stood on top of the hill, which was a long distance from Saul's camp. (David's camp and Saul's camp were far apart.) And David shouted to the army and to Abner, the son of Ner: "Abner, answer me."

Abner answered, "Who are you? Who is calling for the king?"

David said to Abner, "You are supposed to be the greatest soldier in Israel. Isn't that true? Then why didn't you guard your master, the king? We came into your camp to kill your master, the king. What you have done is not good. As surely as the Lord lives, you and your men should die. You have not guarded your master, the Lord's anointed king. Look, where are the king's spear and the water jug which were near his head?"

Saul recognized David's voice, and said, "Is that your voice, David, my son?"

David answered, "Yes, it is, my master, O king." David also said, "Why are you chasing me, my master? What wrong have I done? What crime am I guilty of? And now, my master, the king, please listen to me. If some advisers have caused you to be mad at me, let the Lord condemn them. Those cursed people have forced me to leave the land which the Lord gave me. They have told me, 'Go serve other gods.' Now do not let me die far away from the Lord's presence. The king of Israel has come out searching for a flea. You are like a man hunting a partridge in the mountains."

Then Saul said, "I have done wrong. Come back, David, my son. Today you regarded my life as precious. So I will not try to harm you anymore. Look, I have acted foolishly. I have made a very big mistake."

Then David answered, "Look, here is your spear. Let one of your young men come over here and get it. The Lord rewards every man for the things he does right and for his loyalty to the Lord. The Lord put you into my power today, but I was not willing to harm the Lord's anointed king. Since I valued your life today, surely, in the same way, the Lord will value my life. Surely He will rescue me from all trouble."

Then Saul said to David, "You are blessed, my son, David. You will do great things and succeed."

So, David went on his way, and Saul went back home.

Psalm 35

Written by David About This time

Lord, I want You on my side
Against those who are out to get me.

Protect my back side against my enemies
>*And oppose their evil plans against me.*

Use their lying tactics to confuse them
>*And give me confidence to deal with them.*

Undermine their arrogance and evil determination;
>*Make them suffer the humiliation they plan against me.*

Cut them down like weeds,
>*And let Your angels blow them away like the wind.*

Blind them so they stagger like a blind person;
>*Let Your angels punish them.*

My enemies didn't have any reason to attack me;
>*I didn't do anything to make them mad.*

So punish them when they don't know it's coming,
>*Just like they attacked me when I didn't expect it.*

I rejoice in You, Lord,
>*Because You have saved me from my enemies.*

I thank You deeply for delivering me
>*From an enemy that was too strong for me.*

They lied about me behind my back,
>*I didn't even know they were plotting against me.*

I had been kind to them and helped them,
>*But they returned evil for the good I did for them.*

When they were in trouble,
>*I spent my time praying for them.*

I went without food fasting for them,
>*Did I waste my time caring about them?*

Lord, let Your followers rejoice because You step in;
  Let them know that You will do the right thing
  And that You will punish those who will not follow You.

Lord, I praise You because You will do right;
  I will praise You all day long.

  Amen.

27

David Lives Among the Philistines

First Samuel 27

But David thought: *Saul is going to catch me and my men some day. The best thing for us to do is to make a quick escape to the land of the Philistines. Saul would give up searching for us within all the territory of Israel. Then I can avoid being captured.* So David and the 600 men who were with him got up and crossed the Philistine border. They went to Achish, the son of Maoch. Achish was the king of Gath. David, his men, and their families stayed in Gath with Achish. David had his two wives with him, Ahinoam of Jezreel and Abigail of Carmel. Abigail was previously married to Nabal. Now Saul was told that David had run away to Gath. So Saul did not search for him anymore.

Then David said to Achish, "If you are pleased with me, let me and my men have a place in one of the country towns. We could live there. We don't need to live in the royal city with you."

On that day, Achish assigned David to the town of Ziklag. (That is why Ziklag has belonged to the kings of Judah ever since.) David lived within Philistine territory for one year and four months.

David and his men went up to raid the people of Geshur, Girzi, and Amalek. (The Amalekites were arch-enemies of ancient Israel.) These people had lived for a long time in the land that reached to Shur and to the land of Egypt. When David attacked that region, he killed all of the men and women. He captured sheep, cattle, donkeys, camels, and clothes. Then David returned to Achish.

Many times, Achish would ask David, "Where did you go raiding this time?" And David would tell him that he had gone to the southern part of Judah. Or David would say that he had gone south to the territory of the Jerahmeelites, or south to the Kenites. David never brought back to Gath a man or a woman alive. He thought: *If we bring back anyone alive, he or she may tell Achish: "This is what David really did."* David did this during the whole time that he stayed within Philistine territory.

Achish trusted David, thinking: *David's own people the Israelites, must now truly hate David. Therefore David will serve me forever!*

Psalm 16

Written by David About This Time

Lord, keep me safe
  Because I trust in You.

My soul said You are my Lord,
  Apart from You I have nothing to hope for.

Those who worship earthly gods will never find peace;
  I will not worship idols, nor confess them with my lips.

Lord, You are my future inheritance;
  You are my satisfaction Who will protect me in death.

You have given me a good life,
  I follow the good heritage of my godly parents;

David Lives Among the Philistines

I bless You, Lord, for guiding me throughout life,
You showed me what to do in dark times.

I have always made You my guide;
    I will not be shaken when death comes
    Because You have been at my right hand.

Amen.

28

SAUL CONSULTS A WITCH AT ENDOR

FIRST SAMUEL 28

Later, the Philistines gathered their armies for war to fight against Israel. Achish said to David, "Surely you understand that you and your men must join up with me in my army, don't you?"

David answered Achish, "Certainly. Then you can know for sure what I can do."

Achish said to David, "Good. Then I will appoint you as my personal bodyguard for life."

Now Samuel was dead, and all the Israelites had mourned for him. They had already buried Samuel in his hometown of Ramah.

And Saul had forced out all the spiritists and fortune-tellers from the land of Israel.

The Philistines gathered together, and came and set up camp at Shunem. Saul gathered all the Israelites, and they set up camp at Gilboa. When Saul saw the army of the Philistines, he was afraid, his heart pounded with fear. He tried to communicate to the Lord, but the Lord would not answer him—either through dreams, or through Urim and Thummim (an ephod which was worn by a priest, not Abiathar, who was with David) or through prophets. Then Saul said to his servants, "Find me a woman who is a spiritist. (A medium who claims to communicate with dead people.) I will go and ask her what will happen."

His servants answered, "There is a spiritist in Endor."

Then Saul disguised himself, putting on different clothes. At night, Saul and two of his men went to see that woman. Saul said to her, "Please talk to a spirit for me. Call up the dead person I name."

But the woman said to him, "Listen, surely you know what King Saul has done? He has forced all the spiritists and fortune-tellers out of the land of Israel. Are you trying to trap me and get me killed?"

But Saul made a vow to the woman in the name of Yahweh, saying, "As surely as Yahweh lives, you will not be punished for doing this."

Then the woman asked, "Whom do you want me to bring up for you?"

He answered, "Bring up Samuel for me."

When the woman saw Samuel, she screamed loudly. She said to Saul, "Why did you trick me? You are *Saul.*"

The king said to the woman, "Do not be afraid. What do you see?"

The woman said to Saul, "I see a spirit coming up out of the ground."

Saul asked her, "What does he look like?"

The woman answered, "An old man is coming up. He is wearing a robe."

Then Saul knew it was Samuel, and Saul bowed down his face low to the ground. He laid there facedown.

Samuel asked Saul, "Why have you disturbed me by bringing me up?"

Saul said, "I'm in a lot of trouble. The Philistines are fighting against
me. God has turned away from me. He does not answer me anymore, either by prophets or in dreams. That is why I called for
you; tell me what to do."

Samuel said, "Since the Lord has left you and became your Enemy, why
do you consult me? The Lord has done for Himself what He
said He would do. He spoke those things through me. The Lord
has torn the kingdom out of your hands. And He has given it to
your neighbor—to David. You did not obey the Lord. You did
not carry out His burning anger against the Amalekites. That is
why the Lord has done this thing to you today. Yes, the Lord
will hand both Israel and you over to the Philistines. And tomorrow, you and your sons will be here with me. (With Samuel in
Sheol, the realm of dead people.) Also, the Lord will allow the
Philistines to defeat the army of Israel."

Saul quickly fell to the ground, and the full length of his body lay there.
He was terrified because of what Samuel had said. He was also
very weak, because he had eaten nothing all that day and all
that night.

Then the woman came to Saul. She saw that he was really scared. She
said, "Look, I have obeyed you. I have risked my life and have
done what you told me to do. Now, please, listen to me. Let me
give you some food. Then you could eat and get enough
strength to go on your way."

But Saul refused, saying, "I will not eat."

The woman, joined by Saul's servants, continued to urge Saul to eat
something. Finally, he was persuaded by them. So he got up off
the ground and sat on the bed.

The woman owned a fat calf at the house. She killed it and butchered it
quickly. She took some flour, and she mixed dough with her

hands, and baked the bread without yeast. She put the food in front of Saul and his servants, and they ate. Then that same night, they got up and left.

My Time to Pray

Still Searching for God in the Wrong Places ♂ First Samuel 28

When Saul saw the vast Philistine army, he became frantic with fear. He asked the Lord what he should do, but the Lord refused to answer him, either by dreams, or by sacred lots (Urim and Thummim) or by prophets. Then Saul said to his advisors, "Find a woman who is a medium (witch), so I can go ask her what to do" (1 Samuel 28:6-7 LB).

King Saul looking from the Mountains of Gilboa, saw the Philistine army assembled before him on the plain of Esdraelon (Valley of Armageddon). He was terrified because he had never seen an army this big and this far north. The Philistines lived to the south of Judah, but now they were going to cut the Promised Land in half—probably so they could branch out in each direction to "mop up" any resistance left. For once and all, God's Promised Land would belong to the Philistines. *Lord, satan's forces are huge as we approach the end of the age.*

The lord of each of the five cities of the Philistines assembled on this large plain, later called the battlefield of the world by the famous general Napoleon and the British general Allenby. Probably the well-disciplined troops of Ekron lined up first in perfect rows. Next Saul saw the flags of Ashdod flopping in the breeze. Then another army from Ashkelon appeared in mass, then the pennants of Gaza could be seen, and finally the army of Gath arrived. "The Lords of the Philistines passed on by the hundreds and by thousands." *Lord, I know, "Greater is He who is with me than he who is with the world"* (1 John 4:4 AMP).

Look to the rear of Gath's army, you'll see David and his 600 men marching by. David was the bodyguard for Achish, King of Gath. If David fights Saul and Hebrew soldiers, will he ever be trusted by Israel again? Probably not! If David is in the Philistine army that kills Saul, will it spoil his reputation when he becomes king of Israel? Probably yes! God uses the fear of the other four lords of the Philistines to send David away. Little does anyone present realize that in a few days, David will be king over one tribe—Judah. *Lord, help me look beyond the details of today to see Your larger plan for my life.*

Saul needed the help of God; he is more scared than he's ever been in his life. He is an example of many today who will disobey God, feed the lust of the flesh, and is unaware of the fact that God has turned His back on them. There were three ways God spoke: 1. By dreams, 2. By the Urim and Thummim, and 3. Through prophets. All three were silent. *Lord, teach me to be fearful when Heaven is silent.*

Saul took two trusted servants and traveled ten miles at night to Endor on the other side of the Philistine army. He disguised himself and requested, "Please use your supernatural power of necromancy to bring up someone from the dead" (1 Sam. 28:8). Usually, a demon-inspired woman like this would make a demon appear to imitate the person requested. *Lord, I know there is an evil spirit world; protect me by the Holy Spirit.*

Saul requested, "Bring up Samuel" (1 Sam. 28:11). The witch shrieked in fear because she didn't expect Samuel to actually appear. Some have said this was only an appearance of Samuel the old prophet—not really him—because no one can come back from the dead. Others say it was actually Samuel because a sovereign God has control over the realm of the dead. When Saul realized it was Samuel, he bowed in respect. Samuel reproved Saul again, as he did in life.

Saul told Samuel, "I am deeply distressed…God does not answer me anymore" (1 Sam. 28:15). Aren't most people afraid of dying when they don't know what's on the other side of death? *Lord, I know You'll be with me when I walk through the valley of death (Ps. 23:4).*

Samuel delivers a message that Saul didn't want to hear. "The Lord…has become your Enemy." Then Samuel explained, "The Lord has torn the kingdom out of your hand and given it to your neighbor, David" (1 Sam. 28:16-17). Further, "Tomorrow you and your sons will be with me" (1 Sam. 28:19).

Does the phrase "with me" mean Saul and some of his ungodly sons went to Paradise? Perhaps not! Perhaps Samuel is saying Saul and his sons will be dead tomorrow, just as Samuel was dead. Even though God chose Saul as the first king of Israel, maybe his continued disobedience demonstrated Saul was never a believer in the first place. We probably won't know the answer whether Saul was saved or not till we get to glory. *Lord, none of us deserves to live with You in glory; we are all saved by Your grace.*

Saul is an illustration of what happens to those who continually reject the will of God and refuse to seek God's glory. Disobedience had continuously hardened Saul's heart until it become impossible for him to turn to God. His unbelief was evidenced in his seeking out a witch, which God expressly forbade (see Deut. 18:10-12). Even the dread of the prophecy of the next day couldn't bring Saul to repent and turn to God. *Lord, keep my heart tender toward You.*

Amen.

29

ACHISH SENDS DAVID AND HIS MEN TO ZIKLAG

FIRST SAMUEL 29

The Philistines gathered all of their soldiers at Aphek. The Israelites army camped at the spring which is in Jezreel. The Philistine lords were marching with their groups of 100 soldiers and 1,000 soldiers. And David and his men were marching at the back, along with Achish. The Philistine commanders asked King Achish, "What are these Hebrews doing here?"

Achish answered them, "This is David, isn't it? He used to be an officer to Saul, the king of Israel. But David has been with me for more than a year now. And I have found nothing wrong with David since the time he deserted Saul and came over to me."

But the Philistine commanders were angry with Achish, saying to him, "No! Send David back. He must go back to the town where you assigned him. He must not go with us into battle. If he stays here, then he would become an enemy during the battle. Thus, David would please his own king by killing our own men. David is the one whom the Israelite women still sing about in their dances: 'Saul has killed thousands of his enemies. But David has killed his tens of thousands.'"

So Achish summoned David, saying to him, "As surely as the Lord lives, you are truly loyal; I would be pleased to have you serve in my army. Since the day you came to me until now, I personally have found nothing wrong with you. However, the Philistine lords do not trust you. Return now to Ziklag and go in peace. Do not do anything to upset the other Philistine lords."

David asked Achish, "What have I done wrong? What terrible thing have you discovered in me since the day that I came to you until now? Why won't you allow me to fight your enemies, my lord, the king?"

Achish answered David, "I know that you have been as pleasing to me as an angel of God. But the other Philistine commanders have said: 'David must not go up with us into battle.'

Now early in the morning, you and your former master's soldiers, the Israelites who came with you, ought to go back immediately. As soon as the sun comes up, leave."

So David and his men got up early in the morning and went back to the territory of the Philistines. But the Philistines went up to Jezreel.

My Time to Pray

Have You Ever Been Fired? ↶ First Samuel 29

The Philistine commanders, however, were enraged with Achish and told him, "Send that man (David) back...He must not go down with us into battle only to become our adversary during the battle"...so Achish summoned David..."The leaders don't think you are reliable." (1 Samuel 29:4,6 CSB).

D avid had been given political sanctuary by Achish the Philistine. So David and his 600 men lived and operated under the protected of a foreign ruler. David used this "covering" to attack the Amalekites, the long standing enemies of God's people, Israel. God knew everything that would happen in the next few months. God knew Saul would be killed in battle, and he didn't want David fighting on the wrong side—fighting with the Philistines who would kill Saul. If David stayed with the Philistine army, his reputation would be tainted. For the rest of his life people might suspect David had a hand in killing Saul to get the kingdom. So God had a role in getting David "fired." He was sent home. *God, help me see the big picture—Your picture—when I get fired.*

David fussed at his boss when he was fired, "What have I done?" (1 Sam. 29:8). Don't we all fuss when our ego is tarnished? Because we are mortal we like to complete our task. David wanted to fight with the Philistines, because he had aligned with them. But did David know he'd be killing Hebrew warriors? Did he know he'd be spilling covenant blood? *Lord, You knew.*

It's hard to disengage. It's hard to leave one job and go to another. What about the "empty nest" when all the children are gone? It's hard to readjust. What about a serious illness that forever changes your life? It's hard to break old connections with long-time friends. It's hard to lose those things that gave us identity, or gave us purpose in life. Or gave us meaning and happiness. We feel lost...empty...alone...and dead. Can you thank God for all the good times you've had, before you had to give them up? Can you thank God after they're gone? *Lord, thank You for past blessings You gave to me. Thank You for future times when there'll be greater blessing.*

God knew David's wife and children had been kidnapped by the Amalekites. God wanted David to get one more victory over His enemies. God knew the families of David's 600 men were also kidnapped. If David didn't get them back, he might have lost the support of the new army he'd need when ruling Israel. They were so angry at David, they talked of stoning him (1 Sam. 30:6). *Lord, help me see Your plan on the other side of being fired.*

Old things stand in the way of growing spiritually when God gives us new spiritual experiences. Yes, David had been running from Saul for 13 years, and Philistines had been his friends. Now David needed new friends—the men of Judah who would make him king. Yes, David was successful in hiding from King Saul, now David must learn to be king. Yes, David had given "spoil" to the non-Israel people, now David had to be the supplier of provision for God's people Israel. So God moved the Philistines to "fire" David, so God could install David on the throne of Israel. God is present in both the endings of old things and the beginning of new experiences. *Lord, I'm waiting for new things.*

God is the Lord of "closed doors." There's always the temptation to return to the past because we were comfortable then. But God closes past doors so He can open new doors. New doors will stretch us, challenge us, and new doors make us uncomfortable. But through new doors we enter into new realms of ministry. We become new people when we pass through new doors. *Lord, I'll walk through Your new door.*

Sometimes old doors close slowly, so we're caught in a slow, methodical squeeze. The more we're squeezed, the more pain we suffer. But would you prefer a swift "firing" on one beautiful day? You are fired when you didn't expect it at all, and the pain crashes down on you all at once. *Lord, help me in my pain.*

The same way with open doors. Sometimes a new door is jerked open and we are instantly thrust into a new position. We drown in the new. We lose our identity, meaning, and happiness. Would you rather have your new doors open suddenly or slowly? Didn't new doors help David become monarch to all of Israel? *Lord, You choose my future. Lord, You open doors for me.*

Amen.

30

DAVID DEFEATS THE AMALEKITES

FIRST SAMUEL 30

On the third day, David and his men arrived at Ziklag. The Amalekites had raided southern Judah, including Ziklag. (Because the Philistine forces and David's men were gathered to the north, these Amalekite marauders seized their opportunity to invade this defenseless region in order to pillage it.) They had attacked Ziklag and set it on fire. They had taken the women and everyone else in Ziklag as prisoners—both young and old. But they did not kill anyone. (Perhaps the Amalekites intended to sell these captives as slaves.) As the Amalekites went their way, they carried off their prisoners.

When David and his men came to Ziklag, they found that the town had just been burned. Their wives, sons, and daughters had been taken away as prisoners. Then David and his army cried out loudly, until they were too weak to weep anymore. David's two wives had also been taken, Ahinoam of Jezreel and Abigail of Carmel who was previously married to Nabal.

The men in David's army were threatening to kill David by throwing stones at him. (They thought that their leader, David, had been negligent by leaving Ziklag unguarded.) This upset David very much. Every man was sad and angry because his sons and daughters had been taken as prisoners. But David strengthened himself in the Lord his God.

Psalm 31

Written by David About This Time

Lord, I trust You to deliver me;
> *Don't let me be embarrassed.*

Come down here to listen to me;
> *I need You quickly.*

I need You to be as strong as a rock
> *To keep me from being defeated.*

I need to hold Your hand
> *So You can lead me out of this trouble.*

Get me out of this predicament,
> *I know You can do it.*

I put myself into Your hands
> *Because You are my Redeemer.*

David said to Abiathar the priest, the son of Ahimelech, "Please bring me the holy vest." (The Urim and the Thummim were kept in a pocket in the ephod.) Abiathar did so. Then David prayed to the Lord: "Should I chase the gang who captured our families? If so, will I catch them?"

The Lord answered, "Chase them. You will surely catch them. And, you will succeed in recovering your families."

So David and the 600 men who were with him left. They got to the Besor Ravine. Some of the men stayed there. But David and 400 men continued the chase. The other 200 men stayed behind, because they were too tired and too weak to cross over the Besor Ravine.

Then David's men found an Egyptian slave in a field, and brought him to David. They gave that slave some water to drink and some food to eat. They gave him a piece of a fig cake and two clusters of raisins. After eating, he felt better. He had not eaten any food or drank any water for three days and nights.

David asked him, "Who is your master? Where do you come from?"

He answered, "I am an Egyptian boy. I was the slave of an Amalekite. Three days ago, my master abandoned me because I got sick. We raided the southern area of the Philistines. We attacked the land of Judah, including the southern area that belongs to Caleb. We also set Ziklag on fire."

David asked him, "Will you bring me down to this gang who took our families?"

He answered, "Yes, if you will swear to me, in the presence of God, that you will not kill me or give me back to my master, then I will take you to them."

So the Egyptian man led David down to the Amalekite gang. They were scattered all over the countryside, eating and drinking. They were celebrating with all the many things which they had taken from the land of the Philistines and from the territory of Judah.

David and his men fought them from dawn until just after sunset. None of them escaped, except 400 young men who rode off on the camels. David got his two wives back. He also recovered everything that the Amalekites had stolen. None of their stuff was missing; David brought back everything—the young people and the old people, the sons and the daughters, the valuable things, and everything which the Amalekites had taken for themselves from other towns. David took all the flocks and the herds of cattle. His men drove those animals out in front. They said, "They are David's prize."

Then David came to the 200 men who had been too exhausted to follow him, who had been left behind at the Bensor Ravine. They went out to meet David and the army who was with him. When David came near, the men at the ravine greeted David and his army. But there were some bad men and troublemakers in the group that followed David, who said, "These 200 men did not go with us. Therefore, we should not give them any of the things we captured. But each man may take back his wife and children, then go away."

But David answered, "No, my brothers. Don't do that—after what the Lord has given us. He protected us, and He has handed over to us the enemy who attacked us. Who is going to listen to anything you say? No, the share will be the same for the man who stayed with the supplies as it is for the man who went into battle. All will share alike." David established this as a law and a rule for Israel. That precedent has continued ever since then until today.

David arrived in Ziklag. Then he sent some of the things which he had taken from the Amalekites to his friends, and to the elders of Judah. He said, "Look, here is a present for you from the things we captured from the enemies of the Lord."

David sent some things taken from the Amalekites to the leaders in Bethel, to those in Ramoth-of-the-Negeb of Judah, in Jattir, in Aroer, in Siphmoth, in Eshtemoa, and in Racal. He also sent some plunder to the elders of the towns of the Jerahmeelites and to the towns of the Kenites, to those in Hormah, in Bor-Ashan, in Athach, and to those in Hebron. He sent some things to all the people in the other places where he and his men had roamed.

My Time to Pray

Facing Stress ⌁ First Samuel 30

We share and share alike—those who go to battle and those who guard the equipment (1 Samuel 30:24 LB).

When you think you're doing what you're prepared to do, the enemy may attack you where you least expect it, or when you're not prepared for it. David was prepared to fight, but politics undermined David, and the Philistines sent him home from battle. This was going to be one of the greatest battles, and David couldn't fight. Maybe the greatest thing you ever wanted to do is blocked and you can't be a part of it. You're stuck at home, and you won't be part of the activities. *Lord, help me see Your plan for my life from shut doors.*

When David got home he found his family had been kidnapped, his home burned, and all the families of his men were also kidnapped. This was the second bad news of the day. It's like being fired from a job and when you get home, your family is gone. *Lord, help me accept reverses when they come.*

David's men wanted to stone him. They were angry; and instead of venting their anger on the Amalekites, they took out their frustration on their leader, David. Have you ever been attacked by a person or group because something terrible happened to him or them? *Lord, help me see beyond the attacks by others.*

David asked for the ephod and immediately got directions from God. David was told what to do and when to do it. Don't we get our directions in life from God's Word? When you are tired, or frustrated, or attacked, go to the principles of Scripture. *Lord, keep me in the time of trials.*

As David was pursuing the enemy, some of the warriors couldn't keep up. Were they too old to run that far? Were they unable to go on because they were out of shape because of poor discipline? You must learn that not everyone will go with you to battle. Some are too weak, some are too fearful, and some haven't paid the price of daily discipline; they know they are not equipped to go to battle. *Lord, I will go to battle even if no one else goes with me.*

David and his men won a great victory over the Amalekites. When they returned to these men who stayed behind, there came a crisis. It's something like a church split, people get mad at other Christians because others won't do what is expected. Here David shows his extraordinary wisdom of share and share alike. *Lord, it's better to give than to complain.*

It seems those who were strong and fit ran ahead to catch the Amalekites who had taken every possession of all the soldiers. It also seems there was an agreement that those who couldn't keep up, stayed behind to guard the equipment of those who were strong. We can almost see the strong stripping themselves of excess weight to run faster to catch the Amalekites. At the end David said all soldiers would "share and share alike" (1 Sam. 30:24 LB). *Lord, You reward those who do the most for You and those who do less.*

Amen.

31

Saul Kills Himself

First Samuel 31

The Philistines were fighting against Israel, and the Israelites ran away
from them. Many Israelites were killed on Mount Gilboa. The
Philistines fought extra hard against Saul and his sons, and
killed Saul's sons—Jonathan, Abinadab, and Malchishua. The
battle was fierce around Saul. The archers started to find their
mark—they hit Saul, and their arrows wounded Saul severely.

Then Saul said to the officer who carried his weapons, "Pull out your
sword and kill me, then those uncircumcised Philistines won't
come and abuse me before they kill me." But Saul's officer
refused to do it, because he was terrified. So Saul took the point
of his own sword and threw himself on it. When the officer saw
that Saul was dead, he fell on his own sword too. And he died
with Saul. So they all died together that day—Saul, Saul's three
sons, the officer who carried Saul's weapons, and all of Saul's
bodyguards who were with him that day.

Some Israelites lived on the other side of the Jezreel Valley, and the
other Israelites who were across the Jordan River, when they saw
that the men of Israel retreated, and that Saul and his sons were
dead, they abandoned the Jewish towns and ran away. (Later,
the Philistines came and lived in those towns.)

On the next day, the Philistines came to loot all the valuable things
from the dead soldiers. They found Saul and his three sons dead
on Mount Gilboa. They cut off Saul's head and removed his
weapons. Then they sent messengers to tell the news throughout
the entire country of the Philistines. They told it in the temple of
their idols and to their people. They put Saul's weapons in the
temple of the Ashtaroth. (They were symbolically claiming victory in the name of the Philistine gods.) They also hung up his
body on the wall of Beth-Shan.

The Jews who lived in Jabesh-Gilead heard what the Philistines had
done to the corpse of Saul. So the brave soldiers of Jabesh-
Gilead marched all night and came to Beth-Shan. Then they
took down the bodies of Saul and his sons off the wall of Beth-
Shan, and brought them to Jabesh. There the people of Jabesh
cremated the bodies. They took their bones and buried them
under the tamarisk tree in Jabesh. (Later, King David had their
remains removed from Jabesh and put in Saul's family burial
grounds in Zela, in the territory of Benjamin, see 2 Sam. 21:12-
14.) Then the people of Jabesh fasted for seven days.

My Time to Pray

Was There Any Regard Left? ↙ First Samuel 31

*And when the men of Israel who were on the other side of the val-
ley...saw that the men of Israel had fled, and that Saul and his sons
were dead, they forsook the cities and fled; and the Philistines came
and dwelt in them* (1 Samuel 31:7).

Saul began well and a beautiful reign lay before him. God was with
him and he won several great victories over the Philistines. He stood
head and shoulders above all in physical stature and in allegiance. He was
a popular king (1 Sam. 11:15).

But when he assembled his army at Gilgal, God delayed Samuel because God was testing Saul. Remember, sometimes when things don't happen on your timetable, God operates on His own timetable. God is more interested in who you are than what you do. Saul invaded the priesthood and offered sacrifices to God. Impatience has destroyed many of God's servants. No religious sacrifice is greater than obedience to God. *Lord, I will obey.*

Later God sent Saul to destroy the Amalekites, a perennial enemy of God. Saul fought for weeks to win a military victory, but it was a hollow victory because Saul didn't obey God. *Lord, remind me that partial obedience is complete disobedience.*

It was because of disobedience that God removed Saul from the line of kings. The Spirit of God left Saul, and then God sent Samuel to anoint David in Saul's place. Saul should have known the end was coming when Goliath challenged Israel to fight for 40 days and Saul could do nothing. Then David killed Goliath and gave Israel a great victory. Then the women were dancing and singing, "David killed his ten thousands, but Saul has killed his thousands." Saul's jealousy ruled his life for the next 13 years, and he spent his attention and energy chasing David, rather than fighting the Philistines. Could we conclude that if Saul had properly dealt with the Philistines, then they wouldn't have killed him? *Lord, when the hour of my death comes, may I have something worthwhile to show for the life I've lived.*

The Philistines searched the battlefield for Saul's corpse, but had a hard time finding it because an Amalekite looter had taken the crown and bracelets and tried to get a reward from David (2 Sam. 1). By his armor size they identified Saul, cut off his head, and probably proudly showed it off on the top of a spear. They probably paraded it through the five capital cities of Philistia. Then they placed his armor in the temple of Ashtaroth and pinned his body on the city wall of Beth-Shan. *Lord, the ungodly love to gloat over Your fallen leaders.*

The men of Jabesh-Gilead remembered Saul had come to their rescue earlier. They traveled 14 miles through the darkness, avoiding Philistine soldiers and guards. Under the cover of night, they silently took down the bodies of Saul and his sons, and brought them back to their home. It was there the body of Saul was buried under a tamarisk tree. *Lord, gratitude motivates men to attempt the dangerous for Your glory. May I always be grateful to others who have helped me, even when it threatens my life.*

Amen.

32

WHO WROTE SECOND SAMUEL?

Now the acts of David the king, first and last, behold they are writ-ten in the book of Samuel the Seer (1 Samuel) and in the book of Nathan the prophet, and in the book of Gad the seer (2 Samuel; 1 Chronicles 29:29).

M ost Bible scholars believe Samuel wrote the book we call First Samuel with an unknown writer who penned Second Samuel after Samuel died. It was probably Nathan or Gad (together or separately) who wrote Second Samuel. Since they had access to David's life, they could compose an accurate historical story of David. Also, since they were prophets who spoke *for God*, they could have written the inspired book *for God*. Still some believe Second Samuel was written by an author known only to God.

David Mourns the Deaths of Saul and Jonathan

Second Samuel 1

After Saul was dead, David defeated the Amalekites, and returned to Ziklag. (The Amalekites were Bedouin nomads who had descended from Esau and lived mostly in the Negev; see Gen. 36:12,16.) He stayed there for two days. On the third day, a man came from Saul's camp to Ziklag, his clothes were torn, and he had dirt on his head. He came, fell down, and bowed face down on the ground in front of David.

David asked him, "Where did you come from?"

The man answered, "I escaped from the camp of Israel."

David asked, "What happened? Please tell me."

The man answered, "The Israelite soldiers ran away from the battle, many are dead. Saul and his son Jonathan are dead, too."

David said to the young man, "How do you know that Saul and his son Jonathan are dead?"

The young man answered, "I happened to be on Mount Gilboa, and I saw Saul leaning on his spear. The Philistine chariots and their chariot drivers were getting closer and closer to Saul. When he looked back and saw me, he summoned me. I answered him, 'Here I am.'

Then Saul asked me, 'Who are you?' I told him: 'I am an Amalekite.' Then Saul said to me, 'Come over here and kill me, I am badly wounded, I'm dying.'

So I stood over him and killed him. He had been wounded so badly that I knew he could not live. Then I took the crown off his head and his arm band. And I have brought them here to you, my lord."

Then David tore his own clothes. And all the men with David did so too, being very sad. They wept and fasted until evening. They cried over Saul and his son Jonathan, and wept for the army of the Lord and the people of Israel who had fallen by the sword.

David asked the young man who brought the report, "Where are you from?"

The young man answered, "I am the son of a foreigner, I am an Amalekite."

David asked him, "Why were you not afraid to kill the Lord's anointed king?" Then David said to the Amalekite, "You are responsible for your own death. You have spoken against yourself. You said: 'I have killed the Lord's anointed king.'" Then David called one of his men, "Go, execute that Amalekite." So the Israelite struck down the Amalekite man. He died. (The Amalekite was probably a looter who believed that David, Saul's rival, would reward him. So the Amalekite fabricated his own version of Saul's demise. David knew that he was lying, and publicly David wanted it known that he never participated in the death of King Saul.)

David Mourns Over the Deaths of Jonathan and Saul

Later, David sang a funeral song (something like a eulogy) about Saul and his son Jonathan. David ordered that the people of Judah must learn this song, called, "The Bow." (See 2 Sam. 1:22.) This song is written in the Book of Jashar.

"O Israel, your heroes have been killed on the hills,
How the warriors have fallen in battle.

Do not tell it in Gath,
Do not announce it in the streets of Ashkelon.

If you do, the women of the Philistines will rejoice,
The daughters of uncircumcised ones will gloat.

May there be no dew or rain upon you, you mountains of Gilboa
(this is a curse that has endured to today),
May their fields not produce crops of grain,

Because the shields of the warriors were dishonored there,
Saul's shield will never be polished again with oil.

Jonathan's bow has killed its share of enemies,
Saul's sword had killed its share, too.

Their weapons had been stained with the blood of dead men,
Their weapons had pierced the flesh of some warriors.

We loved Saul and Jonathan,
We enjoyed knowing them while they were alive,
They died together—side by side.

They were faster than eagles,
They were stronger than lions.

O you women of Israel, weep over Saul,
Saul clothed you with beautiful, red dresses,
And he put gold decorations on your clothes.

How the warriors have fallen in the middle of the battle,
Jonathan was killed on top of the hills of Gilboa.

I am grieving over you, O Jonathan, my brother,
You were so dear to me.

Your love for me was so wonderful—
More wonderful than the love of women.

How the warriors have fallen in battle,
How the weapons of war are lost.

My Time to Pray

Between The End and The Beginning ⁊ Second Samuel 1

After David returned from defeating the Amalekites and stayed in
Ziklag two days... (2 Samuel 1:1).

When you walk away from a "closed door," begin looking for the next challenge from God. Look for an "open door." It was two days of waiting for David before the next new door would begin to open, but it would begin with bad news. Saul was dead. Everyone will have a new beginning. So cooperate with the process, don't fight it. It was the new beginning for David and his 600 men. It was now the men of Judah who would make David king. It was now for Saul's followers who wouldn't give up their fixation on "Saul." *Lord, help me to focus on the things You focus on.*

An Amalekite came to bring news to David of Saul's death. David was out of the loop and hadn't heard about it yet. David had fought for the Philistines and was still in an Amalekite city, so the young man thought he could get on David's good side—and perhaps get a reward. The young Amalekite had been a "looter" on the battlefield and evidently lied about his role in Saul's death. David quickly pronounced his death sentence, "Your blood be on your own head." *Lord, may I never "lie" or "stretch the truth" to get on anyone's good side.*

David immediately showed his inner character, he mourned, wept, and fasted. There's no sign of "Saul had it coming because of the scandalous way he treated me." David rose above 13 years of bitterness to pen one of the great eulogies of Scripture. No sign of revenge or self-exaltation. Because David's integrity shines through, no one could suspect David had anything to do with Saul's death. *Lord, may I be forgiving.*

David sang of the exploits of Saul's battles and how Saul had increased the standard of living for Israel. David forgot about all the "wounds" Saul inflicted on him in the past 13 years. David was so different from others who condemn their enemies, and criticize their attackers. David commended Saul. *Lord, I'll do it too.*

David had every right to grieve over Jonathan. After all, Jonathan—Saul's firstborn—had been good to David. He protected David physically, and he defended David from the verbal assaults of Saul. David loved Jonathan as a brother, and in death, weeps for him. But the greatness of David is revealed in his praises to God for Saul. *Lord, I too want to be great in Your sight.*

We begin a new life, only by closing out the old life. David closes out 13 hard years by praising God for Saul. Then he began his new life when

"David inquired of the Lord" (2 Sam. 2:1). This meant David prayed about his future. *Lord, I will pray about my future.*

Amen.

33

DAVID BECOMES KING OF JUDAH

SECOND SAMUEL 2:1-7

Later, David inquired of the Lord, saying, "Should I go up to any of the towns of Judah?" And the Lord said to David, "Go up." Then David asked, "To which one?" The Lord answered, "To Hebron." (It was in the center of the territory of Judah. It would make an excellent capital city, high in the mountains where Philistine chariots could not be effective, and the inhabitants were very sympathetic to David.)

So David went up to Hebron with his two wives. One wife was Ahinoam from Jezreel. The other was Abigail, the previous wife of Nabal in Carmel. David brought his men up there too—each man and his family. They all made their homes in the villages around Hebron.

Then the men of Judah came to Hebron, where they chose David as king over the people of Judah. They told David that the men of Jabesh-Gilead had given a proper burial to Saul. So David sent messengers to the men of Jabesh-Gilead, telling them, "May the Lord bless you. You have shown loyalty to your master, Saul, by burying him with honor. And now, may the Lord be kind and true to you. I will also treat you well because you have done this great deed. (David is diplomatically and clearly communicating to these Benjaminites that he would not seek revenge on anyone who had formerly loved and supported Saul.) Now therefore, be strong and be brave. Your master, Saul, is now dead, and the people of Judah have chosen me as king over them." (David is informing the men of Jabesh-Gilead that he will support them militarily if the Philistines attack them as a reprisal because of their daring raid upon Beth-Shan.)

My Time to Pray

Finding God's Will ᔕ Second Samuel 2

And the men of Judah came and there they anointed David king over the house of Judah (2 Samuel 2:4).

Do you face a decision similar to the one faced by David? He had to leave his home among the Philistines. David had to find a place in Israel to live. He had not had a permanent home in Israel for 13 years. *Lord, find a home for me when I need one.*

David asked God, "Shall I go up to one of the cities of Judah?" God said to him, "Go up." Then David asked, "Where shall we go up?" The Lord answered, "To Hebron" (2 Sam. 2:1). *Lord, I want You to direct my life.*

We are not told how God communicated with David. It could have been with the Urim and Thummim (see Exod. 28:30, Lev. 8:8), or it could be by casting lots (see 1 Sam. 14:37, 23:9-12, 30:7-8; 2 Sam. 5:19, 5:23). Remember, Abiathar the priest had been with David in the wilderness, and he had the ephod the high priest used to determine God's will. Also, God could have used prophetic utterance to guide David. Then too, God could have spoken audibly to David. However God did it, He guided David in this crucial decision. *Lord, guide me just as carefully as You guided David.*

God does not use all these means to guide us today. We can find God's will in the Scriptures. The Bible gives us God's principles on how to live; we must apply these principles to each of our life's situations. While God does not make personal decisions for us in Scripture, we can never be in God's will if we go against Scripture. *Lord, I will live by Scripture.*

Once we read Scripture to find God's will, we then have the indwelling Holy Spirit to help us understand and apply Scripture to our life. Also, the Holy Spirit will lead us (see Rom. 8:14-16). But to get His leading, we must yield to the Spirit's guidance. Yielding may not find God's will, but we cannot find it without yielding. Then we also can pray for God to lead us. *Lord, I pray for You to lead me.*

Circumstances have a lot to do with finding God's will, both for us and David. Saul was dead, David didn't have to hide any longer. He could go home. The question was "where"? The victorious Philistines had not yet gone back home, they were still plundering the towns of Israel after killing Saul. So the Philistines left David alone for the meantime. David probably wanted to go to a city with protective walls. Using his common sense to determine God's leading, it seemed natural for David to choose a place like Hebron. One last point, within the past week David had sent the spoils of his victory over the Amalekites to several Israeli cities, including Hebron (1 Sam. 30:26-31). David's gracious gifts opened them to his leadership. *Lord, help me see the open doors in my life.*

The next phase of David's life was before him. He moved his two wives, Abigail and Ahinoam, into Hebron. His 600 men were added to the defenses of that city. Once David arrived in Hebron, he was made king over Judah. For the next seven and a half years, this would be his home. *Lord, help me see Your plan in my life as clearly as we see Your plan in David's life.*

Did you see the word "there" in the previous text? David was anointed king "there" in Hebron. What if David hadn't gone to Hebron, would the men of Judah go to where he was to anoint David king? Probably not! If David hadn't been led of God to go to Hebron, he might have missed the next step in God's plan for him to rule all Israel. *Lord, may I not miss my step You have for me in my life.*

Amen.

34

ISH-BOSHETH BECOMES A KING TEMPORARILY

SECOND SAMUEL 2:8-32

Now Abner, the son of Ner, was the general of Saul's army. He got Ish-Bosheth, Saul's son, and helped him cross the Jordan River over to Mahanaim (in the territory of the tribe of Gad). There Abner set him up as king over Gilead (the territory to the east of the Jordan River, the only safe region left to the Jews after their stunning defeat by the Philistines at Mount Gilboa) and over the people of Asher, over Ephraim, over Benjamin, and over all the rest of the territory of Israel (North Israel). (Since the Philistines were in control of large sections of the northern tribes of Israel, Abner set up his weak puppet-king Ish-Bosheth in a rival, refugee capital.) Saul's son, Ish-Bosheth, was 40 years old when he became "king" over Israel. He ruled for only two years. (This may mean that Abner took over complete control of Ish-Bosheth's kingdom after the first two years of figure-head existence. Or, it could mean that Ish-Bosheth's "reign" could not begin until after about five years of fighting with the Philistines. If so, that would correspond roughly with the last two years of David's reign in Hebron.) However, the people of Judah followed David. The length of time that David was king in Hebron over the people of Judah was seven years and six months.

War Between Judah and Israel

Abner and the servants of Ish-Bosheth left Mahanaim and went out to Gibeon. Joab, David's general, and David's men also went out there. They met Abner and Ish-Bosheth's men at the pool of Gibeon. Abner's group sat on one side of the pool, Joab's group sat on the other side.

Abner said to Joab, "Let's have the young men get up and have some hand-to-hand combat." (Like the brutal "game" of the Roman gladiators.)

Joab said, "Yes, let them have a contest" (to the death).

Then the young men got up. The two groups counted for the contest. Twelve men were chosen from the people of Benjamin for Ish-Bosheth, the son of Saul, and 12 men were chosen from David's men. Each man grabbed his enemy's head. Then he stabbed his enemy's side with a knife. And the men fell down together. So that place in Gibeon is called "The Field of the Sharp Edges." On that day, it turned into a horrible battle. And David's men defeated Abner and the men of Israel.

Zeruiah, David's sister, had three sons—Joab, Abishai, and Asahel, who were all there. Now Asahel was a fast runner, as fast as a deer in the field. So Asahel chased Abner, going straight toward him.

Abner looked back as he ran and asked, "Is that you, Asahel?"

Asahel said, "Yes, it's me."

Then Abner said to Asahel, "Turn to your right or to your left. Catch one of the young men and take his armor" (as a trophy of warfare). But Asahel refused to stop chasing Abner.

Again, Abner said to Asahel, "Stop chasing me. Turn away. If you don't stop, I'll have to kill you. Then I won't be able to face your brother Joab again." (Abner was reluctant to kill young Asahel, because Abner knew that this would invoke a fanatical vengeance from Joab, Asahel's older brother.)

But Asahel refused to stop chasing Abner. So Abner plunged the butt-end of his spear into Asahel's stomach, and the spear came out his back. Asahel died right there. When everyone came to the spot where Asahel's body lay, they stopped.

But Joab and Abishai continued chasing after Abner. The sun was going down when they arrived at the hill of Ammah. This is near Giah on the way to the isolated land near Gibeon. The men of Benjamin came to assist Abner, banding together as a group at the top of one hill.

Abner shouted to Joab: "Must the sword kill forever? Surely you must know that this will only end in bitterness. Tell the people to stop chasing their own Jewish brothers." (Abner pleads with Joab not to let this skirmish escalate into a very destructive civil war.)

Then Joab said, "As surely as the one true God lives, if you had not challenged them to a fight." Then Joab blew a trumpet, and his small army stopped chasing the Israelites. They did not try to fight them anymore.

Abner and his men marched all night through the Jordan Valley, then crossed the Jordan River. After marching all day, they arrived at Mahanaim.

Joab came back after he had stopped chasing Abner, and gathered all of his small army together. Asahel and 19 of David's men were missing. But David's men had struck down 360 Benjaminites who had followed Abner, and they died.

David's men picked up Asahel's corpse and buried it in the tomb of his
father at Bethlehem. Then Joab and his men marched all night,
reaching Hebron as the sun came up.

My Time to Pray

Like Father, Like Son ∂ Second Samuel 3

*Now there was a long war between the house of Saul and the house
of David. But David grew stronger and stronger, and the house of
Saul grew weaker and weaker* (2 Samuel 3:1).

When the minister visited in the home of a member who had been
missing from church, the father told the pastor, "I spend my
Sundays on prayer vigil." The minister seemed to nod in approval when
the little boy piped up, "His boat is called Prayer Vigil, but God doesn't
answer his prayers; he hasn't caught many fish."

Whether we admit it or not, our children are chips off the ol' block. And
the sons of Saul reflected their father. When Saul was a young king, he
named his first son *Jonathan*, which means "gift of God." This shows the
faith in the Lord that Saul had as a young father. When Saul got older, he
named his last son, "Ish-Bosheth," which means "son of Baal." How could
Saul name his son after a heathen idol? The answer is easy, between the
birth of Saul's first son and last son, he disobeyed Jehovah, violated his
covenant of the monarchy, and became infatuated with heathen gods.
Lord, may I never embarrass the name "Christian."

Ish-Bosheth tried vainly to rule the kingdom, just like his father. Saul held
on to the throne out of selfish pride, and tried to kill David out of jealous
anger. Ish-Bosheth hated David for the same reason as his father.
Children will follow the example of their parents, unless there is an excep-
tion. The only thing to transform a child is the grace of God and the
power of Christ. *Lord, thank You that I am different from my father.*

My (Elmer Towns) father met my mother at a dance, and she knew he drank heavily, but married him anyway, saying, "I can change him." She didn't, and as I got older, my father came more and more under the power of liquor. Once when Daddy fell in the street and couldn't get up, Mother sent me to help him up out of the street. People on their porches were laughing at him and the little boy who couldn't get his father up. Standing in that street, I determined, "I'll never be a drunk like my father." Then years later I was saved, and the power of Christ transformed my outlook on life. *Lord, I promised I'd never drink liquor, and I've kept that promise. May others make the same commitment.*

It's said "fruit doesn't fall very far from the roots of the tree." May every reader plant himself by rivers of living water (see Ps. 1:3) and bring forth the fruit of holiness in its season. *Lord, I'll do that.*

Amen.

35

THE SONS OF DAVID
WHO WERE BORN IN HEBRON

SECOND SAMUEL 3

There was a long war between the people who supported Saul's household and those who supported David's household. The supporters of David's household were growing stronger, while the supporters of Saul's household were getting weaker.

Sons were born to David in Hebron. The firstborn son was Amnon, born to Ahinoam from Jezreel. The second son was Chileab, born to Abigail, the previous wife of Nabal from Carmel. The third son was Absalom, born to Maacah, the daughter of Talmai, the king of Geshur. The fourth son was Adonijah, born to Haggith. The fifth son was Shephatiah, born to Abital. The sixth son was Ithream born to Eglah. These sons were born to David in Hebron. (Not all of David's children are mentioned here. The polygamy of David was wrong; monogamy was God's original intent for marriage [see Gen. 2:18-24].)

Abner Decides to Join David

Abner strengthened himself in the household of Saul during the war between the supporters of Saul's household and the supporters of David's household. Now Saul once had a concubine named

Rizpah, the daughter of Aiah. Ish-Bosheth said to Abner, "Why did you have sex with my father's concubine?"

Abner became very angry because of what Ish-Bosheth said. Abner replied, "Am I on Judah's side? I am not a traitor working for Judah. I have been loyal to the household of Saul and his family and friends. I didn't hand you over to David. But now you are saying I did something wrong with this woman. May God punish me terribly if I don't help David now. I will make sure that what the Lord has promised does happen. I will take the kingdom away from the household of Saul and cause David to be king of Israel and Judah. He will rule from Dan to Beer-Sheba."

Ish-Bosheth could not say anything more to Abner, because he was so afraid of Abner.

Then Abner sent messengers to David at Hebron, saying, "To whom does the land really belong? Make a deal with me. Listen, I will help you become the king of all Israel."

David answered, "Good! I will make a deal with you. But I ask one thing of you. I will not meet with you (you will not see my face) unless you first bring Saul's daughter Michal to me."

Then David sent messengers to Saul's son, Ish-Bosheth, saying, "Give me my wife, Michal. She was promised to me when I killed 100 Philistines to get her."

So Ish-Bosheth sent men to take Michal from her second husband, Paltiel, the son of Laish. Michal's husband went with her, weeping as he followed her to Bahurim. But Abner said to Paltiel, "Go back home." So he went home.

Abner sent a message to the elders of Israel, saying, "You have been eager to crown David as king over you. Now do it. The Lord has spoken about David. The Lord said: 'I will save My people, the

Israelites, through My servant, David. He will save them from the control of the Philistines and all of their enemies.'" (Abner's forces had not been very successful in breaking the stranglehold of the Philistines over most of Northern Israel. But Abner knew that David had the military strength to vanquish the Philistines. It was time for Abner to switch sides.)

Abner also said these things to the people of Benjamin. (This tribe was the most resistant to the idea of David being their new king because Saul and Ish-Bosheth were Benjaminites.) Then Abner went to Hebron to tell David what the Benjaminites and Israel wanted to do. Abner came with 20 men to David at Hebron. There David prepared a banquet for them. Then Abner said to David, "O my master, the king, I will go and bring all the Israelites to you. Then they will make a covenant with you. You will rule over all Israel." So, David let Abner go, and he left in peace.

Joab Kills Abner

Then the soldiers of Joab and David came back from a battle and brought much plunder with them. Abner was no longer with David at Hebron when Joab arrived. David had sent Abner away in peace.

When Joab and all his army arrived back in Hebron, some people told Joab, "Abner, the son of Ner, came to see King David, and David allowed him to leave in peace."

Then Joab went to the king and said, "What have you done? When Abner came to you, why did you let him go? Now he's gone. He came here to deceive you! He wants to find out about everything you are doing."

Then Joab left David and sent messengers after Abner (probably having some of David's representatives tell Abner that he needed to return to David's capital for some urgent "official business"). They brought Abner back from the well of Sirah. (Joab knew that he could not kill Abner inside Hebron, because it was a city of refuge. Sirah was about two miles away from Hebron.) However, David did not know this.

When Abner arrived near Hebron, Joab took him aside at the gate of Sirah, and acted as though he wanted to talk with Abner in private. But Joab stabbed Abner in the stomach, and Abner died. (Abner had killed Joab's brother, Asahel.)

Later, David heard about Abner's death, and said, "My kingdom and I are innocent—forever. (David did everything he could to disassociate himself from Joab's vile deed.) The Lord knows this. We did not kill Abner. Joab and his family are the ones who did this. May many problems swirl like a storm around his head. May his family always have someone with running sores or who has leprosy. May they always have someone who leans on a crutch. May some of his family be killed in war. May they always have someone without food to eat."

Joab and his brother Abishai had killed Abner because Abner had killed their brother Asahel at the battle at Gibeon.

Then David spoke to Joab and all the people who were with Joab, saying, "Tear your clothes and wear sackcloth. Weep for Abner." At the funeral, King David himself walked behind the coffin of Abner. So they buried Abner in Hebron, and David raised his voice to cry at Abner's grave. And all the people wept with him.

King David sang this funeral song for Abner:

"Should Abner have died like a fool? No!
His hands were not tied.
His feet were not brought in bronze chains.

He fell as a person falls in front of evil men."
Then all the people wept for Abner even more.

They came to encourage David to eat something while it was still daytime. However, David had vowed: "May God punish me terribly if I eat bread, or anything else, before the sun sets." All the people noticed this and approved everything the king did. On that day, all the people of Judah and all the other Israelites understood. They knew that it was not David who had killed Abner. David said to his soldiers, "Don't you realize that a very important general in Israel has died today? Even though I am the anointed king, I am weak today. These sons of Zeruiah (Joab and Abishai, nephews of David) are too harsh for me. Accordingly, may the Lord pay them back for the wrong they did."

My Time to Pray

Not Everything Happens At Once ✑ Second Samuel 3

And David grew steadily stronger, but the house of Saul grew continually weaker (2 Samuel 3:1).

Have you ever noticed that most of the big things we hope for and pray for and plan for don't happen suddenly? Rather, the big things we want usually come in stages, or if not in small steps; big things like the dawning of a new day come gradually. The sun doesn't come up instantly, like switching on a light in a dark room. *Lord, give me patience to accept things that come slowly.*

221

Saul was killed and that should have ended the hostilities against God's chosen man to lead Israel. But it would be another seven and a half years before David was crowned king over all Israel. It wasn't that people intentionally thwart God's plan, it's just that people have their own agenda that's different from God's plan. Also, things take time. News travels slowly, and even when people heard new news—good news—it takes time to assimilate it and act on it. Don't forget, people change their minds slowly. *Lord, help me understand how new things happen.*

Saul was dead, and almost everyone knew David was to be king. But notice, "Abner was making himself strong in the house of Saul" (2 Sam. 3:6). Abner could not have the power of king, so he grabbed the power of king-maker, he put Ish-Bosheth on the throne over the tribes of the north. Look at the puppet-king, "And he (Ish-Bosheth) could no longer answer Abner...because he was afraid of him" (2 Sam. 3:11). So Abner kept the war going between the northern tribes and David. *Lord, may none of my sins thwart Your plans.*

Notice the patience of God. He sits in Heaven, allowing sinful men to carry out their selfish plans. It looks like sinful men are thwarting God's plans. But in God's sovereignty, He works behind the scenes to accomplish His will. God never seems to be in a hurry, but He always works with determination. *Lord, teach me Your patience, and put within my heart a spirit of determination to do Your will.*

Notice what David did in his period of transition. He didn't just wait for God to do everything for him. David moved to a fortified city, so that his base of operations made a statement to his enemies. David acted graciously to those who followed Saul, he was not motivated by revenge or anger. David was gracious to all, knowing he would rule all one day. *Lord, help me live today at the level I want to live in the future.*

Amen.

36

A HARMONY OF SECOND SAMUEL AND FIRST CHRONICLES

I have attempted to harmonize Second Samuel and First Chronicles 11-29 because they cover the same period of time from two perspectives. If anything, Second Samuel emphasizes David as king, while First Chronicles emphasizes the priestly line, and includes the work of the Levites in the new Temple to be built by Solomon. Obviously, I've not repeated a section of Scripture when both cover the same event.

Since we're *Praying the Heart of David* we will emphasize First and Second Samuel and leave out First Chronicles, except where the Chronicles' version is a fuller text, or where Chronicles includes events left out of Second Samuel.

There is a long genealogy in Second Chronicles 1-11 that is also left out, not because it is unimportant. The opposite is true, the genealogy shows the line of Christ from Adam to the end of the Old Testament. Matthew 1:1-17 is the legal line to Joseph proving Jesus has the political right to rule. And Luke 3:23-38 is the biological line of Mary proving he has the human qualifications to rule. The genealogy was left out of this volume because it's hard to pray the family tree.

Who Wrote First and Second Chronicles?

The Book of Chronicles was originally known by its opening line, *Dibere ayyamin*, "The Annals of the Days," and was considered one book. The Hebrew version contained no vowels, hence it was originally one large book. But when Chronicles was printed into Greek, vowels were added that significantly lengthened the book, so two bindings were needed. In the fourth century Jerome in his Latin Vulgate gave it the title *Chronicon*

Totius Divinae Historiae (A Chronicle of the Whole Sacred History). From then on it's been known as First and Second Chronicles.

Who wrote the Books of Chronicles? Obviously, we don't know because an author is not noted in the books. Almost every scholar says Ezra wrote First and Second Chronicles, who also wrote a book by his name. Ezra was from the line of Aaron through Phinehas (see Ezra 7:1-5). That makes him a priest. He was a skilled expositor of Scripture (Ezra 7:6,12). He had the skill, temperament, and desire to write these books.

Ezra lived in Babylonia, and gained permission from the Persian King Artaxerxes to lead a group of exiles back to the Holy Land (458 B.C.). Prayer and sacrifice had not been celebrated in Jerusalem by the priest he found there. Since he was committed to God, he instituted these things.

When Jewish laymen came back to the Holy Land from Babylon and other places where they had been dispersed, they needed to establish their lineage. Were they true Jews? What was their lineage? Ezra includes a lineage of Jewish people from the beginning of the return of the Jews to the Holy Land.

Note Second Chronicles ends with a reference to the decree of Cyrus King of Persia to allow Jews to emigrate back to the Holy Land (2 Chron. 36:22-23). The Book of Ezra begins with the same information and continues the history of God's people. Thus, volumes 1 and 2 of Ezra's history were First and Second Chronicles, then Ezra's volumes 3 and 4 were the two Books, Ezra and Nehemiah.

Ezra is described as one having a large library of the kings and prophets and the writings of David, (2 Maccabees 2:13 Apocrypha). Then compare this to all the writings (books) that the author of Chronicles cites in his work: *The Book of the Kings of Judah and Israel, Story of the Book of the Kings, Works of Uzziah,* a book by Isaiah, the works of Shemiah the prophet, and of Iddo the seer, a midrash of the prophet Iddo, the work of Jehu the son of Hanani, the words of Hozai, and the *Book of Nahum* the prophet.

Therefore, since Ezra had all the human ability to write First and Second Chronicles, plus all the written resources, added to his passion to demonstrate

the Messianic line through the Old Testament, I've come to the sensible conclusion that Ezra wrote First and Second Chronicles.

First Chronicles 12:23-40

These were the leaders who joined David at Hebron. They came ready
for battle, to transfer the kingdom of Saul over to David. The
Lord has said that this would happen.

There were 6,800 men from the people of Judah ready for battle. They
carried shields and spears.

There were 7,100 men from the people of Simeon, brave soldiers ready
for battle.

There were 4,600 men from the people of Levi. (They would not fight
but they supported David.) Jehoiada, a leader from Aaron's
household, was in that group. There were 3,700 men with him.
Zadok was also in that group. He was a strong, brave, young
man who came with 22 leaders from his father's household.

There were 3,000 men from the tribe of Benjamin who were Saul's relatives. Most of them had remained loyal to Saul's family until
then.

There were 20,800 brave soldiers from the half-tribe of Ephraim. They
were famous men in their own family groups.

There were 18,000 men from the western half-tribe of Manasseh. Each
man was especially chosen to accept David as king.

There were 200 leaders from the tribe of Issachar. They knew what
Israel should do, and they knew the right time to do it.

There were 50,000 trained soldiers from the tribe of Zebulun. They
could handle any weapon. They followed David completely.

There were 1,000 officers from the tribe of Naphtali, who had 37,000 men with them who carried shields and spears.

There were 28,600 men from the tribe of Dan, ready for war.

There were 40,000 trained soldiers from the tribe of Asher, ready for war.

There were 120,000 men from the east side of the Jordan River, from the tribe of Reuben, Gad, and the eastern half-tribe of Manasseh. They had every kind of weapon for warfare.

All of these fighting men were ready to go to war. They came to Hebron fully agreed to proclaim David as king over all Israel. And also the rest of Israel was of one heart to make David the king. The men spent three days there with David, and ate and drank, because their Jewish relatives had prepared food for them. Also, their Jewish neighbors brought more food from as far away as the areas belonging to Issachar, Zebulun, and Naphtali. They brought food on donkeys, on camels, on mules, and on cattle. They brought much flour, fig cakes, raisins, wine, oil, cows, and sheep. This was because the people of Israel were very happy that David would be their king.

37

Ish-Bosheth Is Murdered

Second Samuel 4

When Ish-Bosheth, the remaining son of Saul, heard that Abner had died at Hebron, he was frightened, and all Israel was terrified. There were two men who were captains in Ish-Bosheth's army. The name of one was Baanah, and the second one was named Rechab. They were the sons of Rimmon, of the sons of Benjamin, from Beeroth. The town of Beeroth belongs with the tribe of Benjamin. The people of Beeroth had run away to Gittaim, and they still live there today.

Now Jonathan, the son of Saul, had a son who was crippled in both feet. His name was Mephi-Bosheth. He was five years old when the news came from the Valley of Jezreel that Saul and Jonathan had been killed. Mephi-Bosheth's nurse picked him up and ran away. However, as she hurried to leave, Mephi-Bosheth fell down and became crippled.

So, Rechab and Baanah went to Ish-Bosheth's house at noon. Ish-Bosheth was lying on his bed. They got inside the house, as if they were bringing some wheat. Rechab and Baanah stabbed him in the stomach, then cut off his head and took it with them. They traveled all night through the Jordan Valley. When they arrived at Hebron, they gave Ish-Bosheth's head to David. They said to the king, "Look, here is the head of Ish-Bosheth, the last son of Saul. He was your enemy. He was trying to kill you. Today the Lord has paid back Saul and his family for what they did to you." (Rechab and Baanah thought that they would be richly rewarded by King David.)

David answered Rechab and Baanah, "As surely as the Lord lives, He has saved me from all troubles. One time, a man thought he was bringing me good news. He told me: 'Look, Saul is dead.' But I grabbed him and killed him at Ziklag. That was the reward I gave him for his news. Even more so, will I require your death. This is because your evil men have killed an innocent man. He was lying down on his bed, in his own house."

So David ordered his men to execute Rechab and Baanah. Then David's soldiers cut off their hands and feet, and hung them over the pool of Hebron. (These mutilated body parts had been the instruments to perpetrate the crime. David wanted to show how abhorrent their deed was to him. This act was a visible warning to others who might be contemplating killing any of David's alleged "enemies.") Next, they took Ish-Bosheth's head and buried it in Abner's tomb at Hebron.

My Time to Pray

It's Wrong To Do Right in the Wrong Way ❧ Second Samuel 4

And (when) the son of Saul (Ish-Bosheth) heard that Abner (was) dead in Hebron, his heart dropped, and all of Israel was terrified (2 Samuel 4:1).

God had predicted almost 20 years earlier that David would be king over all His people—note all the evil men who tried to thwart God's plan: Saul, Abner, Ish-Bosheth, and other lesser names. But God uses even the evil deeds of men to bring about His plan, demonstrating what Paul said, "All things work together for good, to them who love God" (Rom. 8:28). *Lord, I trust Your plan, work Your guidance in my life.*

After Abner was killed, the real power in the northern tribe was eliminated. Ish-Bosheth never had the power; he was a puppet king, even though he was an existing legitimate heir to Saul's throne. The story of Mephi-Bosheth is introduced here to remind readers there were no more legitimate heirs (challengers) to David's throne. A person who was infirmed, such as Mephi-Bosheth's lameness, was prohibited from being king.

Two brothers, Rechab and Baanah, who had risen through the ranks in the army to captain, plotted to murder King Ish-Bosheth. God allowed them to fulfill His plan, even though they committed premeditated murder to do it. Notice God didn't *direct* them to commit murder, God allowed them to do it. It is never right to do wrong, even when you think what you do is right. In other words, "the end does not justify the means." *Lord, may I always do right, in the right way, at the right time, for the right reasons.*

The crime had been done outside David's jurisdiction. But David wanted everyone to know he was not part of any plot to assassinate his rival. Just as David acted honorably toward Saul, so he acted honorably toward Ish-Bosheth. He pronounced the execution of Rechab and Baanah. Their hands and feet (what had been swift to shed innocent blood) were hung in a tree by the pool in Hebron. This was where the population came daily to get water, therefore the news of their execution would spread quickly throughout the city. David's reputation of graciousness to the northern tribes would also be spread in quick fashion. *Lord, I marvel at Your work.*

The bodies of the two assassins were dumped on a burning trash heap, probably a picture of Gehenna, and Ish-Bosheth's head was buried in dignity in the tomb of Abner. The northern tribes could see that David honored their leaders and punished their criminals. The stage is now set for God to complete His prediction for David to reign over all Israel. *Lord, thank You for working Your plan for David, I trust You to work Your plan for me.*

Amen.

38

DAVID BECOMES KING OVER ALL ISRAEL

SECOND SAMUEL 5

Then all the tribes of Israel said to David at Hebron, "We are your family (literally, we are your own flesh and blood). In the past, Saul was king over us, but you were the one leading us out in battle and bringing in Israel. The Lord said to you, 'You will be like a shepherd for My people, Israel. You will become the ruler over them.'"

All the elders of Israel came to King David at Hebron and he made a covenant with them in Hebron in the presence of the Lord. (The Tabernacle and the altar may have been at Hebron at this time, though the Ark of the Covenant was still at Kiriath-Jearim.) Then they poured oil on David to make him king over Israel.

David was 30 years old when he became king. He ruled for 40 years. In Hebron, he was king over Judah for seven years and six months. Then, in Jerusalem, he was king over all Israel and Judah for 33 years.

The king and his men went to Jerusalem to attack the Jebusites who lived there (though Joshua's men had "conquered" the Jebusites [see Josh. 11:3; Judg. 1:8], a resistant pocket of them still occupied this fort at Jebus. Jerusalem made an ideal new capital for the whole country.). One of the Jebusites shouted to David: "You cannot come in here. Even our blind people and those who are crippled could stop you." They said this because they thought David could never enter their city. Nevertheless, David did capture the city of Jerusalem, along with its strong walls. (The stronghold of Zion, the ancient hill upon which the city stood, about 60 acres.) It became "The City of David."

On that day, David said to his men, "To defeat the Jebusites, someone must go up through the water tunnel. (This was a protected water shaft [probably the entrance near the Gihon Fountain] which supplied a natural, perennial spring of water at the eastern foot of the mountain ridge.) Then you can reach my so-called 'crippled' and 'blind' enemies. That is why people say: 'The blind and the crippled cannot enter the palace.'"

So David lived in the city, within its strong walls. He called it "the City of David," and he built more buildings around it. (Thus, it had to be well-fortified by man-made walls.) He began where the land was filled in on the east side of the city, and built more buildings inside the city. He became stronger and stronger, because the Lord, the God of Heaven's armies, was with him.

Hiram, the king of the city of Tyre, sent messengers to David, along with cedar logs, carpenters, and men to cut stones for walls. They built a palace for David. Then David realized that the Lord had truly made him king over Israel. And he knew that the Lord had made his kingdom very important. This was because the Lord loved His people, Israel.

In Jerusalem, David took for himself more concubines and wives from Jerusalem. This was after he moved there from Hebron. More sons and daughters were born to David. These are the names of the sons born to David in Jerusalem: Shammua, Shobab, Nathan, Solomon, Ibhar, Elishua, Nepheg, Japhia, Elishama, Eliada, and Eliphelet.

David Defeats the Philistines

Now the Philistines heard that David had been anointed king over
Israel. So all the Philistines went to invade David's united king-
dom, because it was much more dangerous to them. But when
David heard the news, he went down to a safe place. So the
Philistines came and camped out in the Valley of Rephaim.

David asked the Lord, "Should I attack the Philistines? Will You help me
defeat them?"

The Lord said to David, "Go, I will certainly help you defeat them."

So David went to Baal-Perazim and defeated the Philistines there.
David said, "Like a flash flood of water, the Lord has broken
through my enemies." That's why David named that place Baal-
Perazim. The Philistines left their idols behind at Baal-Perazim.
And David and his men carried those idols away. (The Law of
Moses directed that they must be burned [Deut. 7:5,25]. After
parading these foreign gods, David's soldiers made a bonfire.
See 1 Chron. 14:10-12.)

Once again, the Philistines came up and camped out in the Valley of
Rephaim. (This probably happened one year later, and this time,
the Philistines had an even larger army.) David prayed to the
Lord. This time, the Lord told David, "Don't attack the
Philistines from the front. Instead, go around and attack them
opposite the balsam trees. (When the leaves rustled with even
the slightest movement of air, they made a sound that threw the
hearts of the Philistine army into panic.) You will hear the sound
of marching in the tops of the balsam trees. Then you must
strike quickly. I, the Lord, will have already gone ahead of you to
defeat the Philistine army."

So David did exactly as the Lord commanded. He defeated the
Philistines and chased them all the way from Gibeon to Gezer.

My Time to Pray

Winning Graciously ⌁ Second Samuel 5

O Lord, truly I am Your servant; I am Your servant, the son of Your maidservant; You have loosed my bonds. I will offer to You the sacrifice of thanksgiving, and will call upon the name of the Lord (Psalm 116:16-17).

Do you know how to win with a humble attitude? When someone has done you wrong and they ask for forgiveness, can you forgive and forget? What about those who have done you wrong, but they've never confessed their wrong; or they've never asked your forgiveness, but now they want to be your friend, or they want to work with you? What is your attitude? *Lord, teach me to be gracious in both defeat and victory.*

Now that both Saul and Ish-Bosheth are dead, the leaders of the northern tribes came to see David. It would be nice if their primary motivation was spiritual, but it's not. When you read carefully, you see they wanted David to fight for them against the Philistines. Their real goal in seeking peace and unification was freedom from Philistine oppression and demanding taxes. This was a case of doing the right thing for an inferior motivation. *Lord, help me do right for the right reason.*

The leaders from the north first appealed to their common heritage, "Look we are your bone and your flesh" (2 Sam. 5:1). Doesn't family always tug on our hearts?

The second appeal was their primary motivation. They wanted a proven warrior who could win battles. "When Saul was king over us, you were the one who led Israel in and out" (2 Sam. 5:2).

The third appeal was spiritual, "The Lord said, 'You will shepherd My people Israel, and you will be a leader over Israel'" (2 Sam. 5:2). They should have mentioned God's will first, but it was lost in their appeal to David. If God's will was so plain to them now, why had they not seen it 22 years earlier? And if they had missed God's will for 22 years, should they have confessed their oversight, or their disobedience? But no! There is no evidence of contrition on their part. *Lord, make me sensitive to those I've offended.*

These men were the leaders of the tribes that willingly oppressed David for 13 years. These were years of hurt, loneliness, and fear. Did they say, "We're sorry"? No; even though Saul was the primary cause, they were complicit by their silence back then for 13 years. And they are twice guilty for not offering their apology now. *Lord, help me overlook those who offend me, just as David overlooked these elders.*

One more observation is necessary. David did not say anything about the 13 "lost" years. His graciousness is seen in all his dealings with the northern tribes. No wonder God said David was "a man after My own heart." *Lord, may it be said of me that I pursued Your heart.*

Bible scholars taught that David wrote Psalm 116 after he was crowned king over all Israel. He wrote, "O Lord, truly I am Your servant,...You have loosened my bonds, I offer You the sacrifice of praise" (Ps. 116:16-17). Instead of complaining about past injustices against him, David does the right thing. He praises God that his past pain and suffering is over. David recognizes no human had done wonderful things for him, so he offers the sacrifices of praise to God with his mouth. *Lord, I praise You for the wonderful things I have in my life.*

Amen.

39

DAVID BRINGS THE ARK OF THE COVENANT TO JERUSALEM

SECOND SAMUEL 6:1-9

Again, David gathered all the chosen men of Israel for the peaceful purpose of bringing up the Ark of the Covenant to Mount Zion. There were 30,000 of them. Then David and all his people got up and went to Baale-Judah. They took the Ark of the Covenant from there and moved it up to Jerusalem. The Name—the Name of Yahweh of the armies of Heaven—is pronounced over the Ark of the Covenant. His throne is between the gold seraphim with wings that are on the Holy Ark.

David's men put the Ark of the Covenant of the one true God on top of a new cart. Then they brought the Holy Chest out of Abinadab's house on the hill. Uzzah and Ahio, the sons of Abinadab, were leading the new cart. From there, this cart had the Ark of the Covenant of the one true God on it. Ahio was walking in front of it. David and all the Israelites were dancing and playing all kinds of musical instruments before the Lord. The instruments were made of pine wood. There were lyres, harps, tambourines, rattles, and cymbals.

When David's men came to the threshing-floor of Nacon, the oxen stumbled, and the Ark of the Covenant of the one true God started to fall off the cart. So Uzzah reached out and took hold of it. The Lord was very angry with Uzzah, and right there, the one true God struck him down for that violation. So Uzzah died there beside the Ark of the Covenant of the one true God. (It was supposed to be carried by long poles, and only on the shoulders of true priests [see Exod. 25:12-15; 37:1-5; Num. 4:15; 7:9; 18:3; 1 Chron. 15:3].)

David became very angry because the Lord had killed Uzzah. So that spot is called "The Punishment of Uzzah" even today.

David became afraid of the Lord that day. He said, "How can the Ark of the Covenant of the Lord come to me now?"

My Time to Pray

Discipline in Disappointment ⌐ Second Samuel 6

The Lord blessed the house of Obed-Edom and all that belongs to him (2 Samuel 6:12).

It seemed everything was set to glorify God. David had involved the people in worshiping God, there would be thousands upon thousands present. He had his army of 30,000 people (in case of an attack from the Philistines). The number was so great that they lined both sides of the road from Kirjath-Jearim to Jerusalem. A new cart was constructed. Musicians were assembled. The priests were there, and David led the parade. *Lord, help me remember to make my plans according to Your will and Your way.*

The motive was right. David wanted to unify the nation around Jerusalem, and he could do it with the Ark of the Covenant. He wanted everyone to worship God. He wanted his emphasis on spirituality to influence the people. This day would be the hinge of history; forever after, Jerusalem would be the center of God's strategy on planet Earth. *Lord, may my plans not focus on things or people, but on You.*

It had been 445 years since Israel entered into the land by following the Ark of the Covenant. Who would have remembered God's command to have the priest carry the Ark on long poles (see Exod. 25:12-15)? The last time the Ark was moved, it came from the Philistines on a new cart. Don't most people do in the present what they've seen done in the past? Israel forgot to read God's requirement for moving the Ark. 'Whatever things were written previously, were written for our teaching" (Rom. 15:4). *Lord, I will search Your Word for instructions how to live.*

The Ark tilted, and Uzzah reached out to prevent its fall. "The anger of the Lord burned against Uzzah" (2 Sam. 6:7). It seems the place where God struck Uzzah could be seen by those around Uzzah. At first David was angry—probably a human reaction of embarrassment or frustration. Then David feared the Lord, the right reaction. *Lord, give me a holy fear of disobeying You.*

The best plans of humans can go askew when God's principles are not included in their planning. David put the Ark in the house of Obed-Edom, and went home. The tent on Mount Zion he had prepared for the Ark was empty. David had an opportunity to rethink the whole experience. He realized that all his elaborate plans to worship God were futile when God was left out of the equation. *Lord, come be at the center of all my plans.*

Then David heard the good news. "The Lord blessed the home of Obed-Edom and all that belongs to him" (2 Sam. 6:12). It was wonderful to have God sitting in the front room of Obed-Edom's house and God pays rent when He borrows a room in the house. So David realized God was not angry at all of Israel. He probably realized God's anger was vented against one disobedience, on one occasion. David wanted God to bless all Israel, so he began to make elaborate plans to bring God to Jerusalem. This time they would follow God's instructions. *Lord, teach me how to please You.*

This time oxen wouldn't be used to pull a new cart; rather, oxen would be sacrificed every six paces. Can you imagine walking six paces, and sacrificing to God, then waiting to see if he would judge them again? But no one was struck dead. God approved, so they continue on a six-pace sequence all the way to Jerusalem. Just as a single punishment upon Ananias and Sapphira in the New Testament brought fear and reverence in the New Testament, so the same thing happened here. The people reverently brought the Ark to Jerusalem. *Lord, I will revere You.*

David took off his royal robes and wore an ephod as a symbol of his humility and service to God. The Lord was recognized as King that day. With overflowing joy, he danced before the Lord. Far from being undignified, David worshiped the Lord. *Lord, I will worship You with all I do. Lord, be King of my life.*

David's wife made two mistakes. First, Michal should have been with David in the road to welcome God into Jerusalem. She had an opportunity to join the throng in worshiping God. It would have been an experience she would have remembered forever. The first mistake was staying home. Have you ever stayed home from church and missed the opportunity of worshiping in the presence of God? Michal's second mistake was criticizing David to his face. "How glorious was the king of Israel today, uncovering himself today in the eyes of the maids of his servants, as one of the base fellows shamelessly uncovers himself!" (2 Sam. 6:20). *Lord, may I never ignorantly criticize anyone worshiping You in the sincerity of their heart.*

Up to that time Michal had five children, but after this blistering criticism of her husband—and God—she didn't have any other children. Was this God's judgment on her reproductive organs? Or was David so disgusted with Michal that he could no longer make love to her. So without sex, she was childless. *Lord, remind me that every careless word has consequences.*

Amen.

40

The Ark of God Is Moved
to Jerusalem

First Chronicles 15:1-29

David built houses for himself in Jerusalem. Then he built a tent for the
Ark of the Covenant of the one true God. And he set up a tent
for it. Then David said, "Only the Levites may carry the Holy
Ark of the Covenant of the one true God. (David had learned
his lesson.) The Lord has chosen them to carry the Ark of the
Covenant of the Lord and to serve Him permanently."

David gathered together all the people of Israel to come to Jerusalem.
He wanted to bring up the Ark of the Covenant of the Lord to
the place that he had prepared for it. David gathered the descen-
dants of Aaron and the Levites. There were 120 men from
Kohath's clan. Uriel was the leader. There were 220 men from
Merari's clan. Asaiah was the leader. There were 130 men from
Gershon's clan. Joel was the leader. There were 200 men from
Elizaphan's clan. Shemaiah was the leader. There were 80 men
from Hebron's clan. Eliel was the leader. There were 112 men
from Uzziel's clan. Amminadab was the leader.

Then David summoned the priests Zadok and Abiathar to come to him.
He also asked these Levites to come: Uriel, Asaiah, Joel,
Shemaiah, Eliel, and Amminadab. David said to them, "You are

the leaders of the families of Levi. You and the other Levites must sanctify yourselves. Then bring up the Ark of the Covenant of the Lord, the God of Israel, to the place where I have prepared for it. Why? Because the last time we did not ask the Lord how to carry it properly. So the Lord our God punished us."

Then the priests and the Levites sanctified themselves, so that they could bring up the Ark of the Covenant of the Lord, the God of Israel. This time the Levites used special poles to carry the Ark of the one true God on their shoulders. This was the way that Moses had commanded. They carried it just as the Lord had said they should.

David told the leaders of the Levites to appoint their brothers as singers. The singers were to play their musical instruments— lyres, harps, and cymbals. And they were to sing joyful songs.

So the Levites appointed Heman and his relatives—Asaph and Ethan. Heman was Joel's son. Asaph was Berechiah's son. And Ethan, from the Merari clan, was Kushaiah's son. There was also a second group of Levites. They were: Zechariah, Ben, Jaaziel, Shemiramoth, Jehiel, Unni, Eliab, Benaiah, Maaseiah, Mattithiah, Eliphelehu, Mikneiah, Obed-Edom, and Jeiel. They were the Levite guards.

The singers—Hemen, Asaph, and Ethan—played bronze cymbals. Zechariah, Jaaziel, Shemiramoth, Jehiel, Unni, Eliab, Maaseiah, and Benaiah played the high pitched lyres. Mattithiah, Eliphelehu, Mikneiah, Obed-Edom, Jeiel, and Azaziah were in charge of playing the low-pitched harps. Chenaniah, the chief of the Levites, was in charge of the singing because he was skillful at singing.

Berechiah and Elkanah were two who guarded the Ark of the Covenant. The priests—Shebaniah, Joshaphat, Nethanel, Amasai,

Zechariah, Benaiah, and Eliezer—had the job of blowing the trumpets. They did this marching in front of the Ark of the one true God. And Obed-Edom and Jehiah guarded the holy Chest.

David, the elders of Israel, and the commanders went to bring up the Ark of the Covenant with the Lord. Each of the commanders was over a group of 1,000 soldiers. They all went to bring up the Ark from Obed-Edom's house and were very happy. The one true God helped the Levites who carried the Ark of the Covenant with the Lord. So they sacrificed seven bulls and seven male sheep. All the Levites who carried the Ark of the Covenant wore robes of fine linen. Chenaniah, the man in charge of the singing and all the singers wore robes of fine linen. David wore a robe of fine linen, also. And he also wore a holy vest (and ephod) of fine linen. So all the people of Israel brought up the Ark of the Covenant with the Lord. They shouted praises and they blew rams' horns and trumpets to celebrate. They played cymbals, lyres, and harps.

So the Ark of the Covenant with the Lord entered Jerusalem. As it entered, Saul's daughter, Michal, watched from a window. When she saw King David dancing and celebrating, she hated him in her heart. (Because she thought that David had put aside his royal dignity, and such behavior was beneath her. After all, she was a princess, and she would not associate like that with commoners.)

Psalm 27: 1-8, 13-14

A psalm written by David about his desire to worship in the house of the Lord.

Lord, You are my light and my salvation;
  Whom shall I fear?

Lord, You are the strength of my life;
  Why should I be afraid?

When evil persons come to eat me up,
  They stumble and fall.

Though a host of evil people attack me,
  I will not be afraid of them
  Because I know You will protect me.

Lord, there's one thing I want from You;
  I want to be in Your house to see Your beauty,
  I want to delight in Your presence.

Lord, when troubles and problems attack me;
  Hide me in Your presence,
  Set me on a rock so my enemies can't reach me.

Lord, lift me up above my enemies;
  I will bring the sacrifices of joy to You,
  I will sing praises to You.

O Lord, hear when I cry unto You;
  Send me the help I need.

When You said to me, "Seek my face,"
  I answered, "Your face will I seek."

I would have fainted and given up
  If it hadn't been for Your goodness to me.

Lord, I will wait courageously for You because
  I know You will deliver me;
  I know You will come to me.

Amen.

41

FIRST CHRONICLES 16:1-41

They brought the Ark of the Covenant of the one true God and put it inside the tent. This was the tent that David had set up for it. (This was not the Holy Tent, the Tabernacle. It was a special tent which David had made to house the Ark of the Covenant.) Then they offered whole burnt offerings and peace offerings to the one true God. David (he was not a priest, but as king, he was supervising the proper activities of Jewish worship, consciously establishing permanent precedents in Jerusalem, the centralized place of worship) finished giving the whole burnt offerings and the peace offerings. Then David used the name of the Lord to bless the people. He gave a loaf of bread, some dates, and some raisins to every Israelite man and woman.

Then David appointed some of the Levites to serve next to the Ark of the Lord. They had the responsibility of leading the worship, praising the Lord, the God of Israel, and giving thanks.

Asaph was the leader who played the cymbals. Zechariah was his assistant. The other Levites were: Jeiel, Shemiramoth, Jehiel, Mattithiah, Eliab, Benaiah, Obed-Edom. They played the lyres and the harps. Benaiah and Jahaziel were priests who blew the trumpets regularly next to the Ark of the Covenant of the one true God. On that day, David led off Asaph and his relatives giving thanks to the Lord.

David's Song of Praise

David sang,

"Give thanks to the Lord; pray to Him,
Make known among the nations what He has done.

Sing to Him, sing praises to Him;
Declare all His wonderful deeds.

Praise in the name of His holiness,
Let the hearts rejoice of those who ask the Lord for help.

Seek the Lord and His strength,
Always be looking for help.

Remember the wonderful things that He has done;
Reflect upon His miracles and His decisions.

You are the descendants of Israel, God's servant;
You are the children of Jacob,
His chosen ones.

He is the Lord, our God;
His decisions are for the whole world.

Keep His covenant forever;
He will always keep His promises.

He will keep the covenant that He made with Abraham;
He will keep His promise that He made to Isaac.

The Lord made it a law for the people of Jacob;
He made it a permanent covenant with Israel.

The Lord said, 'I will give the land of Canaan to you;
The Promised Land will belong to you.

Your people were few in number then,
*   There were only a few foreigners in the land.*

You wandered from one nation to another,
*   And from one kingdom to another people.'*

But the Lord did not let anyone hurt you;
*   He warned kings not to harm you.*

He said, 'Don't touch My anointed ones,
*   Don't harm My prophets.'*

Sing to the Lord, all the earth;
*   Every day proclaim the news of how He saves us.*

Tell about God's glory among the nations,
*   Declare His wonderful deeds among all peoples;*
*   Why? Because the Lord is great; He should be highly*
*   praised,*
*   He should be honored more than all the gods.*

All the gods of the other nations are only idols,
*   But the Lord made the skies.*

The Lord has glory and majesty,
*   He demonstrates strength and joy in His Temple.*

Give praise to the Lord, O you families of the peoples,
*   Give glory and honor to the Lord.*

Give the glory of the name of the Lord;
*   Bring your offerings and come before Him,*
*   Worship the Lord with the adornment of holiness.*

The whole earth should tremble before the Lord,
*   Yes, the earth is established; it will not be moved.*

Let the skies rejoice, and let the earth be glad;
> *Let those among the nations say:*

> *'The Lord is King.'*

Let the sea and everything in it roar,
> *Let the fields and everything in them show their joy.*

Then the trees of the forest will shout in the presence of the Lord,
> *Because the Lord is coming to judge the world.*

Give thanks to the Lord, because He is good;
> *His constant love continues forever.*

Say to Him: 'Save us, O God of our salvation,
> *Bring us back and deliver us from the nations.*

We will thank You
> *And we will gladly praise you.*

Blessed be the Lord, the God of Israel,
> *Forever and forever.'"*

All the people said, "Amen" and "Praise the Lord."

Then David left Asaph and the other Levites in front of the Ark of the Covenant of the Lord. They were to serve there every single day. David also arranged for Obed-Edom and 68 other Levites to serve with them. Hosah and Obed-Edom, the son of Jeduthun, were guards. David set Zadok the priest and the other priests who served with him in front of the Holy Tent of the Lord. This was at the place of worship in Gibeon. (While the priests were officiating in Jerusalem, where the Ark of the Covenant had been brought. More priests [under Zadok the priest] were conducting a sacred service at Gibeon, where the ancient Tabernacle still remained. During the time of the judges, the Tabernacle had been at Shiloh [see Josh. 18:1]. During King Saul's reign, it was at Nob [see 1 Sam. 21:1-6], from where it was probably moved hastily before the slaughter of the priests by Doeg [see 1 Sam. 22:18-19]. Later, King Solomon reverently stored it within the Temple [see 1 Kings 8:4; 2 Chron. 1:13; 5:5].)

Every single morning and evening, they offered up whole burnt offerings on the original Altar of Burnt Offerings to the Lord. They did this to follow all the rules written in the Law (Torah) of the Lord, which He commanded to Israel. With them were Heman and Jeduthun and other Levites chosen by name to give praises to the One Who Is Always Present, because the Lord's constant love endures forever.

My Time to Pray

God in the Back Yard

After this I will return and will rebuild the tabernacle of David, which has fallen down; I will rebuild its ruins, and I will set it up; so that the rest of mankind may seek the Lord, even all the Gentiles who are called by My name, says the Lord who does all these things (Acts 15:16-17).

Did you see what God called it in the New Testament—the Tabernacle of David. That's not a mistake, although some think so. Usually, the Tabernacle was called "the tent of Moses" because he set it up. But David set up a separate Tabernacle to worship God. *Lord, I will come to David's Tabernacle to worship You.*

There were two tents during the reign of King David. One in Gibeon where the Brazen Altar of Sacrifice was located. That was the tent called the Tabernacle. Israel went there to offer sacrifices for their sin. The second tent contained the Ark of the Covenant and was placed in Jerusalem on Mount Zion. Israel went there to worship God. This second tent was

249

called the Tabernacle of David. *Lord, I go to the Cross for forgiveness, and I come to Jesus at Your right hand to worship You.*

At night, David could look out the windows of the palace to see the tent on Mount Zion, it was figuratively in his back yard. What could David see? He could see the Tabernacle surrounded by worshipers with their hands raised to God in praise. So David described in Psalm 134:

> *"Behold, bless the Lord, all you servants of the Lord,*
> *Who by night stand in the tent of the Lord.*

> *Lift your heads in the sanctuary, and bless Him*
> *The Lord who made Heaven and earth,*
> *Bless you from my back yard on Zion."*

Some Christians sin so often, that they spend their time at Gibeon, several miles from Jerusalem. They have to go to the Brazen Altar because of their continual sin. Too bad they don't enjoy the presence of God in David's tent on Zion where the Lord lives between the Seraphim, among the praises of Israel (see Ps. 22:3). But then again, if they sin, they need grace. *Thank You, Lord, for continued love and grace.*

Look again at the reference in Acts that predicts the Lord will raise again the Tabernacle of David—not Moses' Tabernacle—in the last day. When will God pitch David's tent? The reference is probably pointing to the future Millennium when David will be the vice-regent and will rule from Jerusalem. But don't count out today. I believe we are in the last days, and God is raising up a praise movement in America and across the world. We see new praise music appearing weekly. It seems more people are lifting their hands in praise than ever before. Is God raising up David's Tabernacle of praise in the 21st century? *Lord, I will praise You, lifting up my heart in worship.* (See Amos 9:11.)

Amen.

42

God's Promise to King David

Second Samuel 7

Later, David the king was living in his palace, and the Lord had given him rest from all of his enemies that surrounded him. And the king said to Nathan the prophet, "Now I am living in a palace made of fine cedar wood, but the Ark of the Covenant of the one true God still remains in a tent."

Nathan said to the king, "Go and do whatever you really want to do. The Lord is with you." (Nathan is speaking to David as a friend, not as a prophet. Nathan did not preface his remarks with, "Thus saith the Lord…" [See 1 Chron. 17:1-2].)

However, that very night, the Lord spoke His word to Nathan. The Lord said, "Go and tell My servant David: 'This is what the Lord says: "You are not the person to build a Temple for Me to live in. I did not live in a house when I brought the Israelites out of Egypt. All this time, I have been moving from place to place in a tent— in My Tabernacle. Wherever I have continued to move with all the tribes of Israel, I have never asked the following question of their leaders whom I ordered to take care of My people Israel: 'Why have you not built for Me a house out of cedar wood?'"'"

The Lord continued speaking to Nathan, "You must tell My servant David: 'This is what the Lord of the armies of Heaven says: "I took you from the pasture, when you were following the flock. I took you to become the leader over My people, over Israel. I have been with you wherever you have gone. I have defeated your enemies for you. Now, I will make you as famous as any of the great men on the earth. Also, I will choose a place for My people Israel. And I will plant them so that they can live in their own home—they will not be bothered anymore. Cruel men will no longer make them suffer as they have in the past.

These men have continued to do this even when I appointed judges to be over My people, Israel. However, I will give you rest from all your enemies. I am also declaring to you that I will make your descendants kings after you.

Your days will come to an end, and you will die. But at that time I will make one of your sons to be the next king. And I will make his kingdom strong forever. I will be his Father, and he will be My son. When he becomes sin (according to Galatians 3:13, on the cross Christ became the sin offering for sin), I will punish him with the rod of men and the lashes of the sons of men. I will never stop loving Him. I withdrew My kindness from Saul. And I removed him when I turned to you. But your family and your kingdom will continue forever because of Me. Your rule will last forever.""

Nathan told David all these words—everything that Nathan had heard and seen from God. That is exactly what Nathan told him.

David Prays to God

Then King David went and sat in the presence of the Lord (near the Ark of the Covenant). David said, "O Lord Who Is Always Present, why have You made me so important to You? Why have You made my family so important? And why have You brought me to this point in life? But that was not enough for You, O Lord Who Is Always Present. You have also said these wonderful things about my future family. I am Your servant. O Lord Who Is Always Present, this is not the usual way that You talk to human beings. What more can I, David, say to You? O Lord Who Is Always Present, You know me, Your servant, so well. You have done this wonderful thing because You said that You would do it—because You wanted to do so. And You have decided to let me know this.

That is why You are so great, O Lord Who Is Always Present. There is no one like You. There is no God except You. We have heard all of this with our own ears. And there is no other people like Your people, Israel. They are the one nation on earth that You chose to be your own people. You used them to make Your name famous. You did great and awesome miracles in the presence of Your people, for Your land. You freed Your people from slavery in Egypt. You saved them from pagan nations and their gods. You made the people of Israel Your special people forever. And You Who Are Always Present became their God.

Now, O God Who Is Always Present, keep the promise which You made about me and my family, and confirm it forever. Do as You have promised. Then You will be honored forever. And people will say: 'The Lord of the armies of Heaven is God over Israel.' And, the family of Your servant David will continue before You.

O Lord of the armies of Heaven, O God of Israel, You have shown these things to me. You have said: 'I will make your family great.' So I am bold enough to pray this prayer to You. And now, O Lord Who Is Always Present, You are the one true God, and Your words are true. And You have promised these good things to me. Now, please bless my family. Let it continue before You forever. O Lord Who Is Always Present, you have said these wonderful things. Let my family be blessed forever with Your blessing."

My Time to Pray

A House for Whom? ↶ Second Samuel 7

And Your house shall be established and your kingdom to the ages before Me, Your throne shall be established to the ages (2 Samuel 7:16 ELT).

When David told Nathan that he planned to build a Temple for the Lord, Nathan told him it was a good idea. Then God spoke to Nathan that night to go tell David, my servant "No." But before we look at God's decline, look at how God addresses David as "My servant." God knew David would do His will, so He called him "My servant." *Lord, I want to be Your servant. I promise to do Your will.*

God asked three questions. First, God asked if David was the one to build the Temple—David had bloody hands. Second, God asked if a house is necessary (2 Sam. 7:7). Finally, God asked if He has ever asked for a house in the past. By God saying "No," He shows His love to David. Can you see God's love to you in your prayers that He has not answered? *Lord, thank You for not giving me all the things for which I pray.*

David went to the tent and sat before the Lord. There's no chair in God's tent, so he must have sat on the floor. This is the only place in Scripture that mentions someone sitting in prayer. I'm personally glad for this illustration because I'm 75 years old as I write this chapter, and my old knees can't hold me for very long. Maybe God is saying, "If you're going to stay a while, sit down." David probably sat on the floor, I don't think he brought a chair with him. *Lord, I bow my heart and humble my spirit before You.*

When you tarry long in God's presence, you think God's thoughts after Him. Isn't that the art of meditation? When you think God's thoughts, you are probably as close to God as you can get. *Lord, I will learn Your Scripture, think Your thoughts, and pray Your words.*

When you sit before the Lord's presence, you are filled with awe and wonder. David asked, "O Lord, who am I, and what is my house?" (2 Sam. 7:18 ELT). This question shows David's humility. He came from one of the smallest towns in Judah, and he was the youngest son in his family. David came from obscurity to be David the king. Perhaps David's humility qualified him to become the greatest king ever. *Lord, I will humble myself so You can use me.*

In His answer to David, the Lord predicted Israel would turn from Him. God is never surprised when His people sin, that's why in God's time, Jesus is the Lamb slain before the foundation of the earth (see 1 Pet. 1:20, Rev. 13:8). *Lord, thank You for forgiving my sin before I commit it.*

God also predicted that His only begotten Son would sit on the throne of David. The angel said to the Virgin Mary, "The Lord God will give unto Him the throne of His father David, and He will be king over Israel forever" (Luke 1:32-33). *Lord, I submit to the rulership of King Jesus.*

Amen.

43

THE MILITARY VICTORIES OF DAVID

SECOND SAMUEL 8

Now David attacked the Philistines and defeated them, and took away control of Metheg-Ammah from them.

He also defeated the people of Moab, forcing them to lie down on the ground. Then he used a rope to measure them. When two men were measured, David had them put to death, but every third man was allowed to live. So the Moabites became the servants of David, and gave him the payments he demanded. As David went to regain power at the Euphrates River, he attacked Hadadezer, the son of Rehob, king of Zobah. From Hadadezer, David captured 7,000 charioteers, as well as 20,000 foot soldiers. David also crippled all but 100 of the chariot horses.

Syrians from Damascus came to help Hadadezer, the king of Zobah, but David defeated those 22,000 Syrians. Then David put groups of his soldiers (garrisons) in Damascus, Syria, so that the Syrians became David's servants and gave him the payments he demanded. Everywhere David went, the Lord made David victorious.

David took the shields of gold that had belonged to Hadadezer's officers, and brought them to Jerusalem. David also took many things made of bronze from Betah and Berothai (cities that had belonged to Hadadezer).

Toi, the king of Hamath (on the Orontes River, about 120 miles north of Damascus), heard that David had defeated the entire army of Hadadezer. So Toi sent his son Joram to greet and congratulate King David. Joram complimented David for defeating Hadadezer. (Hadadezer had fought wars against Toi.) Joram brought things made of silver, gold, and bronze. David took these things and dedicated them to the Lord. David also had given additional silver and gold to the Lord which he had taken from the nations that he had defeated—from Edom; from Moab; from the Ammonites; from the Philistines; and from Amalek, as well as the valuable things which he captured from Hadadezer, the son of Rehob, the king of Zobah.

After David returned from the Valley of Salt (located at the southwestern extremity of the Dead Sea), he became famous. He had defeated 18,000 Edomites there. David put groups of soldiers throughout all the land of Edom so that the people of Edom became his servants. The Lord made David victorious everywhere he went.

David was king over all Israel. His decisions were fair and right for all his people. Joab, the son of Zeruiah, was the general over the army. Jehoshaphat, the son of Ahilud, was the historian. Zadok the son of Ahitub and Ahimelech the son of Abiathar were priests. (Previously, Zadok served as priest under King Saul, and Ahimelech aligned himself with David. When David became king, he upheld the priestly dignity of both men. Zadok officiated at Gibeon, and Ahimelech served in Jerusalem where the Ark of the Covenant was kept.) Seraiah was the royal assistant (the Secretary of State). Benaiah the son of Jehoiada was over the Cherethites and the Pelethites (the king's bodyguards). And, David's sons were chief officials (administrators).

My Time to Pray

We Always Have Opposition ⁊ Second Samuel 8

And the Lord helped David in all places wherever he went (2 Samuel 8:6 ELT).

We do not have Heaven on this earth. As soon as we win one victory there is always another attack, from a different source, with a different threat, and a different strength, than we've experienced before. David finally became victorious over Saul and over Ish-Bosheth. Then David captured the one place he always wanted, Jerusalem. He was set in his mountain stronghold, Jerusalem. Maybe David thought no enemy could reach him behind impregnable walls. But Moab cut off the trade route from the south, the Philistines cut off the trade route from Egypt, and Syria cut off the trade route from the east, the Euphrates River regions. Like David, we must be ever vigilant because the world is inspired by satan to hate us and attack us, and he will try to defeat us in many different ways. *Lord, I will be watchful of temptation and trials.*

Hadad was the Syrian god; so the leader of Syria was named Hadadezer which meant, "Hadad is my helper." So this was a spiritual battle, the gods of Syria against the Lord God of Israel. We know from First Corinthians 10:19-21 that idol worship is inspired by demons because they hate God and will divert worship from God. *Lord, my strength is in You.*

David defeated Syria, killed 22,000 soldiers, burned 1,000 chariots, and hamstrung all the horses so they couldn't be used in an uprising against Israel again. He left garrisons of soldiers in Syria to collect levies or taxes. *Lord, help me get as complete a victory over the enemy as possible.*

No matter what tactic the enemy used, whether chariots, or soldiers, or difficult terrain, God gave David the victory. *Lord, I claim victory no matter what strategy the enemy uses against me.*

Satan's strategy of stirring up the kings against Israel had failed. Psalm 60 was written by David about this time, where he exclaims, "Through God we shall do valiantly, for He shall tread down our foes" (Ps. 60:12). *Lord, You are the source of my victories.*

Since it was spiritual warfare, then David gave tribute to God after the victory. He took the shields of gold that belonged to Hadadezer to Jerusalem, and dedicated them to God. The shields were probably not used in battle because gold was too soft; they were symbolic of Hadadezer's victory, now they were symbolic of the God of Israel's victory. *Lord, I give You all credit for all my victories.*

The majority of satan's attacks against you are indirect. That was the strategy used against David. And in the same way God works indirectly behind the scenes to give us victory. If God worked directly like striking people down with lightning or sending angels with flashing swords, then everyone would only follow the Lord outwardly for the wrong reason. It would be outward submission with inward complaining and inward rebellion. But God wants a pure heart response. He wants our faith and love. *Lord, I will follow You sincerely with all my heart.*

Amen.

44

DAVID BEFRIENDS MEPHI-BOSHETH

SECOND SAMUEL 9

David asked (about the tenth year of David's reign), "Is there anyone in Saul's family still surviving? I want to show love to this individual for the sake of Jonathan."

Now from Saul's household, there was a servant named Ziba. So David's servants summoned Ziba to David. The King said to him, "Are you Ziba?"

He answered, "Yes, I am Ziba, your servant."

The king asked, "Is there anyone still left in Saul's family? I want to show the kindness of God to that person."

Ziba answered the king, "Jonathan has a son who is still living. He is crippled in both feet."

The king asked Ziba, "Where is he?"

Ziba answered, "He is at the house of Machir, the son of Ammiel, in Lo-Debar."

Then King David sent servants and got Jonathan's son from the house of Machir, the son of Ammiel, in Lo-Debar. Mephi-Bosheth, Jonathan's son and the grandson of Saul, came to David, and he bowed face down on the floor.

David said, "Mephi-Bosheth?"

Mephi-Bosheth said, "I am your servant."

Then David said to him, "Don't be afraid. I will surely be kind to you for the sake of Jonathan, your father. I will give back to you all the land of your grandfather, Saul. And, you will always eat at my table."

Mephi-Bosheth bowed down to David again, and said, "You are being very kind to me, your servant. I am no better than a dead dog."

Then King David summoned Saul's servant, Ziba, and told him, "Everything that once belonged to Saul and his family I have given to your master's grandson. You, your sons, and your servants are to farm the land for Mephi-Bosheth. You will harvest the crops. Then Mephi-Bosheth, your master's grandson, will have food to eat. But he will always eat at my table."

Now Ziba had 15 sons and 20 servants. He said to King David, "I am your servant. I will do everything that my master, the king, commands me."

So Mephi-Bosheth ate at David's table as if he were one of the king's sons. And Mephi-Bosheth had a little boy named Mica. Everyone in Ziba's family became servants to Mephi-Bosheth. Mephi-Bosheth was crippled in both feet. He stayed in Jerusalem because he always ate at the king's table.

My Time to Pray

Kindness Reflects Inner Character ~ Second Samuel 9

Now David said, "Is there still anyone who is left of the house of Saul, that I may show him kindness for Jonathan's sake?" (2 Samuel 9:1)

The tough battles had not hardened David's heart, the heart of the shepherd boy (see Ps. 23) was not lost in battle. David still had tenderness for his friend Jonathan. So David asked if any children of Jonathan then still existed, he wanted to be kind to them. *Lord, keep me kind.*

David exercised the opposite of craftiness or expediency. Most kings would have killed any heir to the throne. Even though Mephi-Bosheth was lame—and a lame man couldn't be king—Mephi-Bosheth could have been the source of a rebellion, or even worse, the son of Mephi-Bosheth could challenge the son of David for the throne. But David's kindness was really grace, which is the opposite of what was deserved. *Lord, thank You for giving me the opposite of what I deserve.*

When David brought Ziba in for information, note how Ziba didn't tell David the name of Mephi-Bosheth; Ziba even tried to tell David how worthless was this very man. Even when Mephi-Bosheth came into David's presence, he called himself a "dog," to show how far down the social ladder he was; Mephi-Bosheth was from Lo-Debar, a town that means "nothing." *Lord, I deserve nothing, but thank You for giving me Your riches in grace.*

Mephi-Bosheth was a prince when born. His father Jonathan was killed, and it was supposed that those who killed Jonathan would also want to kill his heir. But at the age of five he was dropped when an attendant ran to hide him, so the boy grew up in an out of the way place with a deformity. He had always known misfortune. *Lord, sin is a hard taskmaster.*

Now Mephi-Bosheth was about 20 years old. He heard David say, "All that belongs to Saul and his house, have I given to you." Then he heard that Ziba would cultivate the fields and harvest them for him (2 Sam. 9:10). Finally, Mephi-Bosheth lived in Jerusalem and sat at the king's table in Jerusalem (2 Sam. 9:13). *Lord, thank You for being a God of mercy, kindness, and grace.*

Amen.

45

DAVID DEFEATS THE AMMONITES AND SYRIANS

SECOND SAMUEL 10

Later, Nahash, the king of the Ammonites, died and his son, Hanun, became king instead. David said, "Nahash was kind to me, therefore, I will be kind to his son, Hanun." So David sent his officers to console Hanun after his father's death, and they went to the land of the Ammonites. But the chiefs of the Ammonites began talking to Hanun, their master: "Do you think David wants to honor your father by sending these men to comfort you? No. David sent them here to study the city and spy it out. They plan to capture it." So Hanun took David's officers and shaved off half their beards. He also cut off their clothes at the hips, then sent them away.

When some people told David what happened, he sent messengers to meet his officers, because these men were humiliated. King David said, "Wait at Jericho until your beards have grown out, then come back to Jerusalem."

Now when the Ammonites realized that they had become David's enemies, they hired 20,000 Syrian foot soldiers from Beth-Rehob and Zobah. They also went and hired 1,000 men from the king of Maacah. And, they hired 12,000 men from Tob.

When David heard about this, he sent General Joab, along with the
entire army of warriors. The Ammonites came out and got ready
for battle, standing at the city gate. The Syrians from Zobah and
Rehob and the men from Tob and Maacah were out in the field
by themselves. Joab saw that there were enemies both in front
and behind him. So Joab chose some of the best men from the
Israelites and got them ready for battle against the Syrians. Then
Joab put the rest of the men under the command of his brother,
Abishai, to fight the Ammonites. Joab said to Abishai, "If the
Syrians are too strong for me, then you must come help me.
However, if the Ammonites are too strong for you, then I will
come and help you. Be strong! Let us fight bravely for our peo-
ple and for the cities of our God. The Lord will do what is best."

When Joab and his men got closer to attack the Syrians, they retreated
from Joab's army. The Ammonites saw the Syrians run away, so
they ran away from Abishai, too. They went into their city. Then
Joab returned from the battle with the Ammonites and went to
Jerusalem.

The Syrians saw that the Israelites had beaten them, so they gathered
together into one big army. Hadadezer sent messengers to bring
the Syrians who lived on the other side of the Euphrates River.
These Syrians went to Helam, their leader was Shobach, the general of Hadadezer's army.

When David heard this, he gathered all the Israelites together, and they
crossed over the Jordan River and went to Helam. There the
Syrians prepared for a battle with David, and they fought with
David's army. But the Syrians ran away from the Israelites.
David's soldiers killed 700 Syrian chariot drivers and 40,000
Syrian horsemen. David's men also killed Shobach, the general
of the Syrian army.

All the puppet kings who served Hadadezer realized that the Israelites had beaten them. So they made peace with the Israelites and served them. And the Syrians were afraid to help the Ammonites anymore.

My Time to Pray

Evil for Kindness ᷙ Second Samuel 10

Then said David, "I will show kindness unto Hanun the son of Nahash, as his father showed kindness to me" (2 Samuel 10:2).

When the king of Ammon (today the kingdom of Jordan) died, David sent representative mourners (much like today our nation sends a representative to attend the funeral of a foreign dignitary). Even though David had shown himself powerful to the nations that attacked him (Philistine, Moab, Syria, Edom), he also had a kind disposition. Ammon had not attacked Israel, so David wanted to keep a good relationship with them. *Lord, may I always be kind to my friends and not ridicule or embarrass them.*

The advisors to young King Hanun said David was sending spies to spy on Ammon, so the immature king cut off half their beards (sign of manhood) and cut off their garments exposing their genitals (the ultimate act of ridicule). Why where the advisors so suspicious and fearful of David? He had not aggressively attacked any nation. David turned his defensive wars into an attack and destroyed Israel's enemies. Immaturity makes us suspicious and fearful. In this case it led to the destruction of their city and slavery of their people to Israel. *Lord, keep me from being suspicious of people, may I live with an open hand and an open heart.*

The embarrassment heaped on David's representatives was done to David as well, plus it was an attack on the entire Jewish people. It was a declaration of war on Israel. So Ammon hastily "bought" Syrian soldiers from the north to come defend themselves from David. It was a good opportunity for the Syrians to get even with David for their recent defeat.

Lord, it seems like when satan attacks in one area, I get trials in several other areas at the same time.

Joab took the army to fight Ammon, but it seems he was unaware that the Syrian soldiers had cut off his retreat. He was surrounded. He divided his army, putting the farmer-soldiers under David's brother Abishai to fight the Ammonites. Joab took the elite warriors and attacked the Syrians. Then he puts trust in God, "Be of good courage, and let us be strong for our people, and for the cities of our God. And may the Lord do what is good in His sight" (2 Sam. 10:12). *Lord, teach me to be strong in the face of attacks and dangers.*

The Syrians ran away, and the Ammonites retreated into their city. Then Joab returned to Jerusalem to report what happened. The Syrians were still angry at David, so they regrouped and rallied a much larger army, and got the well-known general Shobach to lead them in battle. So David went out with Joab and all the fighting men of Israel. David led this larger army across the Jordan River and entered a battle evenly matched. But Israel won, and destroyed 700 chariots, 40,000 soldiers, and killed Shobach. Then the nations that paid taxes to Syria quickly changed their allegiances and made peace with Israel. *Lord, win battles for me that I can't win alone.*

Amen.

46

DAVID AND BATH-SHEBA

SECOND SAMUEL 11

The following year, in the spring, when the kings would go out to war, David sent Joab and his officers, and all Israel. They destroyed the Ammonites and surrounded the city of Rabbah. (A siege lasted a long time; it was designed to starve the inhabitants of a city into submission.) However, David stayed in Jerusalem.

One evening, David got up from his bed and walked around on the roof of his palace. (Literally, "the king's house." The roofs in the East were flat.) While up there, he looked out and saw a woman taking a bath. She was very beautiful. So David sent a man to find out who she was. The man said, "That woman is Bath-Sheba, the daughter of Eliam. And she is the wife of Uriah the Hittite." (Uriah had a high rank in David's royal bodyguard.) Then David sent some messengers to bring Bath-Sheba to him. When she came to him, he had sex with her. Now Bath-Sheba had purified herself from her monthly period. Then she went back to her house.

But Bath-Sheba got pregnant, so she sent a message to David, "I am pregnant."

Then David sent this order to Joab: "Send Uriah the Hittite to me." So Joab sent Uriah to David, and he asked him how Joab was doing, how the soldiers were, and if the war was succeeding. Then David said to Uriah, "Go home and rest." (David thought that Uriah would go home and have sex with his wife, thus covering up the identity of the true father of the baby.)

Uriah left the king's palace, and David sent a special gift to him. However, Uriah did not go home. Instead, he slept just outside the gate of the king's palace. All of his master's officers slept there.

The officers told David: "Uriah did not go home."

Then David said to Uriah, "You have just arrived from a long trip. Why didn't you go home?"

Uriah said, "The Ark of the Lord and the soldiers of Israel and Judah are staying in huts, and my master Joab and his officers are camping out in the open fields. It would not be right for me to go home to eat and drink and to have sex with my wife. I swear, I could never do such a thing."

So David said to Uriah, "Stay here today. Tomorrow I will send you back to the battle lines." So Uriah stayed in Jerusalem that day and the next day. Then David invited Uriah to eat and drink in his presence. David caused Uriah to get drunk. Nevertheless, Uriah did not go home, but went to sleep with the king's officers outside the king's gate.

So the next morning, David wrote a letter to Joab and set it by Uriah. (Uriah unknowingly carrying his own death warrant.) In the letter, David wrote, "Put Uriah on the front lines where the fighting is the worst. Then pull back, leaving him there alone. Let him be killed in battle."

Joab watched the city of the Ammonites and saw where its strongest defenders were, and that is the place where Joab put Uriah. The men of the city came out to fight against Joab. Some of David's men were killed, and Uriah the Hittite was one of them.

Then Joab sent a report to David telling about everything that was going on in the war. Joab ordered the messenger to say: "Tell King David what has happened in the war. After you finish that part, the king may become angry. He may get up and ask you, 'Why did you go so close to the city to fight? Didn't you know that they would shoot arrows from the city wall? Do you remember who killed Abimelech, the son of Gideon? It was a woman on the city wall. She threw an upper millstone used for grinding grain on top of Abimelech. He died there in Thebez. Why did you get so close to the wall?' If King David asks that question, you must answer: 'Your servant Uriah the Hittite is also dead.'"

So the messenger went in and informed David of everything that Joab had told him to say. The messenger said to David, "The Ammonite men were winning. They came out to us into the field, and they attacked, but we drove them all the way back to the city gate. The men on the city wall were shooting arrows at us. Some of your men were killed. Your servant Uriah the Hittite also died."

Then David said to the messenger, "Say this to Joab: 'Don't be upset about this. People die by the sword all the time. Launch a stronger attack against the city and capture it. Encourage Joab with these words.'"

When Bath-Sheba heard that her husband was dead, she cried over her husband, Uriah. After the time of mourning was over, David sent some servants to bring her to his palace. She became David's wife, and she gave birth to David's son.

However, this thing which David had done was wrong, and the Lord saw it.

My Time to Pray

Doing the Wrong Thing at Night ~ Second Samuel 11

And when her mourning was over, David sent and brought her to his house, and she became his wife and bore him a son. But the thing that David had done displeased the Lord (2 Samuel 11:27).

For some reason we think the sin we do is wrong, and we know we should not do it. But have you ever realized that your sin displeases the Lord? Think of doing something your spouse doesn't want you to do, or think of hurting them. Think of intentionally hurting a child of yours, or anyone else's child. The worst thing of all is to displease the Lord. *Lord, I am ashamed of myself for the sin I do, but it's worse than that. My sin breaks my fellowship with You because it displeases You. Lord forgive me.*

Think of the greatness of David, "A man after God's own heart." Think of the spirituality of David, "Lord, You are my Shepherd, I shall not want" (Ps. 23:1). Yet in spite of his walk with God, David sinned. That gives every sinning saint hope, for all saints sin. If the greatest among us sin—David—then the Lord can have compassion on us and forgive us. *Lord, I have sinned, just as David sinned. I sinned in a different way, at a different time, to satisfy a difficult selfish reason. Forgive me, cleanse me, and restore me. Just as You used David after his sin, use me again.*

You are not above temptation. No matter how many battles you've won for God, and David won many; no matter how many good things you've spoken or written for God, and David had written many psalms at this time; no matter how old or how young you are in the Lord, and David was considered old in his spiritual pilgrimage at this time, you can be tempted. "Therefore let him who thinks he stands take heed lest he fall" (1 Cor. 10:12). Not only can you be tempted, you can get victory. "No temptation has overtaken you except such as is common to man; but God

[is] faithful, who will not allow you to be tempted beyond what you are able, but with the temptation will also make the way of escape, that you may be able to bear [it]" (1 Cor. 10:13). *Lord, I intend never to give in to temptation, I will keep myself pure for You.*

The one thing missing in this chapter is David's repentance. God had to send a powerful prophet to announce, "You are the man?" Why didn't David feel himself drifting from God? Why didn't those cold shivers that came from the enemy alert his soul? Why wasn't David praying on that roof top instead of satisfying the lust of the flesh in looking at a naked woman? Long before David sinned, he should have felt the coolness of his walk with God. Was David slouching away from God? *Lord, You know me better than I know myself. When I drift from Your fellowship, rattle my cage. When I begin to cool off, burn my soul with conviction. If I turn around, hit me in the back. If I wander from You, YELL. Don't let me trip into sin.*

Amen.

47

The Results of David's Sins

Second Samuel 12

So the Lord sent Nathan to David. When Nathan came to him, Nathan said, "There were two men in a certain city, one man was rich, but the other man was poor. The rich man had many flocks and herds of cattle. But the poor man had nothing—except one little female lamb he had purchased. This poor man fed that lamb as a pet and it grew up together with him and his children. It shared his food, it even drank from his cup and slept in his arms. The lamb was like a daughter to him.

Then a traveler came to visit the rich man, who wanted to give some food to the guest who had come to him. However, he did not want to take one of his own sheep or cattle to feed the traveler. So he took the lamb from the poor man instead. The rich man butchered that lamb and cooked it for his visitor."

Then David became very angry at the rich man. He said to Nathan, "As surely as the Lord lives, the man who did this thing should die. He must pay for the lamb four times more than its original price for doing such a thing. That man showed no mercy."

Then Nathan said to David, "You are the man. This is what the Lord, the God of Israel says: 'I anointed you king over Israel, and saved you from Saul. I gave you his kingdom and his wives. And

I made you king of Israel and Judah. And if that had not been enough, I would have given you even more. So why did you ignore the command of the Lord? Why did you do what He says is wrong? Using the sword of the Ammonites, you murdered Uriah the Hittite. And you took his wife to become your wife. Therefore, there will always be individuals in your family who die by the sword. Why? Because you showed that you had no respect for Me at all. You took the wife of Uriah the Hittite for yourself.'

This is what the Lord says: 'I will bring nothing but trouble to you from within your own family. As you watch, I will take your wives away from you and give them to somebody else—to someone who is very close to you. He will have sex with your wives—and everyone will know about it. You had sex with Bath-Sheba in secret, but I will do this thing in such a way that all the people of Israel will be able to see it plainly.'"

Then David said to Nathan, "I have sinned against the Lord."

Psalm 51

Written by David at This Time ⌁ A Prayer-Seeking Restoration to Fellowship With God After You Sin

Lord, have mercy on me according to Your loving nature;
Because of Your mercy blot out my transgressions,
Wash me completely from my sin
So I will be clean of my guilt.

For I acknowledge my terrible deed,
I cannot get it out of my mind.

Against You and no one else have I sinned
In doing what was evil in Your sight.

You are absolutely right to convict me,
  And Your punishment is just.

I was born a sinner,
  And I have sinned since the beginning.

But You want us to be inwardly truthful,
  Because that is where You communicate with us.

Cleanse me from my sins so I can be clean,
  Wash me so I can be whiter than snow.

I want to be happy like I was before,
  I want my broken spirit to rejoice again.

Hide my sin from Your face,
  Cleanse my guilty conscience from guilt.

O God, create in me a clean heart
  And renew a right spirit in me.

Don't kick me out of Your presence,
  And don't take Your Holy Spirit from me.

Restore to me the joy of Your salvation,
  And give me a new spirit to obey You.

Amen.

Nathan answered David, "The Lord has indeed removed your sin, you will not die. Nevertheless (the sinner must suffer the consequences of his or her sin) what you did has caused the Lord's enemies to lose all respect for God. That is why the son who will be born to you will surely die."

Then Nathan went home. Next, the Lord caused the little boy of David and Bath-Sheba to become very sick. David prayed hard to the one true God on behalf of the baby, and refused to eat or drink.

(David fasted a fast.) He went into his palace, and did not leave, lying on the floor all night every night. The older men of David's household came to him, and tried to pull him up from the floor, but he refused to get up. And he would not eat anything with them.

Despite all this, on the seventh day, the baby died. David's servants were afraid to tell David that the baby was dead, reasoning: "We tried to talk to David while the baby was still alive, but he refused to listen to us. If we tell him that the baby is dead, then he might harm himself."

But when David saw his servants whispering to each other, he concluded that the little boy was dead. So he asked them, "Is the little boy dead?"

They answered, "Yes, he's dead."

Then David got up from the floor, washed himself, put some lotion on his skin, and changed his clothes. Then he went into the house of the Lord (David had erected a special tent to house the Ark of the Covenant, see 2 Sam. 6:17) and worshiped. After that, he went home and asked for something to eat. His servants set some food in front of him, and he ate.

David's servants said to him, "Why are you doing this now? When the little boy was still alive, you refused to eat. You wept. But when the little boy died, you got up and ate food."

David answered, "While the little boy was still alive, I fasted and I wept, because I thought: 'Who knows, maybe the Lord will feel sorry for me and permit the little boy to live?' But now the baby is dead. So why should I continue to fast? I cannot bring him back to life. Someday I will go to him, but he will not come back to me."

Then David comforted Bath-Sheba, his wife, slept with her and had sex
with her. She became pregnant again and had another son.
David named the boy "Solomon." (This proper name means
"peaceable" in the sense of "completeness.") And the Lord loved
Solomon. The Lord sent a message through Nathan the prophet
to also name the baby Jedidiah. (This name in Hebrew means
"loved by Yahweh.") This was because the Lord loved the child.

News of the War

Meanwhile, Joab continued to fight against Rabbah, the most important
city of the Ammonites. Joab was about to capture their royal
city. So he sent some messengers to David and said, "I have
fought against Rabbah, and have captured its water supply. Now
bring the rest of the soldiers here to attack this city. Capture it
before I capture it myself. If I capture this city, it will be called
by my name. That must not happen."

Therefore, David gathered all the army together to travel to Rabbah.
David fought against Rabbah and captured it. David removed
the crown from the head of the Ammonite king. It was made of
gold and weighed about 75 pounds and also had precious jewels on it. They put the crown on David's head. And David took
many valuable things (plunder) out of that city. King David also
brought the Ammonite people out of the city and put them to
work with saws, iron picks, and iron axes. David also forced
them to bake bricks and to build buildings. David did the same
things to all the other Ammonite cities. Then David and all his
army returned to Jerusalem.

My Time to Pray

Grace Abounds ⌁ Second Samuel 12

David said to Nathan, "I have sinned against the Lord."And Nathan said to David, "The Lord also has put away your sin; you shall not die" (2 Samuel 12:13).

Do you have a tender heart toward God when it comes to your sin? Throughout his life, David's heart had been tender and sensitive first to God, and second it kept him from sinning against God. David walked in awe and reverence to God with a consciousness of God's presence and leadership in his life. *Lord, strengthen my awe of You.*

Notice God gave David about two years to struggle with his sin. There was the nine months of pregnancy, but David didn't repent of adultery. Then the little boy was almost one year old, still David hadn't faced the consequences of his sin. Aren't we like that? We don't face the horribleness of our sin until the Word of God convicts us. God spoke to Nathan, then the prophet said to the king, "Thus says the Lord God of Israel" (2 Sam. 12:7). *Lord, speak to me through Your Word.*

You cannot sin with impunity. David lost fellowship with God, but did he know it? Did David feel guilt, anger, or was he depressed? The text doesn't tell us. Maybe if David had dealt with his sin, the baby boy wouldn't have died. *Lord, help me repent early and completely.*

David had tender mercy for the hypothetical poor man in the parable, but with malice and sin in his heart, David sinned (1) in adultery, (2) in deception to get Uriah drunk, (3) in deception to murder Uriah, (4) in hypocrisy to marry Bath-Sheba and pretend he was the father of the baby. Then we hear the thunderous words of Nathan, *"Thou art the man!"* All we can do is say with David, "I have sinned against the Lord" (2 Sam. 12:13). Remember we don't sin against our neighbor, our job, or our spouse; rather, we sin against God. *Lord, forgive.*

It must have been an agonizing vigil as David fasted and prayed for the life of the baby. Think of his fear of God, his anger toward himself, his loneliness and despair. *Lord, keep me from sin so I don't have to suffer as did David.*

It's terrible for our sin to cause the death of another. The sin of David and Bath-Sheba caused their little one to die. Some have thought it was unfair for God to allow a baby to die when the parents sinned. That is the shame of David and Bath-Sheba. But look on the positive side. God took the child to Heaven to be with Him—which is better and the ultimate goal of us all—than to leave the child with the seared memory of his birth and the consequences to the kingdom. *Lord, You work all things to Your glory.*

We see in this picture of grace what happens to children who die before the age of accountability—the age before they are responsible for their deliberate, willful sin. David said, "I shall go to him, but he shall not return to me" (2 Sam. 12:23). This means the child wouldn't come back from Heaven and death, but that David would go to be with the child in Heaven when he dies. Jesus seems to reinforce the idea that children before the age of accountability have a special relationship to God. Jesus describes children, "For of such is the kingdom of heaven" (Matt. 19:14). Is Jesus saying these little ones belong to the kingdom of Heaven? Then Jesus said, "These little ones...for their angels always see the face of My Father in heaven" (Matt. 18:10). *Lord, thank You for taking little ones who die before their age of accountability to Heaven.*

Where is the first place David went after receiving the awful news of the child's death? "David arose from the ground, washed and anointed himself, and changed his clothes, and he went into the house of the Lord and worshipped" (2 Sam. 12:20). The presence of God is the first place, the last place, the ultimate place for any child of God. When is the last time you've entered His presence in His house? *Lord, I will worship You in Your house.*

Amen.

48

AMNON RAPES TAMAR

SECOND SAMUEL 13

Now David had a son named Absalom and a son named Amnon. Now
Absalom had a full sister named Tamar. She was beautiful.
Amnon fell in love with her. (He was consumed by lust for
Tamar's beautiful body.) Tamar was a virgin. Amnon wanted her
sexually, but he couldn't see how he could get her. Amnon made
himself sick just thinking about her all the time.

Now Amnon had a friend named Jonadab, the son of Shimeah. And
Jonadab was a very shrewd man. He asked Amnon, "Why do
you look so sad day after day? You are the king's son. Tell me
what's wrong."

Amnon told him, "I'm in love with Tamar, but she is the sister of my
half-brother, Absalom."

Jonadab told Amnon, "Go to bed. Act as if you are sick. Then your
father will come to visit you. Tell him, 'Please let my half-sister,
Tamar, enter and give me food to eat. Let her make the food in
front of me. Then I will see it and eat it right from her hand.'"

So Amnon lay down in bed and pretended that he was sick. King David
did come in to see him. Amnon said to him, "Please let my half-
sister, Tamar, come in here. And let her make two of her special

cakes for me while I watch. Then I will eat them from her own hand."

So David sent messengers to Tamar in the palace, telling her, "Please go to the house of your half-brother Amnon and make some food for him." So Tamar went to her half-brother Amnon's house where he was lying down. Tamar took some dough and pressed it together with her hands. She made some special cakes while Amnon watched. Then she baked them. Next, she took the baking pan and presented it to Amnon, but he refused to eat.

He said to his servants, "All of you, leave me alone." So everyone left the room.

Amnon said to Tamar, "Bring the food into the bedroom. Then I will eat from your own hand."

So Tamar took the cakes that she had made and brought them to her half-brother, Amnon, in the bedroom. She got closer to him, so that he could eat. Amnon grabbed her and said, "Come and have sex with me."

But Tamar said, "No, don't rape me. Such a thing should never happen in Israel. Don't do this disgraceful thing. I could never get rid of my shame. And you would become like one of the fools in Israel. Please talk with the king, he might permit you to marry me." But Amnon refused to listen to her. He was stronger than she was, so he forced her to have sex with him.

After that, Amnon hated Tamar. He hated her much more than he had previously loved her. Amnon said to her, "Get up and get out."

Tamar said to him, "No. Sending me away would be an even greater evil. That would be worse than what you have already done." But Amnon refused to listen to her. He summoned his young servant, saying, "Get this girl out of here—right now, and lock the door behind her." So Amnon's servant brought her outside, and bolted the door.

Now Tamar was wearing a royal robe with long sleeves (the king's virgin daughters wore this type of robe). Tamar put ashes on her head, and she tore her special robe and put her hand on her head. (Tamar did the best she could to cover her exposed face.) Then she went away, crying loudly.

Absalom, Tamar's full-brother said to her, "Has Amnon forced you to have sex with him? He is your half-brother. So for now, my sister, be silent. Don't focus your heart on this thing." So Tamar lived in her brother Absalom's house, and was sad and lonely.

When King David heard about all these things, he was very angry. But Absalom did not say a word to Amnon—either good or bad. But Absalom hated Amnon for raping his sister, Tamar.

Abaslom Kills Amnon

Two years later, some of Absalom's sheep shearers came to Baal-Hazor, near Ephraim. Absalom had invited all of the king's sons to come, too. Absalom went to the king and said, "I have some men coming to cut off the wool. Please come, along with your officers, and join me."

But King David said to Absalom, "No, my son. We won't all go. It would be too much trouble for you." Absalom begged him to come, but David did not want to come, but he did give his blessing.

Absalom said, "If you don't want to go, then please let my half-brother Amnon come with us."

King David asked Absalom, "Why should he go with you?"

Absalom kept pleading with David until he allowed Amnon and all the king's sons to go with Absalom.

Then Absalom gave a command to his servants, saying, "Watch Amnon. When he is drunk, I will tell you: 'Kill Amnon.' Right then, put him to death. Don't be afraid. I have commanded you. Be strong and brave." So Absalom's young men killed Amnon, just as Absalom commanded. But all of David's other sons got on their mules and rode away. Each one of them escaped.

While the king's sons were on their way, the news came to David, "Absalom has killed all of the king's sons. Not one of them remains alive." Then King David got up and tore his clothes. Then he laid on the ground, and all of his servants standing nearby tore their clothes, too.

Jonadab was the son of Shimeah, David's brother. Jonadab said to David, "Don't think that all of your sons have been murdered. Only Amnon is dead. Absalom planned this since the day that Amnon raped his half-sister, Tamar. Now, O my master, the king, don't think that all of the king's sons are dead. Only Amnon is dead."

In the meantime, Absalom had run away.

There was a guard standing on the city wall who looked up and saw how many people from the west, coming down on the side of the hill. Then Jonadab said to King David, "Look, I was right. The king's sons are coming."

As soon as Jonadab had said this, the king's sons arrived. They were crying loudly and weeping. David and all his servants wept, too.

Now Absalom ran away to Talmai, the king of Geshur (his father-in-law).

David mourned for his son Absalom every day. Absalom was there for three years. And the spirit of King David yearned for Absalom, after David got over Amnon's death.

My Time to Pray

Wrong Choices ~ Second Samuel 13

Then Amnon hated her exceedingly, so that the hatred with which he hated her was greater than the love with which he had loved her. And Amnon said to her, "Arise, be gone!" (2 Samuel 13:15)

There were a number of bad choices described in this chapter, and most of them could have been avoided. Amnon could not control himself, he had lust for his half-sister Tamar, who was quite beautiful. He chose by the eye of desire, not by the rule of family or by the rule of God. The law forbade marrying his sister, the law forbade sex before marriage. *Lord, help me do Your will which is greater than my desire.*

There was Absalom who was probably 18 or 19 years of age, ambitious and vain. His half-brother was heir to the throne, so Amnon stood in his way to the power he desired. Absalom lied to his father David about a feast, and knew his father would send the crown prince, Amnon, to represent the king. Absalom planned murder to get to the throne.

Jonadab, David's nephew, is described in the *New King James* as "a very crafty man" (2 Sam. 13:3). The Hebrew word *hakam* means "shrewd, or clever, or subtle" (a word used to describe satan). He doesn't tell his cousin Amnon what is right, but rather, he tells Amnon what he wanted to hear. Jonadab must have known that Amnon would try to seduce Tamar. Amnon wanted something illegal, more than anything in the world. *Lord, may I counsel people according to truth.*

King David probably kept his virgin daughters sequestered in a private place. So Amnon had to deceive her father to get Tamar to come to his apartment. Amnon pretended to be sick and asked for his beautiful sister to be allowed to come cook for him. Fifty-year-old David probably coddled his sons and made a bad decision. He sent Tamar to Amnon's apartment. Probably any of David's wives would have seen through the "subterfuge" and said, "No!" *Lord, help me see both sides of issues when I have to make decisions.*

Amnon thickens the plot. He wanted his food cooked in his sight. He wanted Tamar to feed him. He sent the servants out of the apartment. He led Tamar into the inner "bedroom." Then he "hits" on her, "Come lie with me" (2 Sam. 13:11). *Lord, help us all control this powerful thing called sex.*

Notice all the "road blocks" Tamar uses to dissuade her half-brother Amnon. First she pleaded, "No my brother, do not force me" (2 Sam. 13:12). Second, she calls his sexual advance what it is, "Do not do this disgraceful thing" (2 Sam. 13:12). In the third place, she appealed to his pity or reason, "Where could I take my shame?" (2 Sam. 13:13). Fourth, she attacked his reputation, "You would be like one of the fools in Israel" (2 Sam. 13:13). Tamar's last resort is to propose marriage, "Please speak to the king, for he will not withhold me from you" (2 Sam. 13:13). *Lord, rape is a hideous crime for it violates everything that is pure and life-giving.*

The sexual lust of Amnon could not be extinguished. He gave in to pleasure and its desire, but got hatred as its result. "The hatred with which he hated her was greater than the love with which he loved her" (2 Sam. 13:15). If only we had the eyes of God to see the result of every sin we commit—not just sexual sins—we could save ourselves grief and anguish. *Lord, open my eyes to see my sin for what it is.*

The anger of Absalom also couldn't be extinguished. Two years later it bubbled up into vengeance. He murdered Amnon. Partly for revenge, partly to get the throne, partly because it satisfied his deceitful nature. *Lord, help me see my nature for what it is.*

Amen.

49

JOAB PLANS THE RETURN OF ABSALOM

SECOND SAMUEL 14

Joab, the son of Zeruiah, knew that King David missed Absalom very
much. So Joab sent messengers to Tekoa to bring a very smart
woman from there. Joab said to her, "Please pretend to be very
sad for someone. Put on clothes to show your mourning. Do
not put lotion on yourself. Act like a woman who has been crying for many days for someone who has died. (Joab wanted
someone who came from far away who would not be recognized
and whose story could not be investigated.) Go to the king. Talk
to him using the words that I tell you." Then Joab told the wise
woman what to say.

So the woman from Tekoa went to the king. She bowed face down on
the ground, saying, "O my king, help me."

King David asked her, "What is the matter?"

The woman said, "I certainly am a widow. My husband is dead. I had
two sons. They were out in the field fighting. No one was there
to stop them. And one son killed the other son. Now the whole
family is against me. They say to me: 'Bring out the son who
killed his brother. We will kill him for taking the life of his
brother. That way, we will also get rid of the one who would
receive what belonged to his father.' My son is like the last spark

of a fire. He is all I have left. If they kill him, my husband's name and property will be gone from the earth."

Then the king said to the woman, "Go home. I will take care of this for you."

The woman of Tekoa said to him, "Let the blame be on me, O my king. My father's family and I are to blame. But you and your throne are innocent."

King David said, "Refer to me anyone who says anything bad to you. Then he won't bother you again."

The woman said, "Please promise that in the name of Yahweh, your God. Then my relative who has the duty of punishing a murderer won't add to the destruction. And he won't kill my son."

David said, "As surely as the Lord lives, no one will hurt your son. Not even one hair from your son's head will fall to the ground."

The woman said, "Please let me say something to you, O my lord king."

The king said, "Speak on."

Then the woman said, "Why have you planned this? (Absalom was next in line to succeed David as king. She intimated that David was logically at fault for not allowing Absalom, the heir to the throne, to return from exile.) It is against the people of God. When you say this, you show that you are guilty. You yourself have not brought back our own son whom you forced to leave home. We will all surely die someday. (Since life is short, no time should be lost in restoring Absalom to Israel.) We are like water, spilled on the ground. No one can gather it back. But God does not take away life. Instead, He plans ways that those who have been sent away will not have to stay away from Him. O my king, I came to say this to you because the people have made me afraid. I thought: 'Let me talk to the king. Maybe he will do what I ask? Maybe he will listen? Perhaps he will save me from the man who wants to kill both me and my son. That man is trying to keep us from getting what God gave us.' Now I say: 'May the words of my lord, the king, give me rest. Like an angel of the one true God, you know what is good and what is bad. May the Lord, your God, be with you in this decision.'"

Then king David answered the woman, "You must answer the question I will ask you."

The woman said, "O my king, please ask your question."

The king said, "Did Joab tell you to say all these things?"

The woman answered, "As you live, O my king, you are right. Your servant Joab did tell me to say all of these things. Why? Joab did it so that you would see things differently. However, my lord, you are wise, like an angel of God. You know everything that happens in the land."

Then the king said to Joab, "I will do what I promised. Now, please bring back the young man Absalom."

Joab bowed face down on the ground and blessed the king. Then he said, "Today, I know you are pleased with me, O my lord the king. I know it, because you have done what I asked for."

Then Joab got up and went to Geshur, and brought Absalom back to Jerusalem. But King David said, "Absalom must go to his own house. He may not come to see me." So Absalom came back to his own house, but he did not go see the king.

Absalom Was Admired

Absalom was a grown man and was highly praised for his handsome appearance. There was no man in all Israel who was as good-looking as Absalom. There was no defect in him from his head to his feet. At the end of every year, Absalom would cut off all the hair of his head, because it got too heavy. He weighed it, and it weighed about five pounds by the royal measure. Absalom had three sons and one daughter whose name was also Tamar. She was a beautiful woman.

Now Absalom lived in Jerusalem for two full years without seeing King David. Finally, Absalom sent a message to Joab. Absalom wanted to send Joab to the king, but Joab did not want to come to Absalom. So Absalom sent him a second message. Joab still refused to come. Then Absalom said to his servants, "Joab's field is next to mine. He has barley growing there. Go, burn it." So Absalom's servants set Joab's field on fire.

That is when Joab got up and went to Absalom's house and said to him, "Why did your servants burn up my field?"

Absalom said to Joab, "Listen, I sent two messengers to you asking you to come here. I want to send you to the king and ask him why he brought me home from Geshur. It would have been better for me to have stayed there. Let me see the king now. If I am guilty, then let him execute me himself."

So Joab went to the king and told him what Absalom said. Then King David summoned Absalom. He came to the king. Absalom bowed his face low to the ground in front of the king. And the king kissed Absalom.

My Time to Pray

Full Repentance ↝ Second Samuel 14

And Absalom dwelt two full years in Jerusalem, but did not see the king's face (2 Samuel 14:28).

Why did Absalom run away to Geshur and was given asylum by King Talmai, his father-in-law? Because Absalom had murdered his half-brother. He was under law to be punished—to be executed. If David asked King Talmai to return a fugitive from justice, he would have had to execute Absalom. But the father's heart of Absalom is torn, "David mourned for his son every day" (2 Sam. 13:37). Yet David waited for the right time to be reunited with his son. *Lord, I too mourn for those who sin and refuse to return to You.*

Note, Absalom did not take the initiative to repent and ask for forgiveness. Instead he returned to his own house—under virtual house arrest—and remains for two years. Would David have forgiven Absalom if he repented and asked for restitution? Probably yes. Is this a picture of God the Father waiting for His children to repent and return to Him? Yes! Think of all the valuable years lost because a sinning believer doesn't repent and return to fellowship with the Father. *Lord, I will always repent quickly.*

Absalom was a vain young man, who was taken with his good looks. He also was power hungry; he was next in line to be the king of Israel. What a dreadful thought; Absalom will be God's king who murdered to get the throne and who refused to repent to be restored to the favor of the king and God. *Lord, may my sin make me tender to You.*

Absalom probably was more hardened after two years, than immediately after murdering Amnon. Habitual rejection makes us even harder of heart. When a person becomes so controlled by his sinful jealousy, or selfish ambition, or bitter hatred, his sinful nature distorts his sense of right and wrong. They will pursue right things in the wrong way, and they will cover evil things with lies and deceitful behavior. When we see Absalom prostrate himself before King David, we listen in vain for repentance (2 Sam. 14:33). Nothing but silence! We listen, but don't hear, "I have sinned, forgive me." When David sinned with Bath-Sheba, he cried for forgiveness (see Ps. 51), as did the prodigal son when he came home and wept, "I have sinned against heaven and in your sight" (Luke 15:21). *Lord, break my heart over my sin.*

It looks like total submission when "Absalom...came to the king and bowed himself on his face to the ground before the king." But David was too quick to forgive. "Then the king kissed Absalom" (2 Sam. 14:33) which is a kiss of reconciliation. So how does Absalom show his gratitude? Absalom stands in the gate to flatter people to get their allegiance. This is Absalom who will deceive the king's cabinet. This is Absalom who will march with an army on Jerusalem against his father, David. *Lord, teach me to submit both outwardly and inwardly.*

David only saw his son's outward submission to authority. But the evil with which he murdered Amnon is also the evil with which he'll murder David if given the chance. *Lord, take every inclination of evil from my heart.*

Amen.

50

THE CONSPIRACY OF ABSALOM

SECOND SAMUEL 15

After this, Absalom provided himself with a chariot and horses. (Prince Absalom was showing off his royalty.) He also got 50 men to run ahead of him. Prince Absalom got up early in the morning and stood near the city gate. That's where a person would go if anyone had a legal dispute which he wanted the king to decide. When anyone came there, Absalom would call out to the man, "What town are you from?"

The man would answer, "I am from such-and-such a tribe in Israel."

Then Absalom would say, "Look, your claims are valid, but the king has no one appointed to listen to you." Then Absalom would say: "I wish someone would make me a judge in this land. Then I could help everyone who comes with a legal dispute. I would help him receive a fair decision for his case."

People would often come near Absalom to bow down to him. However, when they did this, Absalom would reach out his hand to take hold of them. Then he would kiss them. Absalom behaved this way toward all the Israelites who came to King David for legal decisions. That is how Absalom won the hearts of all the men of Israel.

After four years of this practice, Absalom said to King David, "Please let me go to Hebron. I want to pay my vow that I made to the Lord. I made it while I was living in Geshur in Syria. I made this solemn promise: 'If the Lord surely brings me back to Jerusalem, I will worship Him in Hebron.'"

The king said to him, "Go in peace."

So Absalom traveled to Hebron, but he sent infiltrators throughout all the tribes of Israel, telling the people: "When you hear the trumpets (this was the signal to begin the revolt) at Hebron, Absalom has become the new king.'"

Absalom had invited 200 men to go with him. They went with Absalom from Jerusalem, but they did not know what Absalom was planning. (Absalom wanted to create the impression that his father was endorsing him as co-regent.) Ahithophel was an advisor to David. He was from the town of Giloh. While Absalom was offering sacrifices, he called Ahithophel to come from his hometown of Giloh. So Absalom's plans were working well (literally, "And the conspiracy was strong"). More and more people began going over to Absalom's side.

David Escapes

A messenger came to tell the news to David, saying, "The Israelites are beginning to follow Absalom."

Then David spoke to all his officers who were with him in Jerusalem, "Get ready. We must leave quickly. If we don't, then we won't be able to get away from Absalom. We must hurry before he catches us. (King David had no standing army to resist a sudden attack, and he wanted to spare Jerusalem from a horrible siege. Also, David feared that Absalom's army might cut off his eastern escape route across the Jordan River. David did not know how

strong Absalom's forces were or how well-organized they were.)
He will destroy us and kill the people of Jerusalem with swords."

The king's officers said to him, "We will do anything you say."

So the king set out with everyone in his entire household. However, he
left behind ten concubines to take care of the palace. As the king
left, all of his people followed him. They stopped at "The Last
House." (Probably not a dwelling, but a pavilion that overlooked
the Kidron Valley. David's bodyguards gathered here and would
only cross Kidron Brook when everything was ready for orderly
progress. Otherwise, confusion would result in this hasty situation and would cause a panic.) Then, all the king's servants
passed by David, all the Cherethites and the Pelethites, the
king's bodyguards, passed by him. Also, all the 600 Gittite men
who had followed him in the wilderness passed by the presence
of the king.

The king spoke to Ittai, a man from Gath, "Why are you going with us
too? Turn back and remain with Absalom. You are a foreigner.
This is not your homeland. You came here only a short time ago.
Should I force you to roam with us to other places today? I do
not even know where I am going. Turn back, and take your
countrymen with you. And may kindness and loyalty be shown
to you."

But Ittai answered the king: "As surely as the Lord lives and as you live,
we will stay with you. We will go with you wherever you go. We
will stay with you whether we live or die."

Then David said to Ittai, "Go ahead then, march on." So, Ittai from
Gath and all his men, along with their little children, marched
on by. All the people of the countryside wept loudly as everyone
passed by. King David also crossed Kidron Brook. Then all the
people headed in the direction of the desert.

And then even Zadok and all the Levites with him were carrying the Ark of the Covenant of the one true God. They set down the Ark of the Covenant. And Abiathar offered sacrifices until all the people had left the city.

However, King David said to Zadok, "Take the Ark of the one true God back into the city. If I find favor in the Lord's sight, then He will bring me back. He will permit me to see both the Ark of the Covenant and Jerusalem again. But, if the Lord says He is not pleased with me, I will accept it. He can do to me whatever He wants." The king said to Zadok the priest, "Are you a seer? Go back to the city in peace. Take your son Ahimaaz and Jonathan with you. I will wait near the ford of the Jordan River (David was preparing to use the Jordan River as a natural barrier against Absalom's advancing forces) near the desert, until I hear from you." So Zadok and Abiathar took the Ark of the one true God back to Jerusalem, and they stayed there.

David was going up Olive Mountain weeping as he went. He covered his head (to the Jews, this was a sign of grief), and he wore no shoes (this was a sign of even deeper humiliation). All the people who were with David covered their heads too. And they were crying as they went up. Someone told David: "Ahithophel is one of the men with Absalom who conspired against you."

So David prayed to God, "O Lord God, please cause Ahithophel's advice to become foolish." David got to the top of that mountain, Hushai the Archite came to meet him. Hushai's coat was torn (this was a sign of mourning), and there was dirt on his head (this was another indication of deep mourning). David said to Hushai, "If you go with me, you will be just one more person to take care of. (Perhaps Hushai was an old man and unfit for life as a fugitive.) However, if you return to the city, you could make Ahithophel's advice useless. Say this to Absalom: 'I am your servant, O king. I served your father David in the past, but now I will serve you.' The priests Zadok and Abiathar will be with you there. Report to them everything you learn inside Absalom's palace. Both Ahimaaz (Zadok's son) and Jonathan (Abiathar's son) are loyal to me, along with the priests. You must use them as instruments to tell me anything you find out." So David's friend, Hushai, entered Jerusalem. About that time, Absalom arrived there, too.

My Time to Pray

The Fickle Followers of David ⟨ Second Samuel 15

Now a messenger came to David, saying, "The hearts of the men of Israel are with Absalom" (2 Samuel 15:13).

We see in this chapter how the people are seduced. Almost immediately after Absalom is reinstated, he begins to take over the throne from his father who had forgiven him. How many selfish children, driven by their greed or sinful nature, have slapped the parent's hands that have embraced them?

First Absalom "prepared for himself a chariot...and fifty men to run before him" (2 Sam. 15:1) Isn't this an ostentatious show of pride? "Look out everyone, here comes the king's son. He will run over you." We've already seen Absalom is handsome in person, now he is powerful in presence. *Lord, You look on the heart, not outward appearances.*

Second, he's plotted to win the confidence of the people. He goes to the gate where judicial matters are settled, and begins to ingratiate himself to the people, then he begins to adjudicate matters to win even more support. Surely King David must have heard by official word, or by gossip, what was happening at the gate. David did nothing. If parents corrected small indiscretions of their children, they wouldn't have to deal with major problems. *Lord, give me eyes to see things as You see them.*

In the third place Absalom went to Hebron—his birth place—to make himself king. It was also the place where his father was made king over Judah. Absalom had to lie to his father to get permission to leave the palace. David said, "Go in peace" (2 Sam. 15:9) not knowing his son will "return in war." Absalom took 200 men with him, up from the 50 men he "sported" daily. *Lord, help me see through the lies that people tell me.*

Then Absalom created a media blitz, "Absalom reigns in Hebron" (2 Sam. 15:10). It's not true, but Absalom wanted it to happen. We know from other sources, that David had had an extended sickness. Maybe the people thought he was near death or dead. *Lord, help me see through propaganda and false media reports.*

Next, Absalom had the ram's horn blown. When the average farmer heard the shophar, they were commanded to rally—bring weapons—prepare for conflict. This gathering army doesn't know if there's an invasion, or some other military activity. These farmer-militias go out to face crisis, but they themselves become the crisis. *Lord, keep me from panicking with the crowd, help me always see things as they are.*

Amen.

51

DAVID AND ZIBA

SECOND SAMUEL 16

When David had gone a short distance beyond the top of Olive
Mountain, Ziba, Mephi-Bosheth's servant, met David. Ziba had
a team of donkeys; they were saddled. They were carrying 200
loaves of bread, 100 bunches of raisins, and 100 cakes of figs.
They also carried a leather bag full of wine. The king asked
Ziba, "What are you going to do with all these things?"

Ziba answered, "The donkeys are for your family to ride on. The bread
and the cakes of figs are for your servants to eat. And the wine is
for anyone to drink, whoever becomes tired in the desert."

The king asked, "Where is Mephi-Bosheth?"

Ziba answered him, "Mephi-Bosheth is staying in Jerusalem. He says:
'Today the Israelites will give back my grandfather's kingdom to
me.'"

Then the king said to Ziba, "Everything that once belonged to Mephi-
Bosheth, I now give to you."

Ziba said, "I bow myself down to you. I hope I will always be able to
please you."

Shimei Curses David

When King David came to Bahurim, a man came out who was closely related to the family of Saul's family. His name was Shimei, the son of Gera, who came out cursing David as he went by. He began throwing stones at David and all of the king's officers. But the soldiers and the people gathered around David to protect him. Shimei cursed David saying, "Get out. Get out, you murderer. You troublemaker. The Lord is punishing you for the people in Saul's family whom you killed. You took Saul's place as king. But now the Lord has given the kingdom to your own son, Absalom. You are now ruined because you are a murderer."

Then Abishai, the son of Zeruiah, said to the king, "Why should this dead dog curse you, my lord the king? Permit me to go over there and cut off his head."

But the king answered, "This is none of your business, you son of Zeruiah. Since he is cursing me, it is because the Lord has told him to do it. Who can question him?"

David also said to Abishai and all his officers, "Listen, my own son, the one who came out of my loins, is trying to kill me. Why wouldn't Shimei want to curse me? He is a Benjaminite. Leave him alone. Let him curse me. Maybe the Lord has told him to do this. Perhaps the Lord will look upon my misery and repay me with something good for the curses which Shimei is speaking today."

So David and his men went on down the road. But Shimei continued to follow David. Shimei walked along on the hillside, on the other side of the road, cursing David. And Shimei threw rocks and flung dirt at him.

The king and all his people who were with him finally arrived near the Jordan River. They were very tired, so they rested there.

Ahithophel and Hushai Advise Absalom

Meanwhile, Absalom and all the Israelites who had joined Absalom's
army arrived at Jerusalem. And, Ahithophel was also with
Absalom. Hushai the Archite (David's friend) went to Absalom
and said, "May the king live forever. May the king live forever."

Absalom asked Hushai, "Is this how you show loyalty to your friend
David? Why didn't you leave Jerusalem with your friend?"

Hushai said to Absalom, "No. Because I belong with you, the one who
has been chosen by the Lord and by these people—all the men
of Israel. I will stay with you. Moreover, I served your father in
the past. So whom should I serve now? I will serve you!"

Then Absalom said to Ahithophel, "Please advise us as to what we
should do." (This request was addressed to several men in his
cabinet of counselors, indicated by the Hebrew plural form.)

Ahithophel answered Absalom, "Your father left behind some of his concubines. He left them here to take care of the palace. Have sex
with them. Then all the Israelites will hear that your father is
truly your enemy. (This public deed was the greatest possible
insult to David. Ahithophel selfishly wanted Absalom to "burn
his bridges" behind him.) And all your people will be encouraged to give you even more support."

So they put up a tent (a wedding canopy) for Absalom on the flat roof
of the palace. And Absalom had sex with his father's concubines. Everyone in Israel could see what was going on.

At that time, people thought that Ahithophel's advice was as reliable as
God's own word. Both David and Absalom thought it was that
dependable.

My Time to Pray

Who Are Your Friends?

Ziba replied, "The donkeys are for your people to ride on" (2 Samuel 16:2).

When David was running for his life from Jerusalem, Ziba met the king with donkeys, 200 loaves of bread, 100 clusters of raisins, 100 fruits, and a skin of wine. That's quite a lot of money to buy the king's good will. Probably, Ziba was giving away produce and donkeys that belonged to Mephi-Bosheth. Ziba also lied about Mephi-Bosheth, saying the lame son of Jonathan was wanting to reclaim the throne of Saul. Deceit, trickery, and lies. *Lord, help me see through the compliments people give me, and help me see beyond the gifts that people give me to get on my "good" side. They usually want me to do something for them. Lord, give me wisdom to see through compliments and bribes.*

Shimei came out cursing David, at least he was honest. But it's wrong to kick a man when he's down. Hurling curses at your enemy is not the way God would have us treat them. God would tell us to forgive them, and do good to them, and bless them. But Shimei revealed his wicked heart with every curse he hurled at King David. Remember, David never forgot and when he was dying as an old man, David warned his son Solomon about Shimei. *Lord, show me how to treat those who curse me outwardly, or at least, hate me inwardly.*

Those who were David's true friends helped him. Abishai's heart was in the right place but his actions were wrong. Abishai wanted to kill Shimei, but "evil for evil" is not the right way. *Lord, I will not give "evil for evil" when people treat me in an evil way.*

Hushai was called "David's friend" (2 Sam. 16:18), and he was. Hushai gave bad advice to Absalom that gave David time to escape and regroup to fight again. *Lord, give me good friends like Hushai who will speak up for me when people try to stab me in the back.*

David had other friends like Shobi, Machir, and Barzilla, who provided for him. They did more than say good things about King David, they provided for his physical needs. *Lord, thank You for many friends who have provided for my needs throughout the year.*

Amen.

52

AHITHOPHEL'S PLAN

SECOND SAMUEL 17

Ahithophel said to Absalom, "Please let me choose 12,000 men, and I will arise and chase David tonight. I will catch him while he is exhausted and discouraged. (Ahithophel knew that he had to act quickly before David had the chance to organize his powerful forces.) I will put fear in him, and all his supporters will abandon him. However, I will kill only the king. Then, I will restore all the supporters of David to you. If the man you are looking for is the only one who dies, everyone else will come back to Jerusalem in peace." This plan seemed good to Absalom and to all the elders of Israel.

But Absalom said, "Please call for Hushai the Archite, too. I especially want to hear what he says." So Hushai came to Absalom and Absalom said to him: "This is the plan that Ahithophel has given. Should we follow it? If not, give us your plan."

Then Hushai said to Absalom, "This time, the plan of Ahithophel that he has laid out is not good. You know your father and his men are strong warriors. Right now, they are as mad as a mother bear that has been robbed of her cubs in the field. And your father is a good fighter. He would not spend the night with his troops. He is probably already hiding in a cave or some other such place. If your father defeats your men first, then people will hear the news, and they will think: 'Absalom's followers are losing the war.' Then even the men who are as brave as lions will lose their courage. This is because all the Israelites know that your father is a great warrior. They know what good fighters his men are.

This is what I advise: Gather up all the Israelites from Dan to Beer-Sheba. There will be as many soldiers as the grains of sand on the beaches. Then you yourself must go into battle. We will catch David wherever he is hiding, and we will subtly fall upon him as the dew falls on the ground. And we will kill him and all of his men. Not one of his soldiers will be left alive. What happens if David escapes to a city? Then all the Israelites will bring hooks and ropes to that city, and we will pull down that city into the valley. Not even a small stone will remain."

Then Absalom and all the Israelites said, "The advice of Hushai the Archite is better than that of Ahithophel." They said this because the Lord had so ordered it to counteract the shrewd advice of Ahithophel. In this way, the Lord could bring disaster upon Absalom.

Divulging Absalom's Plans to David

Afterward, Hushai informed Zadok and Abiathar, the priests, all about Ahithophel's plan for Absalom and the elders of Israel. He also reported to them what he himself had advised. (Hushai was warning David to get his men across the Jordan River as rapidly as possible.) Hushai said, "Quick, send this message to David: tell him not to spend the night at the crossings of the desert. Tell him to cross over the Jordan River immediately. If he crosses the river, then he and his army will not be caught."

Now Jonathan and Ahimaaz (two sons of the priests) were waiting at
En-Rogel. They did not want to be seen going into the city of
Jerusalem. Therefore, a servant girl went out to them and told
them a secret message. Then Jonathan and Ahimaaz went to tell
King David.

Nevertheless, a young man saw Jonathan and Ahimaaz, and he
informed Absalom. So Jonathan and Ahimaaz ran off quickly to
a man's house in Bahurim. He had a well in his courtyard, and
they climbed down into the well. The man's wife spread a sheet
over the opening of the well and covered that with barley grain.
No one suspected that Jonathan and Ahimaaz were hiding
inside.

Absalom's servants came to the woman at the house, searching for
them. They asked, "Where are Ahimaaz and Jonathan?"

She answered, "They have crossed the Jordan River."

Then Absalom's servants went to look for Jonathan and Ahimaaz, but
they could not find them. So they returned to Jerusalem.

After Absalom's servants had left, Jonathan and Ahimaaz climbed out of
the well and went to inform King David. They said to him,
"Hurry, cross over the river quickly. Why? Because Ahithophel
has made such-and-such plans against all of you." So David and
all his troops got up immediately and crossed the Jordan River.
By dawn, every single person had crossed over the Jordan River.

When Ahithophel saw that the Israelites did *not* take his advice, he saddled his donkey, and he got up and went to his hometown. He
gave instructions regarding his household. Then he hanged himself. After Ahithophel committed suicide, he was buried in his
father's tomb.

Much later, David got to Mahanaim (a fortified, mountainous city which was about 50 miles from the Jordan River.) And Absalom and all his Israelites crossed over the Jordan River. Now Absalom had put Amasa (David's nephew; Amasa was a first cousin of Absalom) in charge of the army instead of Joab. Amasa was the son of a man named Jether the Ishmaelite who had married Abigail, the daughter of Nahash and the sister of Zeruiah (David's sister). Zeruiah was Joab's mother. The Israelites and Absalom camped out in the land of Gilead.

When David arrived at Mahanaim, Shobi, Machir, and Barzillai were there waiting. Shobi the son of Nahash was from the Ammonite town of Rabbah. Machir the son of Ammiel was from Lo-Debar. And Barzillai was from Rogelim in Gilead. They brought bedding, bowls, and clay pots—and much-needed wheat, barley, flour, roasted grain, beans, and lentils. They also brought honey and milk curds, the meat of sheep, and cheese made from cows' milk. They brought these things to feed David and his men. Beforehand, they had reasoned: "These troops have become very hungry and tired and thirsty in the desert."

Psalm 3

Written by David About This Time ↵ A Prayer for God to Defeat Your Enemies

> *Lord, I have many enemies*
> > *Who are trying to destroy me.*
>
> *They tell me not to look to You,*
> > *Because there is no help in God. Selah!*
>
> *But You, Lord, are my protecting shield;*
> > *You lift me up with encouragement.*

I cried out to You for help,
> *You answered me from Your holy mountain. Selah!*

I was able to lie down and sleep
> *Because You protected me during the night.*

Now I am not afraid of ten thousand enemies
> *Because You are on every side to protect me.*

Smite my enemy on his head,
> *Shut the mouth of those who criticize me.*

Deliverance comes from You, O Lord;
> *Bless Your people with victory. Selah!*

> *Amen.*

My Time to Pray

Now or Later Makes a Difference ⁊ Second Samuel 17

So Absalom and all the men of Israel said, "The advice of Hushai the Archite is better than the advice of Ahithophel." For the Lord had purposed to defeat the good advice of Ahithophel, to the intent that the Lord might bring disaster on Absalom (2 Samuel 17:14).

Hushai gave bad advice to Absalom, that he should wait before attacking David, and the young Absalom did what was counseled. Ahithophel gave good advice, but Absalom didn't follow it. Ahithophel advised young Absalom to hurriedly pursue David and attack him before the older David could organize his warriors, or get support from the people across the Jordan. Absalom's delay gave David time to choose a new capital—David chose Mahanaim, a mountainous fortress that could be defended. David was given time to choose the place of battle, and the time of battle. If Absalom attacked immediately, David would have had to fight a defensive battle with an unprepared army. But Absalom's delay gave David time to organize. David divided his army into three sections and took the initiative. David drove Absalom's troops into Ephraim's forest, "The woods devoured more people that day than the sword devoured" (2 Sam. 18:8). *Lord, teach me how to use time effectively.*

There's another lesson on time. When David retreated from Jerusalem, he settled the first night without crossing the Jordan River. Perhaps David didn't realize the river would be a protection against Absalom's army. But David probably saw the river as just another obstacle in his otherwise "upsetting day" when everything had gone wrong. *Lord, teach me when it's best to settle down to wait and when it's best to keep going.*

The spies left in Jerusalem heard the advice of Ahithophel to attack David immediately. They got word to David that Absalom would attack, and that the deposed king should cross the Jordan that night (2 Sam. 17:22). Sometimes a quick move will win a battle before the fighting begins. *Lord, give me the ability to move quickly according to circumstances.*

There's another thing about time; David was getting old, he was too old to fight a battle where young men excel. The people answered, "You shall not go out to battle...you are worth ten thousand of us now. For you are more help to us in the city" (2 Sam. 18:3). We must all help where we can make the greatest contribution. David was more helpful back in the city as a "cheerleader" and strategist, than just another soldier in battle. *Lord, teach me how to best use my spiritual gifts in Your service.*

Amen.

53

THE DEATH OF ABSALOM

SECOND SAMUEL 18

David counted the soldiers who were with him. Then David put commanders over groups of 1,000 soldiers and officers over groups of 100 soldiers. He sent the troops out in three groups. Joab was in charge of one-third of the men. Joab's brother, Abishai, was in charge of another third. And Ittai from Gath was in charge of the last third of the army. King David said to the army, "I myself will surely go out with you to fight too."

But the soldiers said, "No. You must not go out with us. If we are ever forced to retreat from the battle, Absalom's men would not care about us. Even if half of us were to be killed, Absalom's men would not care. You are worth more than 10,000 of us. It is now better for you to stay in this fortified city. Then if we need support, you could send help."

The king said to them, "I will do whatever you men think is best." So the king stood beside the gate while the army was leaving. They marched out in units of 100 and units of 1,000.

The king gave this command to Joab, Abishai, and Ittai, "Be gentle with young Absalom for my sake." Everyone heard the king's orders to each of the commanders regarding Absalom.

David's army marched out into the field to fight against the Israelites of Absalom. They fought in the forest of Ephraim. There David's soldiers defeated those other Israelites. Many soldiers died that day—20,000 men. From there, the battle spread throughout all the countryside. However, on that day, more men died because of the forest than in the actual fighting.

Then Absalom happened to encounter some of David's troops, and he was riding his mule. As it went under a large oak tree, Absalom's head got caught in the thick oak branches of the tree, and his mule ran out from under him. So Absalom was suspended in mid-air above the ground.

When one of David's men saw this happen, he told Joab, "I just saw Absalom hanging in an oak tree."

Joab said to him, "What? You saw him? Why didn't you kill him, and let him fall to the ground right then and there? I would have been glad to give you a reward—a warrior's belt containing four ounces of silver."

The man answered Joab, "I would not dare to harm the king's son! I would not do it, even if you paid me 25 pounds of silver. We ourselves heard the king's command to you, Abishai, and Ittai. The king said: 'Be careful not to harm young Absalom for my sake.' If I had killed him, then the king would find out. (Nothing is hidden from him.) And you would not protect me."

Joab said, "I'm not going to waste any more time here with you."

Now Absalom was still alive in the middle of the oak tree. So Joab took three spears and ran Absalom through the mid-section. Then young men who carried Joab's weapons also gathered around Absalom. They hit him too and killed him.

Then Joab blew the trumpet as a signal to stop the pursuit. So the troops quit chasing after those other Israelites. Then Joab's men took Absalom's corpse and threw it into the large pit in the forest. Then they filled in the pit with a huge pile of rocks. All the Israelites who had followed Absalom ran away; each one went home.

While Absalom was alive, he had set up a monument in the King's Valley. It was an obelisk that he had dedicated to himself. He thought: "I have no son to keep the memory of my name alive." Absalom had named the pillar after himself. That pillar is still called "Absalom's Monument," even today.

David Learns About the Death of His Son Absalom

Then Ahimaaz, the son of Zadok, spoke to Joab, saying, "Please, let me run and take the news to King David. I will tell him that the Lord has saved David from his enemies."

Joab answered Ahimaaz, "No, you are not the one to take this news today. You may bring news at another time. But do not do it today, because the king's son is dead."

Then Joab said to a man from Cush, "Go tell the king what you have seen." The Cushite man bowed down to Joab. Then he ran off to tell David the news.

But Ahimaaz, the son of Zadok, begged Joab again, "No matter what happens—along with the Cushite man—please let me go too."

Joab said, "My son, why should you run to carry the news? You will not receive any reward for the news that you bring."

Ahimaaz answered, "It doesn't matter; just let me run."

So Joab told Ahimaaz, "Run." Then Ahimaaz ran by way of the Jordan Plain. And Ahimaaz outran the Cushite runner.

Now David was sitting between the two gates of the city. The watchman went up to the roof, by the gateway wall. As he looked out, behold, he saw a man running alone. The watchmen called out to report it to King David.

The king thought: "Since he is alone, he is bringing good news."

The man got closer and closer to the city, the watchman saw another man running too. The watchman called out to the gatekeeper, saying, "Look, another man is running separately."

The king thought: "He must also be bringing good news."

The watchmen said, "I think the first man is running like Ahimaaz, the son of Zadok."

The king said, "Ahimaaz is a good man. Surely he must be bringing good news!"

Then Ahimaaz called out a greeting to the king: "Shalom." And he bowed to the king, low to the ground. He said, "Praise the Lord, your God. The Lord has defeated the men who revolted against you, O my king."

The king asked, "Is young Absalom safe?"

Ahimaaz answered, "When Joab sent me, I observed some big commotion, but I don't know what it was all about."

The king said, "Step over here and wait." So Ahimaaz stepped aside and stood there.

Then, the Cushite man also arrived. He said, "O my master and king, listen to the good news. Today the Lord has rightfully punished those people who revolted against you."

Then the king asked the Cushite man, "Is young Absalom safe?"

The Cushite man answered, "May your enemies be like that young man, O king. May all who rise up to harm you be like him."

King David Mourns

Then the king knew that Absalom was dead. David was very upset. He went up to the room over the city gate and wept. As he went, he continued to cry out, "My son Absalom. My son, my son, Absalom. I wish I had died instead of you. O Absalom, my son, my son."

Second Samuel 19

Some people told Joab, "The king is weeping. He is grieving openly for Absalom." David's army had won the battle that day. However, the entire army was disgusted because they heard: "The king is grieving openly for his son." The army sulked and acted like embarrassed people who had been defeated, or like those who had deserted during the battle. The king covered his face and cried loudly, "My son, Absalom, Absalom, my son, my son."

Then Joab went to the king's house and said to him, "You have shamed all your soldiers today. They saved your life, and they saved the lives of your sons (Absalom would have killed all likely competitors), your daughters, your wives, and your concubines. Yet you have shamed them. Why? Because you love those who hated you. And you hate those people who loved you. Today you have made it clear that your commanders and your men don't really mean anything to you. What if Absalom were still alive, and all of *us* were dead? Would that make you happier? Would you be more pleased? Now get up, and go out and speak to the hearts of your soldiers. I swear by the Lord if you do not go out there in plain view, not one soldier will stay loyal to you by tonight. And that would be worse than all the troubles you ever had since you were a young man until now."

King David Returns to Jerusalem

So the king got up and sat next to the city gate. The news spread to everyone—"*Look*, the king is sitting at the gate." Then all the troops marched past the king proudly.

All the Israelites who had followed Absalom had run away to their homes.

David as Their King

Later, all the people among all the tribes of Israel began to argue, saying, "The king saved us from the Philistines and our other enemies, yet David left the country because of Absalom. We crowned Absalom as our king, but now he has died in battle. So we should restore David as king."

King David sent a message to Zadok and Abiathar, the priests, saying, "Tell the elders of Judah, even in my house, I have heard what all the Israelites are saying, 'So why are you the last tribe to bring back the king to his palace? You are my brothers. You are my flesh and bone. Why are you the last tribe to restore the king?' And tell Amasa: 'You are part of my own family. May God punish me terribly if from now on, I do not make you my general of the army instead of Joab.'" (By this time, David had probably found out that it was Joab who killed Absalom, thus disobeying David's direct order.)

David touched the heart of every individual in Judah. The tribe agreed with one another, as if they were one man. They sent this message to the king: "Return to Jerusalem with all of your soldiers."

When the king came back, he got as far as the Jordan River, and the men of Judah came to Gilgal to meet him, because they wanted to escort the king across the Jordan River.

Shimei and the Others

Shimei also hurried down with the men of Judah to meet King David. Shimei, the son of Gera, was the Benjaminite who lived in Bahurim. One thousand Benjaminites came with Shimei. Ziba, the man over Saul's estate, also came. He brought his 15 sons and 20 servants with him. They all hurried to the Jordan River to wait for the king. The people went across the Jordan River to help bring the king's family back to Judah. They wanted to please the king. As the king was just about to cross the river, Shimei, the son of Gera, came up to him, and bowed himself down low to the ground in front of the king. He said to the king, "O my master, please do not hold me guilty. Please forget the terrible things I did when you were leaving Jerusalem. I beg you, do not hold that against me. I know I have sinned. That is why I am the first person from Joseph's family (this was a common way of referring to the northern tribes) to come down and meet you today, my master and king."

But Abishai, the son of Zeruiah, said, "Shimei should die. He cursed you, the Lord's anointed king."

David said, "I am so different from you, you sons of Zeruiah. Today you are opposing me. No one will be put to death in Israel today. Today I know I am still king over Israel."

Then the king said to Shimei, "I promise you will not die."

Mephi-Bosheth

Mephi-Bosheth, Saul's grandson, also went down to meet King David. Mephi-Bosheth had not bandaged or trimmed his beard, or washed his clothes while David had been gone. He had not done any of these things—from the time King David had left Jerusalem until the day David returned safely. When Mephi-Bosheth came from Jerusalem to meet the king, the king asked him, "Mephi-Bosheth, why didn't you leave with me?"

Mephi-Bosheth answered, "My lord, O king, my servant Ziba tricked me. I said to Ziba, 'I am crippled. So saddle a donkey for me. Then I will ride it, so that I can leave with the king.' But Ziba lied to you about me. You, my master and king, are like an angel of the one true God. Nevertheless, do whatever you think is best. You could have killed all of my grandfather's family. Instead, you put me among the people who eat at your own table. So I don't have any right to ask anything more from you, O king."

The king said to him, "Do not say anything more. I have decided that you and Ziba will split the land."

Mephi-Bosheth said to the king, "Let Ziba take all the land! I am merely happy that you, my master, the king, have arrived safely at your own home."

Barzillai

Barzillai was from Gilead. He had come down from Rogelim for the king's crossing of the Jordan River. Barzillai wanted to give David a good sendoff over the Jordan River. Now Barzillai was a very old man. He was 80 years old. He had supported King David while David was staying at Mahanaim. (Barzillai could afford to do this, because he was a very rich man.) King David said to Barzillai, "Cross the river with me. Come with me to Jerusalem, and I will take care of you."

But Barzillai answered the king, "Do you realize how old I am? Do you really think I can go up with you to Jerusalem? Today I am 80 years old. I cannot enjoy anything. I am too old to taste whatever I eat or drink. And I am too old to hear the voices of male or female singers. Why should you be bothered with me anymore? I am not worthy of any reward from you. However, I will cross the Jordan River with you. Then please let me go back, so that I may die in my own city. Let me die near the grave of my father and my mother. Chimham, your servant, is here. Let him go with you, my master and king. Do whatever you wish for him."

King David answered, "Chimham will go with me. I will do for him anything you want. Yes, I will do for him anything you would have liked to do." So the king and all the people crossed the Jordan. And King David kissed Barzillai and blessed him. Then Barzillai returned home.

When the king crossed the Jordan River near Gilgal, Chimham also crossed with him. All the people of the tribe of Judah crossed, too. Half the troops of Judah and half the troops of Israel led David across the river.

Tribal Trouble Was Brewing

Soon all the men of Israel came to the king and said, "Our brothers, the men of Judah, stole you away from us. They brought you and your family across the Jordan River with your men. Why did they do this?" (In other words, this act of David's tribe made the Israelites look bad, as if the non-Judahites were reluctant to receive their king back.)

All the men of Judah answered the Israelites, "We did this because the king is our close relative. Why are you angry about this? We have not eaten food at the king's expense. He did not give us any special favors."

The men of Israel answered the men of Judah, saying: "We have ten tribes in the kingdom. So we have more right to David than you do. But you ignored us. We were the first ones to talk about bringing our true king back."

But the men of Judah spoke even more harshly than the men of Israel.

My Time to Pray

We Love Our Fleshly Ways ⌁ Second Samuel 19

The King (David) had commanded..."Deal gently for my sake with the young man Absalom" (2 Samuel 18:5).

The King (David) cried with a loud voice, "O my son Absalom! O Absalom, my son, my son" (2 Samuel 19:4).

It's a fact of Christianity, the old self dies hard. By that is meant, we should "crucify" our egotistical pride that loves attention and praise from others. Some love fleshly satisfaction; it's hard to "crucify" the lust of the flesh that wants to please the body in immoral ways. Also, it's hard to "crucify" our lust of the eyes, which is greed for money, things, and the trappings of pleasure. We are warned of these three evils in First John 2:16: "For all that is in the world—the lust of the flesh, the lust of the eyes, and the pride of life—is not of the Father but is of the world." *Lord, help me separate myself from evil temptations.*

When David's men marched into battle, he told his generals (2 Sam. 18:5) in hearing of all his army (2 Sam. 18:12) not to hurt Absalom. This is preposterous! David was blind to reality. Absalom had an army chasing David to kill him. Absalom had lied to David before the rebellion, and if David allowed him to live, Absalom would again try to undermine the reign of David. Absalom is an enemy of his father, but David is blind to the realities of life. *Lord, may I always see clearly the subtle temptations that will destroy my walk with You.*

Just as Absalom is an extension of the physical flesh of David, so our old sinful "fleshly" nature is an extension of our desires and longings. Just as David wept over his son, so we weep when we think about losing the pleasure that our old nature gives us. *Lord, forgive me for weeping over my sin, when I should be crucifying my old nature.*

Paul reminds us, "Those who are Christ's have crucified the flesh with its passions and desires" (Gal. 5:24). A Christian must treat his evil desires as though they are dead. Killing them is a good thing, but we, like David, weep when we lose them. *Lord, I will obey You, I will crucify the old flesh.*

David did these three wrongs. First, he actually wept openly for a rebellious son (which is a reflection of the natural life). Second, he refused to go meet and congratulate his troops that had defeated Absalom's army. Third, David wept so loudly over his loss it demoralized his army. We do the same thing as David. When God "takes" away the fruitage of our flesh, we complain bitterly and refuse to recognize what God has done. Then we cry longingly because God crucifies our old nature so that we confuse other believers who see our tears or hear our anguish. *Lord, may I long for You with tears, not long for the flesh and its satisfaction.*

It took Joab's initiative to stop David's morbid weeping for a rebellious son. Joab lost patience with David, he called David back to his duty as king of the nation and commander and chief of the army. Joab rebuked David harshly, "If you do not go out, not one will stay with you this night" (2 Sam. 19:7). Sometimes it takes another to rebuke us about our compromise with the flesh. Another may point us in the right direction and tell us what to do. *Lord, may I listen to those You send to rebuke me about my failings.*

Amen.

54

SHEBA'S REVOLT AND DEFEAT

SECOND SAMUEL 20

It happened that a troublemaker named Sheba, the son of Richri, from the tribe of Benjamin, blew the trumpet. (Apparently, those who still supported Saul's dynasty were very numerous, and favored a revolt against David as king.) Sheba said:

"We have no share in David. We have no part in the son of Jesse. O people of Israel, let us go to our own homes." So all the Israelites deserted David and followed Sheba. But the men of Judah stayed with their king all the way from the Jordan River to Jerusalem.

David came to his palace in Jerusalem. Earlier, he had left there ten of his concubines to take care of the palace. Now David put them in a house where they would be guarded. They were kept there for the rest of their lives. David gave them food, but he never had sex with them again. They lived like widows until they died.

The king said to Amasa (King David had appointed Amasa to be commander-in-chief of David's army, thus bypassing Joab, his former, veteran general), "Tell the men of Judah to meet with me in three days. And you must also be there." So Amasa called the men of Judah together, but he took longer than the time which the king had told him. (We do not know precisely why Amasa delayed.

Perhaps Amasa was unable to muster a military force from the tribe of Judah that would be sufficient to put down the growing insurrection.)

David said to Abishai (not to Joab, whom David no longer trusted), "Sheba, the son of Bichri, is more dangerous to us than was Absalom. Take my available men and chase him. Hurry, before he escapes to strong, walled cities. If he gets there, then he will save himself from us." So, Joab's men, the Cherethites and the Pelethites (who were the king's bodyguards) and all the soldiers went with Abishai from Jerusalem to chase Sheba, the son of Bichri.

When Joab and the army came to the Great Rock at Gibeon, Amasa came out to meet them. (Trying to re-assume command of the whole army.) Joab was wearing his uniform. At his waist, he wore a belt that held his sword in its case. As Joab stepped forward, his sword fell out of its case. (Joab appeared to drop his sword accidentally. Instead of saluting, Joab deliberately planned to stab Amasa. Amasa would be caught off guard.) Joab answered Amasa, "Brother, is everything all right with you?" Then, with his right hand, Joab took Amasa by the beard to kiss him. Amasa did not guard against the second sword that was hidden in Joab's hand. So Joab plunged the sword into Amasa's stomach. This caused Amasa's intestines to spill on the ground. Joab did not have to stab Amasa again. He was already dead. Then Joab and his brother Abishai continued to chase Sheba, the son of Bichri.

One of Joab's young men stood by Amasa's body. The young man said, "Everyone who is for Joab and David should follow Joab!" Amasa lay in the middle of the road, covered with his own blood. The young man saw that everyone was stopping to look at the body. So he dragged Amasa's body from the road and laid it in a field. Then he put a sheet over it. After Amasa's body was taken off the road, all the men followed Joab. They went with him to chase Sheba, the son of Bichri.

Sheba went through all the tribes of Israel to Abel of Beth-Maacah. (This fortified city was located at the extreme northern boundary of Israel.) All the Bichrites came together and followed him. (Sheba was only able to rally support from his own kinsfolk. His rebellion had fizzled.) So Joab and his men came to Abel of Beth-Maacah and surrounded it. They piled dirt up against the city wall, so that they could attack it. And they began digging under the city walls to make them fall down.

But a clever woman shouted out from the city, "Listen. Please tell Joab to come here. I want to talk to him." So Joab came near her. She asked him, "Are you Joab?"

He answered, "Yes, I am."

She said, "Listen to what I say."

Joab said, "I'm listening."

Then the woman said, "In the past, people would often say: 'Ask for good advice at Abel.' Then the problem would be solved. I am one of the peaceful, loyal people of Israel. You are trying to destroy an important city of Israel. Why should you destroy what belongs to the Lord?"

Joab answered: "I don't want to destroy or ruin anything. That is not what I want, but there is a man here from the mountains of Ephraim. His name is Sheba, the son of Bichri. He has turned against King David. If you will bring him to me, then I will leave the city alone."

The woman said to Joab, "His head will be thrown over the wall to you."

Then the woman spoke very shrewdly to all the people of the city. They cut off the head of Sheba, the son of Bichri, and threw it over the wall to Joab. So Joab blew the trumpet, and the army left the city. Every man returned home. And Joab went back to the king in Jerusalem.

Joab was the new general of the entire army of Israel. Benaiah, the son of Jehoiada, led the Cherethites and the Pelethites. Adoniram led the men who were forced to do hard work. (This official policy of conscripting labor gangs would eventually break up King Solomon's empire.) And Jehoshaphat, the son of Ahilud, was the historian, or recorder. Sheba was the royal assistant. Zadok and Abiathar were the priests. And Ira the Jairite was David's high official.

My Time to Pray

Why God Uses Some Evil Men to Do Good ⌁ Second Samuel 20

Whoever favors Judah and whoever is for David, follow Joab (2 Samuel 20:11).

If it wasn't for Joab, David's reign might have not been as successful as it was. Even in victory, David was a slobbering father and disillusioned leader who didn't have the strength to face his soldiers. It was Joab who told him to do the right thing, "Get out there before your men and congratulate them, or they will all leave you before the sun goes down." Joab did right on many occasions, but that did not make Joab a man of good character (doing the right thing constantly in the right way). *Lord, I want inward character.*

David knew Joab was unscrupulous, so on his death bed he warns Solomon, "Do not let (Joab's) grey head go down to Sheol in peace" (1 Kings 2:6). Joab murdered Abner, who was appointed by David. Joab murdered Absalom. Joab murdered Amasa (2 Sam. 20:10). Joab saved the kingdom, yet did it in an evil way. Why would God later in history use liquor-drinking, cursing generals to win wars for good nations? Because a sovereign God sets up nations and takes them down according to His will. God uses evil men for good purposes. *Lord, help me see Your overall plans.*

Did you see in today's lessons how David originally overlooked Joab to appoint Amasa as his general? But Amasa couldn't get an army to follow him. Maybe David thought Amasa had defected to Sheba. Does David appoint Joab in the second place? No! David appoints Abishai—Joab's brother—to be the second to raise an army. Then Joab appears on the scene, murders Amasa (maybe Joab also thought Amasa had defected), and assumes leadership. David doesn't appoint Joab, Joab appoints himself. No matter what you think of Joab, he was loyal to David, and loyal to the monarchy, even though he was blind to doing the right thing in the right way. *Lord, help me learn a negative lesson from Joab. Help me never do the right thing in the wrong way.*

Joab would have destroyed the Jewish city of Abel-Beth-Maachah to get Sheba. A wise woman out debated Joab, "You seek to destroy a city and a mother in Israel. Why would you swallow up the inheritance of the Lord?" (2 Sam. 20:19). Then she convinced the people of the city to throw Sheba's head over the wall to Joab. Ruthless Joab would stop at nothing to get a job done. With Sheba's head in hand, he returns triumphantly to Jerusalem. He saved the kingdom for David. *Lord, I will pray for people who do right in a ruthless way.*

Amen.

55

THE GIBEONITES ARE AVENGED

SECOND SAMUEL 21

During the time that David was king, there was a time of famine that
continued for three years in a row. So David prayed to the Lord
who answered, "Saul and his family of murderers are behind the
reason for this famine. Saul killed the Gibeonites." (An unrecord-
ed massacre of the Gibeonites which occurred sometime during
Saul's reign, in spite of the solemn oath which Joshua had made
to the Gibeonites many years before [see Josh. 9].) Now the
Gibeonites were not Israelites. They were Amorites who were left
alive. The Israelites had sworn an oath not to hurt the
Gibeonites. But Saul, in an eager attempt to impress the people
of Israel and Judah, tried to kill all the Gibeonites.

King David called the Gibeonites together and asked them, "What can I
do for you? What can I do to make amends, so that you can
bless the Lord's people?"

The Gibeonites said to David, "Saul and his family don't have enough
silver and gold to pay for what they did. And we don't have the
right to execute anyone in Israel. Saul was the Lord's chosen
king. So bring some of his descendants to us. (Saul's sons and
grandsons may have participated in the bloody raids upon the
Gibeonites.) Then we will kill them and hang them up on stakes.

We will put them in front of the Lord at Gibeah, Saul's hometown."

King David said, "I will hand them over to you." But the king protected Jonathan's son, Mephi-Bosheth. David did this because of the vow he had made to Jonathan by the name of Yahweh. But the king did take Armoni and Mephi-Bosheth (this was a different man named "Mephi-Bosheth," who was not the son of Jonathan), sons of Rizpah, and Saul. (Rizpah was the daughter of Aiah.) And the king took the five sons of Saul's daughter Merab. Adriel was the father of Merab's five sons. (Adriel was the son of Barzillai the Maholathite.) (This is not the same "Barzillai" who helped David at Mahanaim [see 2 Sam. 19:31-40].) David handed these seven sons over to the Gibeonites. Then the Gibeonites killed them and hung them on stakes on a hill in front of the Lord. All seven men died together. They were put to death during the first days of the harvest season.

Aiah's daughter, Rizpah, rook some rough cloth and she spread it out on a rock for herself. She stayed there from the beginning of the harvest until the rain fell on her sons' bodies. (This vigil would have been for about six months.) At night, she did not let the wild animals scavenge them.

Some people told David what Aiah's daughter, Rizpah, Saul's concubine, had done. Then David took the bones of Saul and Jonathan from the men of Jabesh-Gilead. (They had taken these bones secretly from the public square of Beth-Shan. The Philistines had hung the bodies of Saul and Jonathan there after they had killed Saul at Gilboa.) David brought up the bones of Saul and his son Jonathan from Gilead. Then the people gathered the bodies of Saul's seven sons who were hanged on the stakes and buried them with the bones of Saul and his son Jonathan at Zela in the territory of Benjamin. They buried them in the tomb of Saul's father, Kish. The people did everything the king commanded.

After this, God answered the prayers of the people in the land.

Wars Between Israel and the Philistines

Again there was another war between the Philistines and Israel. And David and his men went down to fight the Philistines. But David became exhausted. Ishbi-Benob had a new sword, and he planned to kill David. But Abishai, the son of Zeruiah, killed the Philistine. So he rescued David.

Then David's men made a promise to David, "Never again will you go out with us into battle. If you were killed, then Israel would lose its greatest leader."

Later, at Gob, there was another battle with the Philistines. Sibbecai the Hushathite killed Saph, another one of the sons of Rapha.

Later, there was another battle at Gob with the Philistines. Elhanan, the son of Jair the weaver, killed Lahmi, the brother of Goliath from Gath. His wooden shaft of his spear was as large as a weaver's rod.

At Gath, another battle took place. A very large man was there who had six fingers on each hand. He also had six toes on each foot. He had a total of 24 fingers and toes. This man also was one of the sons of Rapha. When he taunted Israel, Jonathan (David's nephew and the brother of Jonadab) killed him. Jonathan was the son of Shimei, David's brother.

These four men were sons of Rapha (giants) from Gath. (These four incidents are grouped together because they are similar, not because they all occurred at or near the same time.) They were all killed by David and his men. (Though these four giants were not felled by the hand of David, he got the credit for it.)

My Time to Pray

Hard Choices ∂ Second Samuel 21

Then the men of David swore to him, saying, "You shall go out no more with us to battle, lest the lamp of Israel is extinguished" (2 Samuel 21:17).

This whole chapter is about *hard choices*. David had to deal with the sin of Saul against the Gibeonites. Apparently Saul had killed a number of Gibeonites and stolen their property to give to his officials (see 1 Sam. 22:7). It was a hard choice for David to turn over seven living offspring of Saul to the Gibeonites. Outsiders may have thought David was trying to get rid of any "son" of Saul who might have claimed David's throne. But David's decision was noble. *Lord, help me make hard decisions.*

David was a warrior and he probably wanted to "die with his boots on," as they say in the old cowboy movies. In this story (2 Sam. 21:15-17), David was almost killed by Ishbi-Benob, a Philistine giant. Probably, Abishai saw the giant head toward David in the battle. Perhaps he saw murder in the eyes of Ishbi-Benob, so Abishai came to David's defense. The way the story records, it appears the giant was about to kill David—and David would have died—if Abishai had not intervened. *Lord, thank You for people who saved me from destruction.*

Notice the phrase "the men of David," this story wasn't about any one soldier who wanted David to retire. They all knew it was time for David to "hang up his spurs," again using an old cowboy metaphor. Sometimes it's hard to know when to quit. *Lord, may I know when to quit every job that I'm doing, and may I know when to move on to the next job.*

Again look at the phrase "the men of David." They were as loyal to him as they were to the kingdom. (And isn't loyalty to the leader the same as loyalty to the movement?) David earned their devotion when he camped out with them under the stars or in a cave. David didn't think he was better than they. Some of them died for David. Why? Because David was the anointed of God to be king. But there is a still deeper reason. He was more than leader, David was their friend. *Lord, help me be a friend to those I lead.*

The "men of David" realized if David died, "the lamp of Israel would be extinguished." How many times has a great church lost its greatness when their great pastor has been removed. Still, "Everything rises and falls on leadership." *Lord, help me respect the leaders You've given me; help me follow them for Your blessing on my life.*

Amen.

56

THE SONG OF DAVID

SECOND SAMUEL 22

David sang to the Lord the words of this song. He sang it when the
Lord had saved him from Saul and all his other enemies (written
during a calmer period of David's later life, when he could
reflect on God's protection over many past years).

"The Lord is my Rock, my place of safety, my Savior,
My God is my Rock.

I can run to Him for safety,
He is my Shield and my Saving Strength.

The Lord is my High Tower, my Safe Place,
The Lord saves me from anyone who wants to harm me.

I will call to the Lord,
I will be saved from my enemies;
The Lord be praised.

The waves of death swirled around me,
The deadly rivers overwhelmed me.

The ropes of death wrapped around me,
The traps of death confronted me.

In my desperation, I called to the Lord;
  I cried out to my God.

From His Temple He heard my voice,
  My call for help reached His ears.

The earth trembled and quaked,
  The foundations of Heaven began to shake and quiver,
  They shook because the Lord was angry.

Smoke came out of His nostrils,
  Consuming fire came out of His mouth,
  Burning coals blazed out of it.

He tore open the sky and came down,
  Dark clouds were under His feet.

He rode an angel-like being, and He flew;
  He soared on the wings of the wind.

He made darkness His canopy around him,
  Surrounded by fog and thick clouds.

Out of the brightness of His presence
  Came flashes of lightning.

The Lord thundered from heaven;
  The Most High God raised His voice.

He shot His arrows and scattered them,
  His bolts of lightning confused them.

The Lord rebuked His enemies
  With the blast of the breath from His nostrils.

The valleys of the sea appeared;
  The foundations of the earth became exposed.

The Song of David

The Lord reached down from above and He took hold of me,
  He pulled me up from the deep waters,

He saved me from my powerful enemies
  From those who hated me.

They were too strong for me,
    They attacked me at my time of trouble,
    But the Lord protected me.

He took me to a safe place;
    Because He delights in me, He rescued me.

The Lord spared me because of the righteous way that I've lived;
    I did what the Lord said was right,
    He has rewarded me.

For I have guarded the ways of the Lord;
    I have not betrayed my God.

I have observed all of His laws,
    And I have not turned away from His decrees.

I was blameless in His presence;
    Therefore, the Lord has rewarded me
    According to my righteousness,
    According to my purity in His sight.

O Lord, You are loyal to those who are loyal;
    You are upright to those who have integrity.

You are pure to those who are pure,
    But You are hostile to those who are morally twisted.

You save those who are humble,
    But You humble those who are proud.

O Lord, You are my lamp;
  You, Lord, brighten the darkness around me.

With Your help, I can attack an army;
  With God's help, I can climb over a wall.

God's way is without fault,
  The Lord's Word is pure;
  He is a Shield to all those who trust Him.

Who is God? None but the Lord;
  Who is the Rock? Only our God.

The one true God is my Protection,
  He guards innocent people in His pathway.

He causes me to be as sure-footed as a deer,
  He helps me stand on steep mountains.

He trains my hands for battle,
  Therefore, my arms can bend a bronze bow.

You provided me with Your saving shield,
  You have stooped down to raise me up.

You gave me a better way to live
  So I don't fall down.

I chased my enemies, and I destroyed them;
  I did not quit until they were finished.

I crushed them, and I devoured them,
  They didn't get up again;
  They fell beneath my feet.

You dressed me with strength for the battle,
  You put my foes under my feet.

You made my enemies turn and retreat,
    I silenced those who hated me.

They called for help
        But there was no one to save them.

They cried out to the Lord,
        But He did not answer them.

I beat my enemies into fine dust,
        They were like the dirt of the streets.

I pounded them down and walked on them,
        You saved me when my own people attacked me;
        You kept me as the leader of nations.

People whom I never knew served me,
        Foreigners obey me;
        As soon as they hear me, they obey me.

They all become afraid,
        They came out of their strongholds, trembling.

The Lord lives,
        May my Rock be praised;
        Exalt God, the Rock, who saves me.

The true God gives me victory over my enemies,
        He brings people under my rule.

He frees me from my enemies;
        Yes, You set me over those who hate me,
        You saved me from cruel men.

So I will acknowledge You, O Lord of the nations,
        I will sing praises to Your name.

The Lord gives great victories to his king;
He honors the king whom He crowned,
To David and his descendants forever."

My Time to Pray

The Psalm of a Senior Saint ⌁ Second Samuel 22

Then David spoke to the Lord the words of this song, on the day when the Lord had delivered him from the hand of all his enemies, and from the hand of Saul (2 Samuel 22:1).

David writes this psalm as an elderly saint looking back over all his life—the word "day" does not refer to a particular victory or a specific day. The word "day" refers to a plateau in David's life. God has done all that God promised to do. "God has fulfilled all of His promises." *Lord, I know You will fulfill all Your promises to me.*

When we realize what God has done for us, what should be our response? We should praise God, as did David. This is a psalm of gratitude, thankfulness, and worship. David realizes God had been present every time David needed him. *Thank You Lord for protecting me, guiding me, anointing me, using me, and allowing me to worship You.*

Throughout the psalm, David talks about "I" and "me" and "my." Yet this is not a psalm of boasting or self-exoneration. None of that. David is not claiming to be perfect, David is not saying everything he did was right. What David is saying is that he trusted the Lord, and God saw him through difficult days. David said he was obedient to God and tried to demonstrate integrity in all that he did. David did not claim perfection, but David was upright and conscientious. *Lord, David claimed for his life what I want for my life.*

We still see David the warrior in this psalm. David fought because people attacked him. God's enemies were his enemies. David's victories were

God's victories because David honored God for saving him time and again. *Lord, Your enemies will be my enemies.*

What we see in this psalm is relationship. David walked with God when he was afraid, and David trusted in God in battle. We do not see the external things of religion. He doesn't tell us how long he prayed, nor does he describe his fast, or what he did when coming to the Tabernacle to worship God. David doesn't even list all the great things he has done for God. David only describes his intimate relationship with God, that's the most important thing now that his life is almost over. *Lord, You are everything in my life.*

Amen.

57

THE LAST PSALM OF DAVID

SECOND SAMUEL 23

These are the last words of psalm by David, the inspired message of
David to the nation from the son of Jesse; the man who was
made great by God.

He was the crowned king by the God of Jacob,
He is the sweet psalmist of Israel.

"The Spirit of the Lord spoke through me,
His word was on my tongue.

The God of Israel spoke,
The Rock of Israel said to me:

'The Person who rules fairly over mankind,
The Person who rules with reverence for God,

He is like the morning light at dawn,
He is like a morning without clouds,

He is like sunshine after a rain because
The sunshine causes the tender grass to grow.'

Even though, my family is not God-fearing, (Note: The sense of this line
is: David is comparing the actual state of his family and kingdom during the latter years of trouble and disaster with the

prophetic description of the righteous King of Second Samuel 7:12-16. And seeing how far his household falls short, David still comforts himself by the terms of God's covenant with him. So David looks forward to the kingdom of the Messiah.)
God has made a lasting covenant with me,
Arranged and secured in every detail.

It is my complete salvation,
This covenant is all I ever needed,

God will surely make it come to pass.

But all evil people will perish like thorns,
People cannot hold on to thorns,

Anyone who handles them
Must use an iron tool or the shaft of a spear,
Thorns will be completely burned up in the end."

David's Strong Warriors

These are the names of David's mighty warriors who made themselves mighty with him: Josheb-Basshebeth, the Tah-Chemonite, was head of the Three. He used his spear to kill 800 men at one time.

Next, there was Eleazar, the son of Dodo, the son of Ahohi. Eleazar was one of the three strongest warriors who was with David when they challenged the Philistines in battle and the Israelites retreated. But Eleazar stood his ground. He fought the Philistines until he was so tired that he could not let go of his sword. So the Lord caused a great victory for the Israelites on that day. The people came back after Eleazar had won the battle, but they came only to scavenge the weapons and armor from the enemy.

Next there was Shammah, the son of Agee, the mountaineer. The
Philistines came together to fight for a field full of lentils. Israel's
troops ran away from the Philistines, but Shammah stood in the
middle of the field to save the crop. He fought for that field and
he killed those Philistines. And the Lord gave another great victory.

One time, three of the Thirty, David's best soldiers, came down to him
during the harvest. Now David was at the cave of Adullam, the
Philistine army had camped in the Valley of Rephaim. David was
in a protected place, and some of the Philistine soldiers were in
Bethlehem.

David had a strong desire for some good water. He said, "O I just wish
someone would get me some water from the well near the town
gate of Bethlehem." So the three warriors broke through the
Philistine camp, drew water out of that well near the town gate
of Bethlehem. Then they brought it to David. However, he
refused to drink it, but poured it out on the ground as a sacrifice
to the Lord. (None but God was worthy to drink it.) David said,
"O Lord, I cannot drink this. It would be like drinking the blood
of the men who risked their lives." So David refused to drink
that water. These were some of the brave things that the three
warriors did.

Abishai was the brother of Joab, the son of Zeruiah. He was captain of
the Three. Abishai used his spear against 300 enemies and killed
them. He became as famous as the Three. Abishai received even
more honor than the Three. He became their commander, but he
was not a member of that elite group.

Benaiah, the son of Jehoiada, was a brave fighter from Kabzeel. He did
many brave things. He killed two of the best lion-like men from
Moab. He also went down into a pit when it was snowing.
There he killed a lion. One time, Benaiah killed a huge Egyptian.

The Egyptian had a spear in his hand, but Benaiah only had a club. Benaiah grabbed the spear from the Egyptian man's hand and killed him with his own spear. These were some of the brave things that Benaiah, the son of Jehoiada, did. He was as famous as the Three Warriors. Benaiah received more honor than the Thirty, but he did not become a member of the Three. David made him leader of his bodyguard.

The following men were among the Thirty: Asahel, the brother of Joab; Elhanan, the son of Dodo from Bethlehem; Shammah the Harodite; Elika the Harodite; Helez the Paltite; Ira, the son of Ikkesh from Tekoa; Abiezer the Anathothite; Sibbecai the Hushathite; Zalmon the Ahohite; Maharai the Netophathite; Heleb, the son of Baanah the Netophathite; Ittai, the son of Ribai from Gibeah, of the sons of Benjamin; Benaiah the Pirathonite; Hiddai from the ravines of Gaash; Abialbon the Arbathite; Azmaveth the Barhumite; Eliahba the Shaalbonite of the sons of Jashen; Jonathan the son of Shammah, the Hararite; Ahiam, the son of Sharar, the Hararite; Eliphelet, the son of Ahasbai, the son of the Maachathite; Eliam, the son of Ahithophel the Gilonite; Hezro the Carmelite; Paarai the Arbite; Igal, the son of Nathan of Zobah, the son of Hagri; Zelek the Ammonite; Naharai the Beerothite, who carried the armor of Joab, the son of Zeruiah; Ira the Ithrite; Gareb the Ithrite and Uriah the Hittite. There was a total of 37 men.

My Time to Pray

The Last Word of a Psalm ᔒ Second Samuel 23

These are the last words (official) of a psalm, written by David, the inspired message of David to the nation from the son of Jesse, the man who was made great by God (2 Samuel 23:1).

These are not the final words of David, for obviously he spoke to Solomon and others after this psalm. These are the last official words of David through a psalm to the nation. Where the previous psalm in chapter 22 looks to the past victories of David, this psalm looks to the future when David's son—Jesus Christ—will rule Israel. *Lord, I look forward to the rule of Jesus Christ, David's Son, who will rule the earth.*

Look carefully at the phrase, "The Spirit of the Lord spoke by me" (2 Sam. 23:2). This is why we believe in the inspiration of Scripture and this phrase teaches the dual authorship of Scripture. The psalm was written by David the human author, but the Spirit of God guided the words so that David wrote exactly what God wanted written. That is called the plenary (complete) verbal (words) inspiration of Scripture. *Lord, I take Your Word at face value.*

The greatness of a leader is made even greater by those around him who made him great. David recalls the rule of the great men who made him great. No one is an island; we all are dependent upon others to help us serve the Lord. But that street goes two ways. The greatness of David made his men even greater than they were. Did you see the translation in verse 8? "These are the names of David's mighty warriors, who made themselves mighty with him." Yes, we help one another become great as we see the Word of God work in one another. *Lord, may I be as great as the wonderful people who want to serve You with me.*

Did you miss Joab? Of all the mighty warriors, Joab's name is missing. Why is that? Joab won many battles, and was instrumental in bringing David to the throne. Joab may have accomplishments, but he did not do them in God's strength, nor did he do them God's way. To be a great person, and to be listed in God's honor role, you must distinguish yourself in one area of life (self-discipline), but you must also be a dedicated follower of God. Joab had the human qualifications, but not the spiritual. *Lord, I will be the best I can be in human ways, and I will wholly follow You in spiritual ways.*

As you read the short stories of these great battles in this chapter, remember: (1) victory never came easy, (2) they always had to fight hard, (3) the enemy kept coming back, (4) they only enjoy peace with strength, (5) but God always worked through them. *Lord, I will remember.*

Amen.

58

A Census Is Taken

Second Samuel 24

The Lord was angry with Israel because David wanted to count the people of Israel and Judah. King David spoke to Joab, the general of the army who was with him, saying, "Go now throughout all the tribes of Israel. Go from Dan to Beer-Sheba (from the extreme north of the country to its farthest point south) and count the people. Then I will know how many there are." (Moses' two censuses were commanded by God. David's order was entirely self-serving.)

But Joab said to the king, "May the Lord your God give you 100 times more people. And may you live to see this happen. But why do you want to do this?" Nevertheless, the king strongly commanded Joab and the officers of the army. So they left the king to count the people of Israel.

After crossing the Jordan River, they camped near Aroer on the south side of the town in the ravine. They went through Gad and on to Jazer. Then they went to Gilead and the land of Tahtim-Hodshi. Next, they went to Dan and around to Sidon. They went to the strong walled city of Tyre, and also to all the cities of the Hivites and the Canaanites. Finally, they went to southern Judah, to Beer-Sheba. After nine months and 20 days, and going through all the land, they came back to Jerusalem.

Joab gave the list of the total number of the people to the king. There were 800,000 able-bodied men in Israel who could use the sword. And there were 500,000 men in Judah.

David has a Change of Heart

Before David got up in the morning, the Lord spoke His word to Gad, who was a prophet and David's seer. The Lord told Gad, "Go and tell David: 'This is what the Lord says: I am offering you three choices. Choose one for Me to do to you.'"

Gad went to David and said to him, "Choose one of these three things. Should three years of hunger come to you and your land? Or, should your enemies chase you for three months? Or, should there be three days of disease in your country? Now think about it. Then decide which of these things I should tell the Lord who sent me."

David felt ashamed after he had counted the people. He said to the Lord, "I have sinned greatly in what I have done. Now, O Lord, I beg You, forgive my sin. I have been very foolish."

David said to Gad, "I am really in trouble! But the Lord is very merciful. So let the Lord punish us. Don't let my punishment come from human beings."

So the Lord sent disease upon Israel. It began in the morning, and continued until the chosen time to stop. The angel raised his arm toward Jerusalem to destroy it also. But the Lord felt very sorry about the terrible things that had happened. He said to the angel who was destroying the people, "That's enough. Put down your arm." At this time, the angel of the Lord was next to the threshing-floor of Araunah the Jebusite.

David saw the angel that killed the people, and said to the Lord: "I have
sinned. I have done wrong. But these people only followed me
like sheep. They did nothing wrong. Please let Your punishment
be against *me* and my father's family."

On that day, Gad came to David and told him, "Go and build an altar
to the Lord. Built it on the threshing-floor or Araunah (who
lived on Mount Moriah where the Temple would be built later)
the Jebusite." So David did what Gad told him to do. He obeyed
the Lord's command and went to see Araunah.

Araunah looked and saw the king and his servants coming to him. So
Araunah went out and bowed face down on the ground. He
said, "Why has my master, the king, come to me?"

David answered, "To buy the threshing-floor from you. I want to build
an altar to the Lord. Then the epidemic on the people will stop."

Araunah said to David, "O my master, the king, you may take whatever
I own that you desire for a sacrifice. Here are some oxen for the
whole burnt offering. Here are the threshing-boards and the
yokes for the wood. My king, I give everything to you." Araunah
also said to the king, "May the Lord your God be pleased with
you."

But the king answered Araunah, "No, I will pay you for the land. I will
not offer to the Lord my God whole burnt offerings which cost
me nothing."

So David purchased the threshing-floor and the oxen for one and a
quarter pounds of silver. (Later, David paid a larger sum—600
shekels of gold [see 1 Chron. 21:25]—for the entire hill. That is
where David made preparation for building the Temple of
Solomon.) Then David built an altar to the Lord there. And he
offered whole burnt offerings and peace offerings. Then the Lord

answered his prayer for the country. Then the epidemic in Israel stopped.

My Time to Pray

We Never Get Too Good That We're Beyond Temptation (see 2 Samuel 24).

Now Satan stood up against Israel, and moved David to number Israel (1 Chronicles 21:1).

We never get too spiritual that we can't be tempted to sin. We never get too accomplished or too promoted in God's kingdom that we are beyond spiritual warfare. At the end of David's reign, David listened to satan and sinned. So the sin of David hurt the entire kingdom. Remember, the higher you are elevated in God's work, the more people you hurt with your sin than if you sinned when you were an infant believer. *Lord, keep me from sin.*

The wrong man tried to talk David out of doing it. Joab was the wrong man to tell David to do the right thing (2 Sam. 24:3). Did Joab know David was sinning? Probably not. Perhaps Joab knew the number of potential soldiers, 1,100,000 would incite envy or rage in an enemy. Perhaps he was afraid the project would anger their enemies. David didn't trust Joab because he murdered Abner, the one David put in charge of the army of the Northern Kingdom. Joab murdered Absalom, knowing he was disobeying David's order. Joab murdered Amasa, even though David made Amasa general over the army. Joab, an un-trustworthy friend, told David the right thing to do. *Lord, may I judge the truthfulness of counsel given to me, and not judge the one who delivers the message.*

Moses numbered God's people twice, therefore taking a census was not wrong. So what did David do that was a sin? When Moses took a census, he received atonement money for those who were numbered (see Exod. 30:12-16). Did we find that David did it? No! Did David not know about the "poll tax" that was required when a census was taken?

Maybe David committed a sin of ignorance. *Lord, may I not be guilty of ignorant sin.*

Maybe David's sin had to do with ego and pride. Maybe David wanted to brag to the other kings how mighty was his kingdom. But Israel was not mighty by "head count," but strong by the Spirit of God.

Maybe David's sin was false defense. He wanted to scare other nations so they wouldn't attack Israel because they had such a large population. If that was his sin, it was the sin of complacency and fake security. Wasn't God the Defender of Israel? *Lord, help me see beyond every temptation to see the sinful motive for what it is.*

This sin comes on the heel of the previous chapter where David spoke of a divine vision of seeing the Messiah ruling the earth. If Christ was going to rule and get the glory, why was David trying to brag about how big was his kingdom? *Lord, may I never try to take Your glory.*

Even though David was a "man after God's own heart," notice the result of his census: "The anger of the Lord burned against Israel." Good men can do evil things. I have seen good pastors fall to adultery, theft, and lying. Being used of God is not a vaccine against evil. *Lord, keep me from being blind to evil, and keep me in the hour of temptation. I purpose not to sin against You.*

When David realized what he had done, he prayed, "Surely, I have sinned, and I have done wickedly..." (2 Sam. 24:17). Just as God forgives the new believer of ignorant sins (see 1 John 1:7), so God forgives the ancient King David of his presumptuous sin. Just as God forgives the fleshly lust of a younger David's sin with Bath-Sheba, so God forgives the egotistical sin of an old man. *Lord, keep me from sin so I don't hurt others, or my own walk with You. But most of all, keep me from sin so I can honor You.*

God directed David to the threshing-floor of Araunah (spelled "Ornan" in 1 Chron. 21:18). This was God's divine chosen place for the Temple that Solomon would build. Usually a threshing-floor was a wide, flat place on the top of a tall hill near the city where the farmers lived. Farmers would beat the grain, or have oxen pull heavy weights over the grain to separate the kernels from the husk. Then in the evening wind the grain was tossed into the air for the breeze to blow away the lighter husk. Here, next to God's city Jerusalem, would be God's Temple, buil on a hill called Moriah where Abraham offered Isaac, and also called Araunah's threshing-floor. *Lord, places are important to You, never let me forget Calvary where my sins were atoned.*

How do we know God forgave David? First, because the death angel was halted after only nine hours of destruction. But second, God approved David's sacrifice by sending fire from Heaven to burn up the sacrifice "Then (God) answered him (David) from heaven by fire on the altar o. burnt offering" (1 Chron. 21:26). *Lord, let Your fire of approval fall on me*

The burnt offering by David was for his sin, but David also offered "peace offerings" (1 Chron. 21:26). The peace offering showed David's gratitude to God for hearing his prayer. It was there David "called on the Lord" (1 Chron. 21:26). *Lord, I worship You for hearing my prayers.*

Amen.

59

DAVID PREPARED TO BUILD THE TEMPLE

FIRST CHRONICLES 22

David said, "The Temple of the Lord, the one true God, will be located here in Jerusalem. And the altar for the whole burnt offerings for Israel will be located here."

So David gave an order for all foreigners who lived in the land of Israel to be gathered together. From that group David chose stonecutters to cut and finish stones for building the Temple of the one true God. David supplied a large amount of iron that was used for making nails, the hinges of the doors of the gates, and the clamps. He also supplied so much bronze that it couldn't be estimated. And he provided countless cedar logs. The people from Sidon and Tyre brought much cedar to David.

David said, "We should build a great Temple for the Lord. It will be famous everywhere for its magnificence and beauty. But my son Solomon is young. (He could not have been more than 25 years old, but he could have been as young as 15.) He has not yet learned what he needs to know. So I will prepare for its construction." Before David died, he made ready vast amounts of building materials for the Temple.

Solomon, Not David

Then David called for his son Solomon, whom he commanded to build
the Temple for the Lord, the God of Israel. David said to
Solomon, "My son, I really wanted to build a Temple to the
name of the Lord my God. But the word of the Lord was against
me saying: 'David, you have killed so many people, and you
have fought so many battles, you must not build a Temple for
My name, because you have killed so many people on earth in
my sight. Behold, a son will be born to you.' (See 2 Sam. 7:12-
14). David failed to understand what God had said about when
that son [the Messiah, the Prince of Peace (see Isa. 9:6)] would
be born; it would not happen during David's lifetime. Therefore,
it could not have been referring directly to Solomon because
Solomon reigned with King David for four years [see 1 Kings
1:32-40; 1 Chron. 23:1].) 'Your son will be a man of tranquility.
I will give him rest from all his enemies around him. His name
will be peaceable. And I will give Israel peace and quiet while he
is king. He (Jesus Christ) will build a Temple for My name (see
John 2:19). He will become My Son, and I will be His Father. I
will establish the throne of His kingdom over Israel forever.'"

David also said, "Now, my son (Solomon), may the Lord be with you.
May you have success. Build the Temple for the Lord your God,
just as He said concerning you. And may the Lord give you wisdom and insight. Then you will be able to obey the teachings
(Torah) of the Lord when He puts you in command of Israel.
Then you will succeed, if you carefully obey the rules and decisions which the Lord gave to Moses for Israel. Be strong and
brave. Don't be afraid or discouraged.

Listen, Solomon, I have worked very hard to get many of the materials
ready for building the Temple of the Lord. I have supplied
100,000 talents of gold (4,000 tons of gold). And I have sup-

plied 1,000,000 talents of silver (40,000 tons of silver). I have supplied so much bronze and iron it cannot be weighed. And I have supplied vast amounts of wood and finished stones. You may add to them. You have many workmen. You have stonecutters, stonecarvers, and carpenters. You have men who are skilled in every type of work. They are experts in working with gold, silver, bronze, and iron. You have more craftsmen than can be counted. So start the work, and may the Lord be with you!"

Then David ordered all the leaders of Israel to help his son Solomon. David said to them, "The Lord your God is with you. He has given you rest from the enemies who surround us. He has put those inhabitants of the land in my control. The Lord and His people have conquered this land.

Now yield yourselves completely to obeying the Lord your God. Start building the sanctuary of the Lord, the one true God. Build the Temple for the name of the Lord. Then bring the Ark of the Covenant with the Lord into the Temple. Also, bring along the holy things that belong to the one true God."

My Time to Pray

Building the Temple ~ First Chronicles 22

Now set your heart and your soul to seek the Lord your God. Therefore arise and build the sanctuary of the Lord God, to bring the ark of the covenant of the Lord and the holy articles of God into the house that is to be built for the name of the Lord (1 Chronicles 22:19).

Notice how carefully David wanted everything in the Temple to be done "decently and in order," just as later Paul would command the church to do everything right (see 1 Cor. 14:40). David knew he was not going to build the Temple; God told him that through the prophet (see 2 Sam. 7:5). In this chapter and the following, David wanted everything to be done rightly as a testimony to the greatness of God. *Lord, give me passion to do everything right so I can live and serve You effectively.*

David recruited the foreigners living in Israel to be the workmen. Why? Probably because Jews were not trained in all the trades, they were farmers and priests. David wanted the best for God. *Lord, I give You the very best of my time, talent, and treasures.*

How did David know what preparations to make? God told him what to do.

> *Then David gave his son Solomon the plans for the vestibule, its houses, its treasuries, its upper chambers, its inner chambers, and the place of the mercy seat; and the plans for all that he had by the Spirit, of the courts of the house of the Lord, of all the chambers all around, of the treasuries of the house of God, and of the treasuries for the dedicated things; also for the division of the priests and the Levites, for all the work of the service of the house of the Lord, and for all the articles of service in the house of the Lord* (1 Chronicles 28:11-13).

It was clear that Temple worship was a continuation of Tabernacle worship. Just as Israel had gone into a tent to worship God, now they would go into an exquisite, expensive Temple to worship God. The Temple "must be exceedingly magnificent, famous, and glorious throughout all countries" (1 Chron. 22:5). But worship is not measured by the place, nor is it the building. It's the worship relationship that's important. Didn't Jesus tell the woman at the well, "You will neither on this mountain, nor in Jerusalem, worship the Father" (John 4:21). What does the Father want? "The Father is seeking worship" (John 4:23 ELT). *Lord, I will focus on You in worship, not on the place, nor the method, nor the music.*

As David speaks to his son, Solomon is probably in his twenties, a young man not yet tested with the weight of responsibility. He has not ministered long enough to make mistakes and learn lessons from the consequences of his actions. David said, "Solomon my son is young and inexperienced" (1 Chron. 22:5). *Lord, help me learn from others so I don't have to learn from painful mistakes.*

David predicts his son Solomon would enjoy peace all his days (1 Chron. 22:9). The Temple would reflect the peace of heart that only God gives. The peace *with* God, means our sins are forgiven (see Eph. 2:14). The peace *of* God is our inner tranquility and rest (see Eph. 2:17). *Lord, I want peace.*

God gave David the blueprint for the new Temple, just as God gave Moses the blueprint for the Tabernacle in the wilderness. The word *plan* is the Hebrew word *Tabnit* (see 1 Chron. 28:11, and Exod. 25:9,40). The pattern for the Temple was more than an oral communication, and more than something David thought up. "The Lord made me understand" (1 Chron. 28:19). The pattern was written, meaning the Spirit spoke to David as he wrote down what the Temple would be like. Maybe David went so far as to draw a blueprint to give Solomon directions in construction. It seems in the public ceremony that David was turning over to Solomon a completed set of drawings. *Lord, thank You for Your written directions in Scripture.*

The written direction also included how the priests would be organized and how they would minister in the Temple. Perhaps David was including the casting of lots in First Chronicles chapters 23-27 to determine what priests would minister and how they would do it. Lord, I will minister to You the way You intended in Scripture.

Amen.

60

THE LEVITES AND THEIR DUTIES

FIRST CHRONICLES 23

David had lived a long time, and was old. So he made his son Solomon
the new king over Israel. David gathered all the leaders of Israel
along with the priests and the Levites. David counted the Levites
who were 30 years old or older. In all, there were 38,000 men.
David said, "Of these, 24,000 Levites will be supervisors over
the work of the Temple of the Lord. And 6,000 Levites will be
officials and judges; 4,000 Levites will be gatekeepers; and
4,000 Levites will praise the Lord with musical instruments that
I made for them to use for praising God."

David separated the Levites into three groups according to Levi's sons:
Gershon, Kohath, and Merari.

So there is no need for the Levites to carry the Holy Tent anymore. They
do not need to carry any of the things in its services any longer.
David's last instructions were to count the number of the Levites
who were 20 years old or older.

The Levites had the responsibility of assisting Aaron's descendants in
the services of the Temple of the Lord. They took care of the
courtyard and the side rooms. They had the responsibility of
making all the holy things "pure," in the Temple of the one true
God. They were responsible for putting out the holy bread on

the table, for the flour in the grain offerings, and for the bread made without yeast. They did the baking and the mixing, too. And they did all the measuring.

The Levites also stood every morning to give thanks and praise to the Lord. And they did the same thing in the evening. The Levites offered up all the whole burnt offerings to the Lord on the special Sabbaths for the New Moon festivals, and at all the appointed feasts. They served in the presence of the Lord every day. They followed the rules for the number of Levites who served each time. So the Levites took care of the Meeting Tent and the sanctuary. And they helped their relatives, Aaron's descendants, with the services at the Temple of the Lord.

My Time to Pray

Everyone has a Task ~ First Chronicles 23

The Levites had responsibility of assisting Aaron's descendants in the service of the Lord (1 Chronicles 23:28).

This chapter could be boring, and may even become inconsequential to you as a child of God. Why? Because this chapter, like those that follow, seem only to introduce the number of Levites and how some of them should serve God. You may think this has nothing to do with your walk with Christ, or your service of Him. But think again, since God has inspired every word in the Bible, we ought to find out why every word is there and what God can say to us through this chapter. *Lord, speak to me through this chapter, and every chapter in Scripture.*

You probably don't care how many Levites were "gatekeepers," or the other details in this chapter or the next. But the Levites cared. It was what they had to do for God. Do you care what God wants you to do, and how you should do it? Of course you do. So this chapter was imperative—more than just important—to the Levites. They wanted to serve God properly. If they didn't, they could be judged with death as the two sons of Eli, Hophni and Phinehas. *Lord, I want to serve You in the right place, and in the right way.*

God had a powerful purpose for each of these Levites mentioned in this chapter. Hebrews remind us, "For every high priest taken from among men is appointed for men in things pertaining to God, that he may offer both gifts and sacrifices for sins" (Heb. 5:1). These priests dealt with the sins of people back then, just as Jesus, my High Priest, dealt with my sins on the Cross. *Lord, thank You for forgiveness.*

Each Levite had a specific duty to do for God. When they did their duty, the Lord used each according to his faithfulness, just as He will use us according to our faithfulness. *Lord, I will be faithful to do today what You have planned for my life.*

Amen.

61

THE PRIESTS ARE ORGANIZED

FIRST CHRONICLES 24

These were the groups of Aaron's sons: Nadab, Abihu, Eleazar, and
Ithamar. But Nadab and Abihu died during the lifetime of their
father, and they had no sons. But Eleazar and Ithamar served as
priests. Zadok was a descendant of Eleazar. And Ahimelech was
a descendant of Ithamar. With the help of Zadok and
Ahimelech, David separated the clans of Eleazar and Ithamar
into two different clans. Each group had certain duties that it
had been given. There were more leaders from Eleazar's clan
than from Ithamar's clan. There were 16 leaders from Eleazar's
clan, and eight leaders from Ithamar's clan. So men were chosen
from Eleazar's clan and Ithamar's clan by lots to serve as priests
of the one true God in the sanctuary.

Shemaiah, the son of Nethanel, was the secretary. He was from the tribe
of Levi. Shemaiah recorded the names of those descendants in
the presence of King David and other important officials: Zadok
the priest, Ahimelech the son of Abiathar, and the leaders of the
families of the priests and the Levites. The work load was distrib-
uted among the families of Eleazar and Ithamar. The following
men were chosen with their shifts:

The first lot chosen was Jehoirib's. The second lot was Jedaiah's. The
third lot was Harim's. The fourth lot was Seorim's. The fifth lot

was Malchijah's. The sixth lot was Mijamin's. The seventh lot
was Hakkoz's. The eighth lot was Abijah's. The ninth lot was
Jeshua's. The tenth lot was Shecaniah's. The eleventh lot was
Eliashib's. The twelfth lot was Jakim's. The thirteenth lot was
Huppah's. The fourteenth lot was Jeshebeab's. The fifteenth lot
was Bilgah's. The sixteenth lot was Immer's. The seventeenth lot
was Hezir's. The eighteenth lot was Happizzez's. The nineteenth
lot was Pethahiah's. The twentieth lot was Jehezkel's. The twenty-
first lot was Jachin's. The twenty-second lot was Gamul's. The
twenty-third lot was Delaiah's. The twenty-fourth lot was
Maaziah's.

These were the groups chosen to serve in the Temple of the Lord. They
obeyed the rules which Aaron had passed down to them. The
Lord, the God of Israel, had commanded those rules to Aaron.

These are the names of the rest of Levi's descendants: Shubael was a
descendant of Amram. And Jehdeiah was a descendant of
Shubael. As for Regabiah, Isshiah was the first son of Rehabiah.
From the Izhar family, there was Shelomoth. Jahath was a
descendant of Shelomoth. Hebron's first son was Jeriah.
Amariah was his second son. Jahaziel was his third son.
Jekameam was his fourth son. Uzziel's son was Micah. Micah's
son was Shamir. Isshiah was Micah's brother. Isshiah's son was
Zechariah. Merari's sons were: Mahli and Mushi. Merari's
descendant was Uzziah. Uzziah the descendant of Merari had
sons named: Shoham, Zaccur, and Ibri. Nahli's son was Eleazar,
but Eleazar did not have any sons.

As for Kish, Kish's son was Jerahmeel.

Mushi's sons were: Mahli, Eder, and Jerimoth.

These are the descendants of the Levites, listed by their families. They
too were chosen for special jobs by lots. They did this just as

their relatives had done before them. The priests were Aaron's descendants. They cast lots in the presence of King David, Zadok, and Ahimelech. The leaders of the families of the priests and the Levites were there, too. The families of the oldest brother and the youngest brother were treated the same.

My Time to Pray

First Chronicles 24

Now there are divisions of the sons of Aaron (1 Chronicles 24:1).

Lord, there is a list of names in this chapter that have no meaning to me today. But they were meaningful to You because they served You in their day. You blessed them, used them, and rewarded them according to their faithfulness. *Lord, I will serve You today according to the task You have given me for this day. Bless me, use me, and reward me according to Your grace.*

Lord, their physical birth into the tribe of Levi determined their service for You. I know it's my spiritual new birth into Your family that determines my service for You. *Lord, use my spiritual service for You to bring fruit into Your Kingdom.*

Lord, help me be careful about my physical family on earth, just as these priests were careful about their physical families on earth. And just as a family gives meaning and identity to its children, help me pass on to my children an identity in Christ and meaningful service for You. *Lord, thank You for my physical family.*

Amen.

Psalm 110

A psalm written by David predicting Jesus would be our Priest interceding for us at the right hand of the Father.

Lord, You said to Jesus;
> *Come sit at your right hand,*
> *While You put His enemies under Your feet.*

Lord, You extended Your powerful scepter out from Zion
> *To rule over all Your enemies.*

Your people will serve You in the day of battle;
> *They will be beautifully dressed in holiness*
> *To serve You from the dawn of the morning*
> *Until the dew finishes the day.*

Lord, You have vowed and will not change Your mind
> *That Jesus will be a Priest forever;*
> *He serves according to the order of Melchizedek.*

Lord, You will be at the right hand of Jesus
> *To crush the kings that oppose Him.*

Jesus will judge all the nations,
> *Those who rebel will die,*
> *The rulers of great countries will be destroyed.*

He will drink from the brook after the task,
> *His head will be exalted in victory.*

62

THE MUSICIANS AND THEIR DUTIES

FIRST CHRONICLES 25

David and the commanders of the army chose some men for ministry.
They chose some of the sons of Asaph, Heman, and Jeduthun.
They were proclaiming with harps, lyres, and cymbals. Here is a
list of the men who served in that way:

Asaph's sons were: Zaccur, Joseph, Nethaniah, and Asarelah. King
David selected Asaph to perform with his sons.

As for Jeduthun, his sons were: Gedaliah, Zeri, Jeshaiah, Shimei,
Hashabiah, and Mattithiah. There were six of them, and
Jeduthun, their father, directed them. He used a harp to give
thanks and praise to the Lord. As for Heman, his sons were:
Bukkiah, Mattaniah, Uzziel, Shubael, and Jerimoth. Also, there
were: Hananiah, Hanani, Eliathah, Giddalti, and Romamti-Ezer.
And there were: Joshbekashah, Mallothi, Hothir, and Mahazioth.
All these men were sons of Heman, the king's seer (prophet).
The one true God promised to make Heman strong. So he had
many sons. God gave him 14 sons and three daughters. Heman
directed all these sons in making music for the Temple of the
Lord. They used cymbals, lyres, and harps in serving in the
Temple of the one true God. And King David supervised Asaph,
Jeduthun, and Heman. These men and their relatives from the
Levites were talented musicians who trained in music for the

Lord. There were 288 of them. Everyone was chosen by lots concerning the time when each one would perform at the Temple. The young and the old were chosen by lots. The teacher and the student were chosen by lots.

First, 12 men were chosen from Joseph's family, his sons and his relatives. Joseph was from the family of Asaph.

Second, 12 men were chosen from Gedaliah's family, his sons and his relatives.

Third, 12 men were chosen from Zaccur's family, his sons and his relatives.

Fourth, 12 men were chosen from Izri's family, his sons and his relatives.

Fifth, 12 men were chosen from Nethaniah's family, his sons and his relatives.

Sixth, 12 men were chosen from Bukkiah's family, his sons and his relatives.

Seventh, 12 men were chosen from Jesharelah's family, his sons and his relatives.

Eighth, 12 men were chosen from Jeshaiah's family, his sons and his relatives.

Ninth, 12 men were chosen from Mattaniah's family, his sons and his relatives.

Tenth, 12 men were chosen from Shimei's family, his sons and his relatives.

Eleventh, 12 men were chosen from Azarel's family, his sons and relatives.

Twelfth, 12 men were chosen from Hashabiah's family, his sons and his relatives.

Thirteenth, 12 men were chosen from Shubael's family, his sons and his relatives.

Fourteenth, 12 men were chosen from Mattithiah's family, his sons and his relatives.

Fifteenth, 12 men were chosen from Jerimoth's family, his sons and his relatives.

Sixteenth, 12 men were chosen from Hananiah's family, his sons and his relatives.

Seventeenth, 12 men were chosen from Joshbekashah's family, his sons and his relatives.

Eighteenth, 12 men were chosen from Hanani's family, his sons and his relatives.

Nineteenth, 12 men were chosen from Mallothi's family, his sons and his relatives.

Twentieth, 12 men were chosen from Eliathah's family, his sons and his relatives.

Twenty-first, 12 men were chosen from Hothir's family, his sons and his relatives.

Twenty-second, 12 men were chosen from Giddalti's family, his sons and his relatives.

Twenty-third, 12 men were chosen from Mahazioth's family, his sons and his relatives.

Twenty-fourth, 12 men were chosen from Romamti-Ezer's family, his sons and his relatives.

My Time to Pray

First Chronicles 25

So the number of them, with their brethren who were instructed in the songs of the Lord, all who were skillful, was two hundred and eighty-eight (1 Chronicles 25:7).

Whereas words in preaching and teaching communicate head to head, Christian music communicates heart to heart. And heart worship is important to God, so He included music and musicians in the Old Testament Temple, and in the New Testament Church (see Col. 3:16). God used a whole chapter in Scripture to tell how to organize musicians for His new Temple. *Lord, even when I don't sing perfectly like professionals, may my singing glorify You and advance Your work.*

God chose singers by lots (see 1 Chron. 24:5) which suggests different families passed before the high priest who wore the ephod vest where the Urim and Thummim determined God's will. That means God knew something about the musical ability of each family. He chose some to sing, some to play musical instruments, and others were gatekeepers, teachers, or ministering priests. That's like my church, people who have some musical ability end up in the choir, those with a tin ear—like me—end up in the pews. *Lord, thank You for those with beautiful voices who glorify You through music.*

The Lord put some men as directors over other musicians. It would be disconcerting if every man sang what he wanted to sing, when he wanted to sing. No! God gave leaders to the musicians to lead them to sing together. Isn't that word *together* a beautiful word? It's wonderful when believers get together to sing together. The word *together* suggests Christian unity that God expects of us all. *Lord, I will sing together with other believers to offer praise to You.*

God has a place for leaders, whether it's in music, the military, or in the king's court. Good leaders bring God's people together to do what God wants them to do (serve effectively) the way God wants us to serve (in unity). God is glorified when His leaders bring His people together in harmony. *Lord, I will sing in harmony with other believers. Amen.*

Psalm 100:1-5

A Psalm written by David about worshiping the Lord.

Lord, I shout with joy to you;
> *Everyone from every nation joins me.*

I worship as I enter Your presence with singing
> *Because You, Lord, are my God.*

Lord, You made us and we belong to You;
> *We are Your people and the sheep of Your pasture.*

Lord, I come into Your gates giving thanks;
> *I enter the courts with praise.*

I bless Your holy name
> *By giving thanks for all you've done for me.*

Lord, You are good, Your mercy is everlasting;
> *And Your truth endures forever.*

> *Amen.*

63

THE GATEKEEPERS AND THEIR DUTIES

FIRST CHRONICLES 26

These are the groups of the gatekeepers: from the clan of Korah, there was Meshelemiah, the son of Kore, was from Asaph's family. Meshelemiah had sons. Zechariah was his first son. Jediael was his second son. Zebadiah was his third son. Jathniel was his fourth son. Elam was his fifth son. Jehohanan was his sixth son, and Eliehoenai was his seventh son.

There were also Obed-Edom and his sons. Obed-Edom's first son was Shemaiah. Jehozabad was his second son. Joah was his third son. Sacar was his fourth son. Nethanel was his fifth son. Ammiel was his sixth son. Issachar was his seventh son, and Peullethai was his eighth son. God had blessed Obed-Edom with many children. (Because of his faithful care of the Ark of the Covenant [see 2 Sam. 6:11-12; 1 Chron. 13:13-14] he had 62 descendants.)

Obed-Edom's son, Shemaiah, also had sons. They were leading in their father's household because they were men of great ability. Shemaiah's sons were: Othni, Rephael, and Obed. And other relatives—Elzabad, Elihu, and Semachiah—were skilled workers. All these men were Obed-Edom's descendants. They and their sons and their relatives were capable men. They were strong enough to do the work. Obed-Edom had 62 descendants in all.

Meshelemiah had sons and relatives who were skilled workers. In all, there were 18 sons and relatives.

These are the gatekeepers from the Merari clan: Hosah had sons. Shimri was chosen to be in charge even though he was not the oldest son, but his father chose him to be in charge. Hilkiah was his second son. Tebaliah was his third son, and Zechariah was his fourth son. In all, Hosah had 13 sons and relatives.

These were the leaders of the groups of the gatekeepers who had special jobs for serving in the Temple of the Lord. Their relatives also had special jobs in the Temple; each family was given a gate to guard. They were chosen by casting lots. Young men and old men were chosen by lots.

Shelemiah was chosen by lot to guard the East Gate. Then lots were chosen for Shelemiah's son, Zechariah. He was a wise counselor, and was chosen by lot for the North Gate. Obed-Edom was chosen for the South Gate. And Obed-Edom's sons were chosen to guard the storehouse. Shuppim and Hosah were chosen for the West Gate. They also were to guard the Shallecheth Gate (through which all the trash from the Temple area was taken out) on the upper road.

Guards stood side by side. Six Levites stood guard every day at the East Gate. (Because more people went through there, being the main entrance.) Four Levites stood guard every day at the North Gate. Four Levites stood guard every day at the South Gate. And Levites guarded the storehouse—two at a time. There were two guards at the western court. And there were four guards on the street to the court. These were the groups of the gatekeepers from the clan of Korah and Merari.

Other Workers

Of the other Levites, Ahijah was responsible for taking care of the treasuries of the Temple of the one true God. He was also responsible for the places where the holy things were kept.

Ladan was Gershon's son. Ladan was the ancestor of several clans. Jehieli was a leader of one of the family groups. Jehiehli's sons were: Zetham and his brother Joel. They were responsible for the treasuries of the Temple of the Lord.

Other leaders were chosen from the clans of Amram, Izhar, Hebron, and Uzziel. Shubael was the leader responsible for the treasuries of the Temple of the Lord. Shubael was the descendant of Gershom, who was Moses' son. These were Shubael's relatives through Eliezer: Eliezer's descendants were; Rehabiah, Jeshaiah, Joram, Zichri, and Shelomith. Shelomith and his relatives were responsible for every sacred thing that had been collected for the Temple. These things had been dedicated to the Lord by King David, and by the heads of families, and by the commanders of 1,000 men and the commanders of 100 men and other army commanders. They also dedicated some of the things to the Lord that they had captured in battles to be used for repairing the Temple of the Lord. Shelomith and his relatives took care of all the holy things. Some things had been dedicated to the Lord by Samuel the seer and Saul, the son of Kish. Some things had been dedicated by Abner the son of Ner, and Joab the son of Zeruiah.

Chenaniah was from the Izhar family. He and his sons worked outside the Temple as officials and judges over Israel.

Hashabiah was from the Hebron family. He and his relatives were responsible for all of the Lord's work and the king's business in Israel west of the Jordan River. There were 1,700 skilled men in

Hashabiah's group. The history of the Hebron family shows that Jeriah was their leader. In David's 40th year as king, the records were searched, and some capable men of the Hebron family were found living in Jazer in Gilead. Jeriah had 2,700 relatives who were skilled men. They were leaders of families. King David gave them the responsibility of directing the tribes of Rueben, Gad, and the eastern half-tribe of Manasseh. They took care of everything concerning the one true God and all of the king's business.

My Time to Pray

First Chronicles 26

And they cast lots for each gate (1 Chronicles 26:13).

Gatekeepers were chosen by lots, which means God made the choice, not David or other men. Remember, men look on the outward appearance (we judge people outwardly), but God chooses by the heart (see 1 Sam. 16:7). God wanted honest men that He could trust to keep the gates. Some people are just not trustworthy, so God passed over these people. *Lord, I will be trustworthy; choose me.*

The Lord loves unity and harmony. That's why the universe works in harmony and that's why God gave laws to work together as a unit. God is glorified when all things work smoothly and calmly. Therefore, God dedicated a chapter in Chronicles to help organize the gatekeepers and other workers. *Lord, help me live in harmony with Your universe. I know sin produces disharmony in so many ways, so I seek unity in all things.*

The Lord knows that the natural heart—unguarded by the Holy Spirit—will give itself to sin and people will steal. They will even steal from a church, or as Ananias and Sapphira did, they stole from You (see Acts 5:1-11). So God directed the Levites to guard the treasury of God. Doesn't that suggest that today the church should get insurance, keep money in a safe place, make individuals responsible and accountable, plus do all they can to protect God's assets? Sure God likes to give money away to the needy, but He punishes those who steal from others or from Himself. *Lord, I will guard Your money, both when it's in my possession, and after I give it to You.*

Amen.

Psalm 118:14-28

A psalm of ascent written by David for pilgrims to sing as they approached the gates of the Lord into the House of God.

You are the strength of my battle, O Lord;
I sing of You in my victory song.

Shouts of joy and victorious songs of praise
Are sung among those who have been redeemed.

Your mighty right arm has done glorious things;
Your mighty right arm has been exalted.

I will not be defeated but I will live,
And I will tell what You have done for me.

You punished me severely for my sin,
But You did not deliver me to death.

Open the gates of righteousness for me,
And I will enter to give thanks to You, O Lord.

Open the gates that lead to Your presence
And the godly will come in to You.

Thank You for answering my prayers
And for saving me from my troubles.

The stone which the builders rejected
     Has now become the cornerstone of the building.

You have accomplished this great thing
     And it is a marvelous thing to see.

This is the day that You have made,
     I will rejoice in it and be glad.

And now, O Lord, please save me;
     And please give me success, O Lord.

Bless the one who comes in Your name,
     Bless him because of the One standing in Your presence.

Lord, you have accepted me into Your light;
     I bring the sacrifice to Your altar.

You are my God, and I offer You thanks;
     You are my God, and I exalt You.

          Amen.

64

THE MONTHLY SCHEDULE
FOR THE MILITARY

FIRST CHRONICLES 27

This is the list of the Israelite men who served the king in the army: each division was on duty for one month each year. There were the leaders of families, the commanders of 1,000 men, the commanders of 100 men, and other officers. Each division had 24,000 men.

Joashobeam, the son of Zabdiel, was in charge of the first division for the first month. There were 24,000 men in his division. He was one of the descendants of Perez. Jashobeam was the general of all the army officers for the first month.

Eleazar, the son of Dodai was in charge of the division for the second month. He was from the Ahohites. Mikloth was a leader in the division. There were 24,000 men in Eleazar's division.

The third army commander was Benaiah, the son of Jehoiada, an important priest. He was the commander for the third month. There were 24,000 men in Benaiah's division. He was the Benaiah who was one of "The Thirty" elite soldiers. Benaiah was an outstanding soldier who was in charge of those men. Benaiah's son, Ammizabad, was in charge of Benaiah's division.

The fourth commander was Asahel, the brother of Joab. He was the commander for the fourth month. Later, Asahel's son, Zebediah, took Asahel's place as commander. There were 24,000 men in his division.

The fifth commander was Shamhuth. He was the commander for the fifth month. He was from the Izrahites. There were 24,000 men in his division.

The sixth commander was Ira, the son of Ikkesh. He was the commander for the sixth month. He was from the town of Tekoa. There were 24,000 men in his division.

The seventh commander was Helez. He was the commander for the seventh month. He was from the Pelonites and one of the descendants of Ephraim. There were 24,000 men in his division.

The eighth commander was Sibbecai. He was the commander for the eighth month. He was from Hushah, from Zerah's family. There were 24,000 men in his division.

The ninth commander was Abiezer, from the town of Anathoth. He was the commander for the ninth month. He was from the tribe of Benjamin. There were 24,000 men in his division.

The tenth commander was Maharai. He was the commander for the tenth month. He was from the town of Netophah, from Zerah's family. There were 24,000 men in his division.

The eleventh commander was Benaiah. He was the commander for the eleventh month. He was from Pirathon, from the half-tribe of Ephraim. There were 24,000 men in his division.

The twelfth commander was Heldai. He was the commander for the twelfth month. He was from the town of Netophah, from Othniel's family. There were 24,000 men in his division.

The Captains of the Tribes

These were the leaders over the tribes of Israel. Eliezer, the son of
Zichri, was the leader over the tribe of Reuben. Shephatiah, the
son of Maacah, was over the tribe of Simeon. Hashabiah, the
son of Kemuel, was over the tribe of Levi. Zadok was over the
priests of Aaron. Elihu, one of David's brothers, was over the
tribe of Judah. Omri, the son of Michale, was over the tribe of
Issachar. Ishmaiah, the son of Obadiah, was over the tribe of
Zebulun. Jerimoth, the son of Azriel, was over the tribe of
Naphtali. Hoshea, the son of Azaziah, was over the tribe of
Ephraim. Joel, son of Pedaiah, was over the western half-tribe of
Manasseh. Iddo, the son of Zecharaiah, as over the eastern half-
tribe of Manasseh in Gilead. Jaasiel, the son of Abner, was over
the tribe of Benjamin. Azarel, the son of Jeroham, was over the
tribe of Dan.

These were the leaders of the tribes of Israel. The Lord had promised to
make the Israelites as numerous as the stars of the sky. So David
only counted the men who were 20 years old and older.

Joab, the son of Zeruiah, began to count the people but he did not finish because God became angry with Israel for taking the census.
So that number of the people was not recorded into the official
royal records about King David's rule.

Those in Charge of the King's Possessions

Azmaveth, the son of Adiel, was in charge of the royal storehouses.
Jonathan was in charge of the storehouses in the countryside, in
the towns, the villages, and the towers. He was the son of
Uzziah.

Ezri, the son of Chelub, was in charge of the field workers who farmed the land.

Shimei was in charge of the vineyards. He was from the town of Ramah.

Zabdi was in charge of storing the wine that came from the vineyards. Zabdi was from Shepham.

Baal-Hanan was in charge of the olive trees and the sycamore trees in the western mountain slopes. He was from the town of Geder.

Joash was in charge of storing the olive oil.

Shitrai was in charge of the cows that grazed in the Plain of Sharon. He was from Sharon.

Shaphat, the son of Adlai, was in charge of the cattle in the valley.

Obil was in charge of the camels. He was an Ishmaelite.

Jehdeiah was in charge of the donkeys. He was from the town of Meronoth.

Jaziz was in charge of the sheep and the goats. He was from the Hagrites.

All these men were the officers who took care of King David's property.

Personal Advisors to the King

David's uncle was named Jonathan, who advised David. Jonathan was a wise man, and a scribe. Jehiel, the son of Hachmoni, took care of the king's sons. Ahithophel also advised the king. Hushai was "the king's friend." He came from the Archite people. Later, Jehoiada and Abiathar took Ahithophel's place in advising the king. Jehoiada was Benaiah's son. Joab was the general of the king's army.

My Time to Pray

First Chronicles 27

This is the list of Israelite generals...(who) supervised the army divisions that were on duty each month of the year. Each division served one month and had twenty-four thousand men (1 Chronicles 27:1).

Lord, You protected the nation of Israel with a militia of farmer-soldiers who each served one month out of the year. Each month these soldiers who reported for duty were organized, trained, and equipped to defend Israel. Most of the time You worked through these soldiers to win battles, You did that by their training, discipline, and their dedication to You. However, at times You won victories supernaturally by sending storms (see Judg. 5:4,21), earthquakes (see 1 Sam. 14:15), and You even kept the daylight around for 24 hours (see Josh. 10:13-14). And we can't forget bringing down the walls of Jericho supernaturally (see Josh. 6:20). *Lord, You protected Israel many different ways, just as You protect me in many different ways. Thank You for a hedge of protection (see Job 1:10).*

Lord, when each man did his job faithfully, Israel was protected. You work the same way when an army attacks. Each man has to do his job faithfully. The same thing happens in the church. *Lord, I will do my job faithfully; give me strength, wisdom, and skill to serve You with all my heart.*

There comes a time when we must learn from the consequences of our sin. David wanted to number Israel—take a national census to find out how strong and big the nation was. God judged David by sending a plague on the nation (see 2 Sam. 24). David repented, "Surely, I have sinned" (2 Sam. 24:17). But not all of the story was told in Second Samuel 24; apparently God began His judgment before Joab got finished taking the census. In First Chronicles 27:24 we read, "Joab...began a census, but did not finish for wrath came upon Israel because of the census." *Lord, I know You punish sin; I will keep myself from sin so I won't be punished.*

We can learn three lessons from this reference to First Chronicles 27:24. First, the sin of leaders hurts the followers. *Lord, keep me from sin.* Second, when we are confronted with our sin, repent immediately; time is vital. *Lord, I will repent immediately when confronted with my sin.* Third, instant repentance will minimize the damage. *Lord, I will quickly repent to stop any damage to my spiritual walk with You, and my spiritual service for You.*

Amen.

Psalm 121

I lift up my eyes to the hills,
 But does my help come from there?

No! My help comes from You, Lord;
 You made the heavens and the earth.

Your foot will not stumble,
 Indeed, You who watch over Israel
 Will not get tired, nor will You sleep.

Lord, watch over me to keep me;
 Stand at my right hand to protect me.

The sun will not harm me during the day,
 Nor will the moon at night.

Lord, deliver me from all evil;
 Preserve my soul.

Lord, watch over me as I come and go,
 Both now in this present age and forever more.

Amen.

65

DAVID TELLS OF THE PLANS FOR THE TEMPLE

FIRST CHRONICLES 28

David gathered all the leaders of Israel to Jerusalem. There were the chiefs of the tribes and the commanders of the army divisions who were serving the king. There were the commanders of 1,000 men and of 100 men. There were the leaders who took care of the property and the animals that belonged to the king and his sons. There were the men over the palace, the powerful men, and all the brave soldiers.

King David stood up and said, "Listen to me, my brothers and my people. I wanted the Ark of the Covenant with the Lord's presence to be God's footstool. And I made plans to build a Temple for worshiping God. But the one true God said to me, 'You must not build a Temple to My name, because you are a soldier. You have shed much blood.' Nevertheless, the Lord, the God of Israel, did select me out of my whole family to be the king of Israel forever. He chose the tribe of Judah to be the leading tribe of Israel. He chose my father's family. And God chose me from among my brothers, to make me king over all Israel. The Lord has given me many sons, and from among all my sons, He has chosen my son Solomon to be the new king of Israel. The kingdom belongs to the Lord. God said to me: 'Your son Solomon will build My Temple. And he will build up the courtyards around it, because I have chosen him to be My son. And I will be his heavenly Father. He is obeying My laws and My commands now. If he continues to obey them, then I will make his kingdom strong forever.'"

David said, "Now, in front of all Israel (the congregation of the Lord) and in front of our God, I am telling you these things: Be careful to obey *all* the commands of the Lord your God. Then you may keep this good land, and you may pass it on to your sons to inherit after you.

And you, O Solomon my son, trust the God of your father. Serve God completely. Be glad to serve Him. Do this because the Lord knows what is in every person's heart. He understands everything you think. If you go to Him for help, then you will get an answer. But if you turn away from Him, then He will reject you forever. Solomon, you must understand this. The Lord has chosen you to build a Temple as a sanctuary. Be strong and finish the job."

Then David gave to his son Solomon the plans for building the Temple complex. Those plans were also for the porch around the Temple. They were for its buildings, its storage rooms, its upper rooms, and its inside rooms. They were also the plans for the spot where the sins of the people were covered. David gave him the plans for everything that the Spirit of God had planned. David gave him the plans for the courtyards around the Temple of the Lord and all the rooms around it. He gave him the plans for the treasuries of the Temple of the one true God. And David gave him the plans for the treasuries of the holy things used in the Temple. And David gave Solomon the directions for the groups of the priests and the Levites. David told him about all the responsibilities of serving in the Temple of the Lord. He told him about all the things to be used in the services of the Lord's

Temple. Many things made of gold or of silver would be used in the various Temple services.

David told Solomon how much gold or silver should be used to make each thing. David told him how much gold to use for each gold lampstand and its lamps. (There was only one lampstand in the Tabernacle, but there were ten lampstands in Solomon's Temple.) David told him how much silver to use for each silver lampstand and its lamps. The different lampstands were to be used wherever needed. David told him how much gold should be used for each table that held the holy bread. And David told him how much silver should be used for the silver tables. David told him how much pure gold should be used to make the forks, the bowls, and the pitchers. He told him how much gold should be used to make each gold dish. He told him how much silver should be used to make each silver dish. David told him how much pure gold should be used for the altar of incense. He also gave Solomon the plans for the "chariot." This is where the golden, angel-like seraphim spread their wings over the Ark of the Covenant with the Lord.

David said, "All these plans were written with the Lord guiding me. God helped me to understand all the details in the plans."

David also said to his son Solomon, "Be strong and brave. Do the work. Don't be afraid or discouraged. God, the One Who Is Always Present, my God, is with you. He will be with you until you finish all the work. He will not fail you or abandon you. You will build it for the services of the Lord.

Now, the groups of priests and the Levites are ready for all the services of the Temple of the one true God. Every skilled worker is ready to help you with all the work. The leaders and all the people will obey every command you give."

My Time to Pray

Seeking ∂ First Chronicles 28

...If you seek Him, He will be found of you; but if you forsake Him, He will cast you off forever (1 Chronicles 28:9).

Many people turn a deaf ear to God's word, and they turn their backs to the love of God. They will not attend church where they hear the Word of God preached. They will not sing praises to God. They will not call on God to guide them or bless them. David reminds Solomon, "Seek Him." Why? Because God can be found. *Lord, early will I seek You.*

The terms *seeking* and *surrender* go hand in hand. When you seek God, it is a process; when you surrender it is the product of having found God. You surrender to Him. So seeking is an active verb. Are you seeking God? How do you know if you are seeking God, or seeking God rightly? If you seek God, He will be found. If you haven't found God, then you're doing something wrong. Usually, your heart is not honestly seeking God. *Lord, I surrender my ideas, I seek You honestly.*

Seeking and surrender usually hopscotch. First you are seeking, meaning you want God with all your heart. Next you surrender all preconceptions of God and preconceptions of how to seek God. You surrender to God and look in the pages of Scripture where the true God is found. Then you seek the God of the Bible in the pages of the Bible. *Lord, I will look in Scripture.*

There are two aspects of seeking God and two aspects of surrendering to God. First, you seek Him in salvation. Usually your sins convict you terribly of something. So you seek Him to be saved. Then once you know Him in salvation, you seek to know God in daily fellowship. You want to walk deeper with Him. The same is true about surrender. When you come to be saved, you make a great big **YES** to God. You repent of all sin and turn to Him with all your heart. Then every day you begin with surrendering that day to God. Every day it's another **YES**. *Lord, because I've said* **YES** *to You once, today I say* **YES** *to You again.*

Amen.

66

OFFERINGS FOR THE HOUSE OF GOD

FIRST CHRONICLES 29

King David said to all the Israelites who were gathered: "God has sin-gled out my son Solomon, even though he is young and inexpe-rienced. But the task is very important. This palace is not for people, but for God Himself, the One Who Is Always Present. I have done my best to prepare for the building of the Temple of my God. I have provided the gold for the things made of gold. I have donated the silver for the things made of silver. I have given the bronze for the things made of bronze. I have given the wood for the things made of wood. I have given onyx for the settings and turquoise. I have given precious jewels of many dif-ferent colors. I have given valuable stones and white marble. I have supplied all these things abundantly. In my devotion to the Temple of my God, I am now also giving my own private treas-ures of gold and silver. I am doing this because I really want the Temple sanctuary of my God to be built. I have given about 225,000 pounds of the purest gold from Ophir. And I have given about 525,000 pounds of pure silver. They will be used to cover the walls of the buildings. They will also be used for all the gold and silver work. Skilled men will use the gold and the silver to make things for the Temple. Now who is ready to dedi-cate his possessions to the service of the Lord today?"

Then the family leaders and the leaders of the tribes of Israel gave their valuable things. The commanders of 1,000 men and the commanders of 100 men gave their valuable things. And the leaders responsible for the king's business gave their valuable things, too.

The following are the things which they gave for the Temple of the one true God: about 375,000 pounds of gold coins; about 750,000 pounds of silver; about 1,350,000 pounds of bronze; about 7,500,000 pounds of iron. People who owned valuable jewels gave them to the treasury of the Temple of the Lord. Jehiel from the Gershonite clan collected them. Because they gave freely, the people rejoiced. They gave freely and with a perfect heart to the Lord. And King David was very happy.

David Praises God

David praised the Lord in front of all of the people who were gathered saying:

"We praise You, O Lord,
You are the God of Jacob our ancestor;
We praise You forever and ever.

O Lord, You are great and powerful,
You have the glory, the victory, and the honor;
Everything in Heaven and on earth belongs to You.

The kingdom is Yours, O Lord,
You are the Ruler over everything.

You have the power and might
To make anyone great and strong.

Now, our God, we thank You,
And we praise Your glorious name.

Yes, these things did not really come
 From me and my people.

Everything comes from You;
 We have given back to You
 Only what You first gave to us.

We are like foreigners and settlers in Your presence;
 Like all of our ancestors,

Our time on earth is like a shadow,
 It doesn't last.

O Lord, our God, all of this abundance that we have collected
 To build You a Temple for Your holy Name,

It really comes from Your hand;
 Everything belongs to You.

I know, my God, that You test the human heart,
 You want people to do what is right.

I was very happy to donate all these things freely,
 I gave them with an honest heart.

And now Your people are gathered here;
 They also are happy to give freely to You.

I am very happy to see their generosity;
 O Lord, You are the God of our ancestors.

You are the God of Abraham, of Isaac, and of Jacob;
 Please help Your people desire
 To always serve You.

And help them desire
 To always obey You.

Now as for Solomon, give my son a strong desire to serve You;
*   May he always obey all Your commands, Your laws, and*
*   Your rules,*
*   And may he construct this palace which I have prepared*
*   for You."*

Then David said to all the people who had gathered, "Now praise
*   the Lord your God!" So the whole congregation praised the*
*   Lord, the God of their ancestors. The people worshiped,*
*   and bowed down on the ground to give honor to the Lord*
*   and to the king.*

The next day, the people gave sacrifices to the Lord. They offered
*   whole burnt offerings to Him: 1,000 bulls, 1,000 male*
*   sheep, and 1,000 male lambs. They also brought drink*
*   offerings and many thanksgiving sacrifices were made on*
*   behalf of all the people of Israel.*

Solomon Becomes King

That day the people ate and drank with much joy in the presence of the
Lord. They made Solomon, David's son, king for the second
time. (Solomon's first appointment may have occurred at the
time of Adonijah's rebellion.) They anointed him as the prince-
king. And they anointed Zadok as high priest. They did this in
the presence of the Lord (in the immediate vicinity of the Lord's
sanctuary). Then Solomon sat upon the Lord's throne as king.
He took his father David's place, and Solomon was very successful. And all the people of Israel obeyed him. All the leaders and
the soldiers, as well as all of King David's sons, accepted
Solomon as the king. They promised to obey him. The Lord
made Solomon great before all the Israelites, and the Lord
bestowed much royal honor upon him. Before Solomon, no king
over Israel ever had such honor.

David, the son of Jesse, had been the king over all Israel for 40 years. He ruled in the city of Hebron for seven years. And he ruled in Jerusalem for 33 years. David died when he was old, having lived a good, long life. He had received many riches and honors, and Solomon, his son, became the king after him.

Everything King David did as king—from the beginning to end—is recorded among the words of Samuel, the seer, and among the words of Nathan, the prophet, and among the words of Gad, the seer. Those writings tell about what David did as the king of Israel, about his power and everything that happened to him, and they tell what happened to Israel and all the kingdoms of the lands around them.

My Time to Pray

The New King ⁊ First Chronicles 29

Then Solomon sat on the throne of the Lord as king instead of David his father, and prospered; and all Israel obeyed him (1 Chronicles 29:23).

Did you notice that David did not ask the people to do what he was not willing to do? He said, "I have given to the house of my God...my own special treasure of gold and silver" (1 Chron. 29:3). He donated an enormous amount from his own money to build the Temple. David gave 225,000 pounds of gold, and 525,000 pounds of silver. So he could ask, "Now, who is ready to dedicate his possessions to the service of the Lord today?" (1 Chron. 29:5). *Lord, I give You everything I have.*

The people gave generously to the Temple, probably because of the generosity of King David, but more because they felt they had a part in building a house for God. The best motivation for giving to a project is to "give to God Himself." *Lord, I give to You because I want to be Your partner in ministry.*

David was so overwhelmed with the people's generosity that they burst into praise, "Blessed be thou, Lord God of Israel our Father, forever and ever" (1 Chron. 29:10 KJV). The word *bless* is from the Hebrew *barak* which originally meant "to bend the knee." It ended up with the people "worshiping the Lord" (1 Chron. 29:20). The word *worship* is from the Hebrew word *shachah* which means "to prostrate oneself." What more can we give to God beyond our money? We can bow our knees to Him and bless Him. We can prostrate ourselves in His presence and worship Him. *Lord, I bless You and worship You.*

Notice young Solomon was "the second time...anointed...unto the Lord to be leader" (1 Chron. 29:22). You will not see the first anointed in this series of *Praying the Scriptures* until you read and pray First Kings 1:32-40—*Praying with the King(s)*. The younger brother of Solomon, Adonijah, tried to seize the throne from Solomon, and even got Abiathar the high priest and Joab to back his usurping of the throne. This second anointing was the official coronation of Solomon to the throne of his father. Did all the people approve? Yes, because "all the leaders, and the mighty men, and also all the sons of King David, submitted themselves to King Solomon" (1 Chron. 29:24). *Lord, help me do all things right, as did David.*

God's three representatives were inducted into office by anointing, such as the President of the United States is inducted into office by placing his hand on a Bible and swearing to uphold the Constitution of the United States. Priests were anointed with oil (Exod. 29:4-7), prophets were anointed by oil (1 Kings 19:15-16), and so were kings. David was anointed as a 16-year-old boy (1 Sam. 16:13), a second time by the men of Judah (2 Sam. 2:4), a third time by all Israel (2 Sam. 5:3). So don't be surprised when the Jews of the New Testament looked for a Messiah (word means "anointed one"). The Messiah (Hebrew) is the Greek word *Christ.* Jesus is the anointed of God. He comes from the line of David. *Lord, I worship Jesus Christ, Your Anointed One.*

Amen.

ABOUT THE AUTHOR

D R. ELMER TOWNS is an author of popular and scholarly works, a seminar lecturer, and dedicated worker in Sunday school. He has written over 125 books, including several best sellers. He won the coveted Gold Medallion Book Award for *The Names of the Holy Spirit*.

Dr. Elmer Towns also cofounded Liberty University with Jerry Falwell in 1971 and now serves as Dean of the B.R. Lakin School of Religion and as professor of Theology and New Testament.

Liberty University is the fastest growing Christian university in America. Located in Lynchburg, Virginia, Liberty University is a private, coeducational, undergraduate and graduate institution offering 38 undergraduate and 15 graduate programs serving over 39,000 resident and external students (11,300 on campus). Individuals from all 50 states and more than 70 nations comprise the diverse student body. While the faculty and students vary greatly, the common denominator and driving force of Liberty University since its conception is love for Jesus Christ and the desire to make Him known to the entire world.

For more information about Liberty University, contact:

Liberty University
1971 University Boulevard
Lynchburg, VA 24502
Telephone: 434-582-2000
Website: www.Liberty.edu

Dr. Towns's e-mail: www.eltowns@liberty.edu.

Additional copies of this book and other book titles from DESTINY IMAGE are available at your local bookstore.

Call toll-free: 1-800-722-6774.

Send a request for a catalog to:

Destiny Image® Publishers, Inc.
P.O. Box 310
Shippensburg, PA 17257-0310

"Speaking to the Purposes of God for This Generation and for the Generations to Come."

For a complete list of our titles, visit us at www.destinyimage.com.